C000172685

THE MIDLAND HOTEL

Morecambe's White Hope

THIS BOOK BELONGS TO

· JOANNE SAVAGE ·

THE MIDLAND HOTEL

Morecambe's White Hope

Barry Guise

Pam Brook

For Sue
who loves the Midland

"Buildings should keep you dry and feed the soul."
Zaha Hadid

First published in 2007, second edition 2008,
third edition 2009
by Palatine Books,
Carnegie House,
Chatsworth Road
Lancaster LA1 4SL
www.palatinebooks.com

Copyright © Barry Guise and Pam Brook, 2007

All rights reserved
Unauthorised duplication contravenes existing laws

British Library Cataloguing-in-Publication data
A catalogue record for this book is available from the
British Library

ISBN: 978-1-874181-55-2 (softback)
ISBN: 978-1-874181-54-5 (hardback)

Designed and typeset by Carnegie Book Production
www.carnegiebookproduction.com
Printed and bound by Gutenberg Press Ltd, Malta

CONTENTS

Perspective Drawing
of the Midland Hotel
by J.D.M. Harvey.
(RIBA Drawings Collection)

ACKNOWLEDGEMENTS

The authors would like to express their gratitude to the many people who have helped in the production of this book.

Particular thanks are due to…

Harry Adams, Sylvester Bone, Dorothy Coombs, Beulah Drinkall, Beverley Hicks, Noel Jeffrey, Peter Johnson, Bobby Parkes and John Wilson for sharing their memories;

Christine Boydell for her knowledge of Marion Dorn;

John Champness for conservation issues;

Anne and Rob Greenham for their stories;

Rennick and Robert Hodgson for their trust;

Tony Overton for all things LMS;

Robert Speirs for his letters;

Ian Thompson for his computer expertise;

Peter Wade for his drawings.

and to…

Glen Cooper and Michael Hill at the *Visitor*;

Kieran Gardiner and Paul Jones at Urban Splash;

Laura Whitton at RIBA;

Everyone at Carnegie Publishing.

Thanks also to those individuals and organisations who have kindly allowed illustrations to be used. Credits are given after the picture captions.

Special thanks to Lesley Guise for reading the text, offering constructive criticism, cutting the pretentious bits and helping with the writing as deadline day loomed.

The authors are grateful for the financial assistance provided by The National Lottery's 'Awards for All' scheme and for the support of the Friends of the Midland Hotel.

Morecambe Midland Hotel
verdigris-green entrance doors.
(RIBA Drawings Collection)

Chapter One

THE FIRST MIDLAND

On 3 August 1933, an envelope postmarked Lancaster arrived at the Kent home of Sir Josiah Stamp, president of the London Midland and Scottish Railway. Its contents must, initially, have left him a little puzzled, for inside was a photograph of a silver trowel. Looking more closely he might have noticed that the trowel had been inscribed but would probably have found the small writing difficult to decipher. Fortunately, an accompanying letter afforded an explanation. It was from Colonel Gerald Sharpe, a director of Storey Brothers, Lancaster, and read:

> In connection with the opening of the new Railway Hotel at Morecambe, the Midland, I thought the enclosed photograph might be of interest. This is a photograph of a Silver Trowel presented to my grandfather on August 5th 1847, on the occasion of his laying the first stone of the old hotel, which was then called The North Western. Morecambe was only a village then, by name Poulton-le-Sands, and my grandfather suggested that what was hoped would eventually become a town, should be called Morecambe, after the Bay of that name. I enclose the typed copy of the wording on the trowel as it is difficult to read on the photograph.

> 'Presented to Edmund Sharpe, Esq. on the occasion of laying the first stone of the North Western Hotel Morecambe as a memorial of the commencement of the first building of a New Town which owes its name and existence to him, and in token of the respect which he has won for himself, by the Public Spirit, the Energy, the Perseverance, and the Ability he has displayed in projecting, organizing and establishing the North Western Railway and Morecambe Harbour Companies, by the Contractors, on Thursday, August 5th, 1847.'

Three weeks before receiving Colonel Sharpe's letter, Sir Josiah had been one of the distinguished guests at the opening of the LMS's new Midland Hotel in the seaside town of Morecambe. This building replaced an earlier Midland Hotel, originally called the North Western, which had been erected by the railway company of that name in 1847–8 and for which Edmund Sharpe had laid the foundation stone.

In reply, Sir Josiah thanked Colonel Sharpe for his interest, adding that he would forward the photograph to the company's Hotels Department 'with a view to seeing whether it would be possible to have it framed and exhibited in the new hotel'. Intrigued by the eulogy engraved on the trowel, he asked for company records to be examined to try to discover more about Colonel Sharpe's grandfather and his connection with the railway company. These revealed that the very first meeting of the Provisional Committee for the establishment of the North Western Railway had been held at the office of Edmund Sharpe on 14 February 1845 and that in the following year he had been made Secretary and General Superintendent of the newly created company. Over the next seven years Sharpe was to play a major role not only in the development of the railway but also in the foundation of Morecambe as a holiday resort.

Born in Knutsford and educated at Cambridge, Edmund Sharpe came to Lancaster in 1836 where he set up as an architect in Sun Street. Gradually he built up a successful practice, taking on Edward Paley as pupil, then partner, to help with the growing number of commissions. Sharpe was a talented man with many other interests beside architecture, chief among which were local politics (he was mayor of Lancaster in 1848) and railways. These two came together in 1845 when, in his capacity as a Port Commissioner for Lancaster, Sharpe was instrumental in devising a scheme to construct a 'harbour of refuge' at the coastal village of Poulton (later to become Morecambe) which would be linked by railway, first to Lancaster and then across the Pennines to Yorkshire.

To promote the scheme, the Morecambe Bay Harbour Company was registered in November 1845 with Edmund Sharpe appointed to sit on its Management Committee. The company's promotional literature claimed:

> No shorter or more economical means of communication can possibly be constructed between the West Coast and the heart of the West Riding of Yorkshire, and this port will therefore be in a position, by reason of its accessible nature and the completion of this railway communication, to command the whole of the import and export traffic of this populous manufacturing district.

Another, more prescient, passage stated:

> When to this traffic is added the present passenger traffic between Poulton and Lancaster, and that likely to be brought in the bathing season to this favourite place of resort by the North Western Railway from Yorkshire, it will be seen that this Railway will prove to be not the least remunerative part of the project.

The Morecambe Bay Harbour Company's plan was for a low water harbour, a dock and seven miles of railway, ¾ mile to the west of Poulton. This was estimated to cost £220,000, the money to be raised by the flotation of £20 shares. With support from the North Western Railway Company the necessary Act of Parliament was secured in

Lancaster architect Edmund
Sharpe was influential in
bringing the railway to Poulton
(Morecambe) from Yorkshire. His
partner, Edward Paley, designed
the first Midland Hotel, originally
named the North Western Hotel
after the railway company
which built it.
(Lancashire County Library)

July 1846. Three months later the two companies amalgamated.

Euphoria gave way to grim reality the following year when an economic recession set in and the company's board of directors, anticipating financial problems, took the decision to shelve the original grandiose scheme for a low water harbour in favour of a single wooden jetty where vessels could tie up and discharge cargo. Under the former plan, a dock would have been cut which would have enabled boats to operate irrespective of the tide. Now, however, they would have access only at high tide, a situation which would have serious consequences for the long term future of the port.

Despite these drawbacks, work continued on the construction of the North Western Railway which by then had acquired the unofficial prefix 'Little' in order to distinguish it from the somewhat larger London and North Western Railway. The line opened on 12 June 1848, just in time for the Whitsuntide holiday. During the day nearly 2,000 people enjoyed the novel experience of a train ride from Green Ayre station in Lancaster to Poulton, adult passengers paying 6d for a 3rd class return ticket, children under ten half price. A social change was on the way. As the *Lancaster Gazette* observed:

With a train running every hour, a trip to the shore of Morecambe is within everybody's reach now, and to such as desire to breathe the fresh air of the seaside, after the business of the day, the opportunity is invaluable.

The main disadvantage of the pared down scheme for the new port was the tidal nature of the harbour. This meant that sailing times would be irregular and that between the arrival of passengers by train and their departure by boat there could be a gap of several hours. To overcome this inconvenience the railway company decided to build a hotel next to the proposed jetty which would not only provide accommodation for those passengers waiting to embark but also for visitors who wished to holiday by the seaside.

Not surprisingly, given Edmund Sharpe's involvement with the railway company, the contract for the new hotel went to his architectural practice. By this time, however, Sharpe's outside interests were leaving little time for architecture and, to all intents and purposes, the firm was being run by his partner Edward Paley. It was he who was responsible for the design of the hotel, as the minutes of the North Western Railway's Executive Committee for 14 June 1847 confirm.

Mr. Paley submitted his plans for the erection of an Hotel on the Company's land at Poulton-le-Sands with tenders for the execution of the works [and] That the sum of Four Thousand Five Hundred Pounds be paid over to the credit of Mr. Paley for the purpose of the said Building, and that he be requested to contract for, and have the works completed as soon as possible.

Although Sharpe had contributed little to the hotel's design, this did not prevent him from taking centre stage at the ceremonial laying of its foundation stone on 5 August 1847. Afterwards 'a number of gentlemen interested in the undertaking dined together at the New Inn' while 'the workmen engaged for the erection of the building were plentifully regaled at the Morecambe Hotel'. Most of the construction work was undertaken by local craftsmen (Christopher Baines – mason, Charles Blades – joiner, Thomas Cross – slater and plasterer, Anthony Hargreaves – plumber and glazier), the building taking just under a year to complete. Its final cost, including furnishings, was £4,795.

Paley's North Western Hotel was a grand Georgian-style edifice with a pale rendered façade and a pitched slate roof topped by tall stone chimneys. In plan, it incorporated a short central section with symmetrical wings set at an angle, giving a flattish U-shape, the convex side facing the sea. Although strictly a two-storey building, a third storey had been provided by utilising the roof space and adding dormer windows. The imposing porticoed entrance was approached by a short flight of steps and surmounted by three arched windows. These differed from the majority of the windows which were rectangular in shape, each with a pair of green louvred shutters which appeared more ornamental than practical. As one of the earliest railway hotels it possessed a distinctly vernacular character, its elegant and well-proportioned lines obviously influenced by the eighteenth-century buildings Paley would have been familiar with in Lancaster. It certainly had little in common with the over elaborate Gothic fantasies so beloved by later Victorian railway architects. The *Lancaster Gazette* was impressed, not least with Paley's orientation of the building.

> One of the first recommendations of the hotel is that the chief entrance is wisely placed at the back, and in the centre, so that, protected by the wings of the building, parties may alight from their carriages without exposure to the rude winds, which in the most favourable seasons, may be expected at the sea-side. On entering the building we find it laid out in convenient suites of apartments, suitable for family parties, whilst for more general purposes there are a sufficient number of large rooms – especially a beautiful drawing-room – where gatherings of visitors may take place. Every care seems to have been taken to provide abundant ventilation; hot and cold baths are at command; and in truth the building may be said to be replete with all that luxury, to say nothing of mere comfort, can desire.

On 11 September 1848 a large marquee was erected on the hotel lawn to accommodate the many local dignitaries invited to the hotel's official opening, an event described in the *Gazette*'s sister paper, the *Lancaster Guardian*.

The opening of the spacious and elegant hotel at Poulton, erected by the North Western Railway Company was celebrated on Monday last by a public dinner, to which upwards of a hundred gentlemen sat down. The Mayor presided. The toast of the evening, "success to the North Western Railway and the Morecambe Hotel", elicited a very interesting response from Mr. E. Sharpe, who took a bird's eye retrospect of what the Company had already achieved, and what they were in hopes of accomplishing when the line was opened throughout, as the facilities thus afforded for a marine trip would induce a still greater number of persons to avail themselves of the invigorating breezes of Morecambe Bay. A pyrotechnical display wound up the activities.

The hotel had actually been in business a few weeks before the above ceremony and from late August was being used to co-ordinate entries for the Morecambe Regatta scheduled to be held on 15 September. Regattas had been a common sight on Morecambe Bay for several summers prior to the opening of the North Western Hotel, early evidence that Poulton was already beginning to evolve from a small fishing village into an embryonic holiday resort even before the arrival of the railway. Sea bathing had been growing in popularity for a number of years and summer days, particularly at weekends, would see the shore at Poulton crowded with day trippers.

However, for those wishing to stay longer, the fishermen's cottages and handful of

Map showing the line of the 'Little' North Western Railway between Morecambe and Skipton.

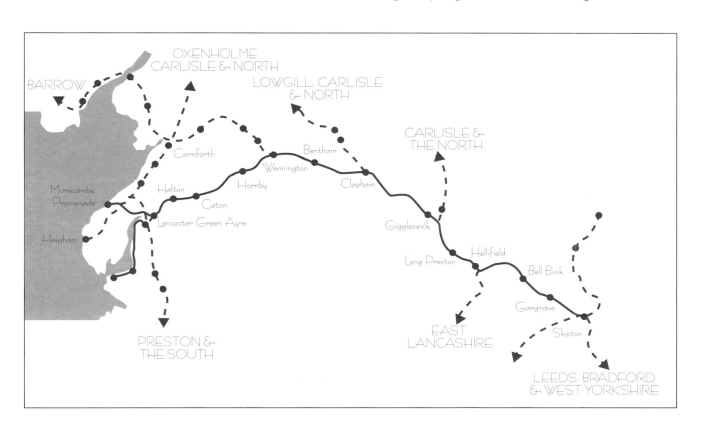

boarding houses were rapidly becoming inadequate to satisfy the steadily increasing influx of holidaymakers. Despite the addition of a number of recently constructed marine villas along the shoreline, accommodation for the wealthier classes was also limited. Such visitors aspired to something more refined than a boarding house – they wanted a high class hotel and expected it to be a little grander than their own homes, preferably some distance away from those parts of the resort frequented by day trippers and their attendant vulgarities.

The new North Western Hotel fulfilled all these requirements, at least in the early years of its existence. Standing in its own spacious grounds it catered principally for a clientele referred to as the 'carriage trade' – wealthy visitors who would arrive by train to be met at the station by their personal horse-drawn vehicles laden with luggage. Re-united, they would then drive the short distance to the hotel. An adjacent stable block provided shelter for the horses and carriages which would then be readily available for excursions during the holiday.

Poulton's first station was a temporary affair but in 1851 a more permanent structure opened in Northumberland Street, about half a mile short of the end of the line. By that time the jetty had been finished and the railway line extended up the valley of the river Lune to Wennington and thence to Skipton and the industrial towns of the West Riding of Yorkshire. All was now set for the transformation of the sleepy fishing village of Poulton into the bustling holiday resort of Morecambe.

The rapid expansion of its network was not without problems for the 'Little' North Western Railway. Struggling to cope with increasing demands on its limited resources, it entered into an agreement with the much larger Midland Railway to manage its daily services to and from Yorkshire, thus effectively making it a part of the Midland Railway even though it was not officially absorbed until 1871. Once the jetty was in operation,

Watercolour print of the North Western Hotel c.1870 by Leighton Bros. (Lancaster City Museum)

Mannex's Directory of 1866 records Robert Hartley as manager of the hotel and commends it to visitors. 'The North Western Hotel, a very extensive building near the pier, is replete with every convenience, and commands a fine view of the bay and the opposite shore. Attached are warm and cold sea-water baths, assembly and billiard rooms.'

vessels started to arrive with a variety of cargoes: timber from Spain, iron ore from Cumberland, cattle from Ireland. From 1851 the cargo boats were joined by a regular weekday steamer service to Belfast whose passengers frequently had to while away a few hours, sometimes a night, in the hotel before embarkation.

The North Western Hotel's first manager was Joseph Sly who came from the Royal Oak Hotel in Lancaster. He was engaged for a five-year term at an annual rent of £100 in the first year rising in £50 increments to £300 in the fifth, plus 'interest at 7½% per annum on the cost of such parts of the furniture as have been agreed upon to be provided by the Company'. An enterprising man, Sly actively sought new customers by using newspaper advertisements to extol the attractions of the hotel. In 1854 he

SEA SIDE
NORTH WESTERN HOTEL
MORECAMBE, POULTON –LE-SANDS
JOSEPH SLY

Begs most respectfully to acquaint the Public that the above commodious and well-arranged Hotel is open for the reception of Company. It is situated close and facing the sea, with an extensive Private Promenade Lawn in front of the Hotel, surrounded by a Sea Wall, and commanding a Picturesque and Panoramic View of the beautiful Bay of Morecambe, the Westmoreland and Cumberland Mountains, &c. It is near to the Poulton-le-Sands Railway Station; and Trains to and from London, Birmingham, Liverpool, Manchester, and all parts of the South; the Lakes, all parts of Yorkshire and the North, arrive and depart nearly every hour. The Hotel has recently been built, and is handsomely furnished, affording the best accommodation for Families and Visitors, as the scale of charges will be moderate and the accommodation very superior.

J.S. relies with confidence upon obtaining a share of public patronage, and assures all who may honour him with their support, that every attention will be paid to promote their comfort, and ensure their approbation.

Families boarded by the week; Hot and Cold Baths; Bathing Machines; Pleasure Boats; Open and Close Carriages; Billiards; Lock-up Coach Houses, &c.

Lancaster Gazette, Saturday 3 August 1850

List of visitors on that day:

Rev. James Pedder, Churchtown

Mrs. Few and family, London

Mrs. De Vitre, Lancaster

Mr. and Mrs. Fidswell, Carlton Place, London

Rev. Mr. and Mrs. Harrison, Boston, Lincolnshire

Mrs. Stevenson and family, Liverpool

Mrs. Batty and family, Hooton Roberts

C. Jenkinson, Esq., Wolverhampton

D. B. Drewis, Esq., Manchester

P. Phillips, Esq., Hartlepool

W. Robinson, Manchester

G. Gaves, Esq., Sheffield

Mr Alcock, Esq., Skipton

W. Brown, Esq., Leeds

Mr. and Mrs. T. Birkbeck, Settle

Mr. and Mrs. Fisher and family, Clapham

was succeeded as manager by Thomas Wesley, 'late of the Swan Hotel at Newport Pagnal', who bought space in the *Lancaster Gazette* 'to inform the Nobility, Gentry, and Public in general, that he has taken the Hotel, and will endeavour to conduct it in such a manner as to give general satisfaction, and he hopes, by strict attention, to merit a share of their patronage and support'. These early years were prosperous ones for the hotel, founded on a combination of well-to-do visitors and steamer passengers en route to Ireland. To be manager of such a prestigious establishment was a coveted position and the railway company had little difficulty in finding suitable tenants when the need arose.

For many years the North Western Hotel remained the most impressive building in Morecambe, detached both physically and socially from the rest of the town. But times were changing. The railway which had brought trade and holidaymakers had also acted as a catalyst for growth and sparked a building boom. In the three decades between 1851 and 1881 Morecambe's resident population tripled and, while the hotel still stood in splendid isolation, the expanding town was advancing inexorably towards it. During this period a significant development took place which was to have an adverse effect on the financial status of the hotel.

Even though port facilities had been improved in 1855 by the construction of a stone jetty parallel to the existing wooden one, the lack of a consistent steamship timetable due to tidal constraints was having economic implications for the Midland Railway which had taken over the steamer service in 1854. In 1867 it transferred its Belfast boats first to Piel Island and then in 1881 to Barrow. Morecambe still retained some sailings, including a service to Londonderry and a twice weekly sailing to Dublin operated by Laird Line, but the loss of the Belfast route dealt a severe blow both to the port and to the hotel.

With one of its main sources of income removed, the hotel must have appeared a less attractive proposition to potential tenants, especially as the annual rent remained relatively high. This proved to be the case in 1878 when the lease of the incumbent manager expired. Despite extensive advertising, the vacancy could not be filled and, faced with this predicament, the General Purposes Committee of the Midland Railway (which now owned the building) 'resolved that the Hotel and the land immediately adjoining be sold'. It is fascinating to conjecture what might have happened had the hotel passed out of railway ownership at this time, but its sale was averted at the eleventh hour when Mr Moore of the County Hotel, Ulverston agreed to take over the tenancy for 21 years at an annual rent of £300, on the condition that the railway company expended a sum of £100 on essential repairs.

Under Moore's management and with a change of name, the Midland Hotel continued to be reasonably profitable, aided by the growth of Morecambe as a holiday destination, particularly for the middle classes. It may have lost something of its original grandeur but still offered a degree of exclusivity and remained the favoured rendezvous for the social elite of the district.

An aerial view of T.W.Ward's shipbreaking yard in October 1921. Note the close proximity of the Midland Hotel. Seven ships of various sizes lie between the wooden and stone jetties. They are, from left to right: Mersey (monitor), Adventurer (cruiser), Kempenfelt (destroyer), Peyton (destroyer), U101 (submarine) next to remains of Albion (battleship), and in foreground Diadem (cruiser). (Lancaster Maritime Museum)

In 1904 the Midland Railway moved its freight services from Morecambe harbour to a new deep water port at Heysham, 3½ miles along the coast. The remaining passenger services followed soon afterwards. Heysham harbour had the advantage of being accessible to shipping at all states of the tide thus enabling a regular time-table to be adopted, something which had not been possible at Morecambe. The redundant harbour did not remain vacant for very long before being leased as a ship-breaking yard by the Sheffield firm of T.W.Ward Ltd. Ward's took over the site in October 1905 and in the course of the next 28 years dismantled a total of 55 vessels, from battleships and German submarines, to excursion steamers and Atlantic liners. Not unexpectedly, the noise and smoke emanating from the demolition process brought numerous complaints from residents, while wagons loaded with scrap constantly disrupted traffic as they were shunted across Marine Road into the goods sidings next to the station. Guests at the Midland Hotel must have found a peaceful stay almost impossible, being only a stone's throw from the centre of operations. Most local councillors were sympathetic towards the concerns of Ward's neighbours but

The first Midland Hotel, photographed in the mid 1920s. (Morecambe Visitor)

This postcard, sent on 5 July 1904, was specially produced for the hotel and shows a typical Edwardian interior with easy chairs, potted plants and vases of flowers. Its sender was not that impressed. 'You will see that the lounges of all these hotels are much the same.' (Barry Guise)

were willing to tolerate the pollution and disturbance as the ship-breaking yard provided much-needed employment for around 200 of the town's workforce. Some, on the other hand, considered the business to be a blight on the seafront and wholly inappropriate for a holiday resort. Ironically, rather than acting as a deterrent to would-be visitors, Ward's became a major tourist attraction, with holidaymakers queuing to look round the condemned ships or crowding into the specially built warehouse where furniture and fittings salvaged from the vessels were offered for sale.

The period immediately after the First World War was a busy time for the ship-breaking yard with an increasing number of vessels arriving for demolition, including several ex-navy warships. Ward's were doing well out of the business and were not particularly anxious to give up their lease. However, Morecambe Corporation had its eye on the old harbour as part of its seafront improvement scheme and had opened negotiations with the railway company with a view to purchasing the site. For its part, the railway company (which had become the London, Midland and Scottish Railway following amalgamation in 1923) was keen to sell, provided that a satisfactory price could be agreed. Although benefiting financially from Ward's tenancy, it had belatedly reached the conclusion that 'since the establishment of the ship-breaking yard … the amenities of the Midland Hotel have been seriously affected'. So too had profits, which had registered a steady decline throughout the 1920s.

In addition, the physical condition of the building was giving cause for concern. On 1 April 1927 Arthur Towle, Controller of LMS Hotel Services wrote to Sir Josiah Stamp describing the run down state of the hotel.

> The Morecambe Hotel is about 70 years old. The walls are practically porous, the roof leaks and although comparatively well furnished the structure is dilapidated and the hotel cannot be said to be any credit to the Company. Had there been no railway considerations I should therefore have been inclined to advise the sale of this hotel whilst it is still a going concern and earning net revenue.

Towle estimated that to carry out the necessary repairs would cost at least £2,000 and felt that, given the age of the building, he could not recommend such an expenditure. If the LMS wished to maintain a presence in Morecambe, he would suggest that the existing hotel be rebuilt with more rooms plus facilities for the casual visitor. Support for this proposal came from H.V. Mosley, the company's Chief Executive Officer, who was concerned that

> whilst an hotel at Morecambe will probably never be a very substantial source of income to the Company it would be a mistake if we closed down altogether there. Our hotel is the only decent one in the place, and I feel satisfied that if closed down it would have a material effect – perhaps not immediately, but in the course of a few years' time – on the status of Morecambe as a holiday resort and residence for Leeds and Bradford business people and consequently on our traffic to and from the place.

Encouraged by this backing, Towle asked the company architect to sketch out a plan for 'a moderate price hotel with about eighty rooms together with a cheap café, etc. to provide for the tripper crowds which frequent Morecambe during the summer'. Although he was pleased with the resultant design and considered it 'would have met the case admirably', Towle was forced to concede that the estimated cost of £100,000 was too high and could not be justified when set against anticipated earnings. Disappointed, he reluctantly dusted off the idea of repairing the existing hotel, with the incorporation of a public café on the site of the old stables. While unhappy with this course of action, he could see no alternative as long as the company did not want to sell the building.

Arthur Towle

One of the principal driving forces behind the building of the Midland Hotel, Arthur Edward Towle came from a prominent railway family. His father, William Towle, had been appointed manager of the Midland Hotel, Derby in 1871 and it was here that Arthur was born on 22 August 1878. Over the next two decades William would be responsible for building up the hotel division of the Midland Railway, gradually grouping all the company's hotels under one general management and demonstrating that they could be profitable enterprises. He was also instrumental in improving the quality of the food and drink served in station refreshment rooms and in the company's dining cars. Such was the railway influence in the Towle household that it was almost inevitable that Arthur and his elder brother Frank would eventually follow in their father's footsteps and pursue careers with the Midland Railway.

Both brothers were educated at Marlborough College but whereas Frank went on to study at Cambridge University, Arthur spent several years travelling, gaining practical experience of the hotel trade in America and on the Continent. On his return to England he entered Midland Railway service, as did his brother, and together they became joint assistant managers under their father, based at St Pancras in London. When William Towle retired in 1914, Arthur and Frank took over full control, each on a salary of £500 per annum plus commission and free accommodation. They were very much 'hands-on' managers and made it their business to visit regularly each of the company's hotels, often once a week, in order to ensure that the high standards set by their father were being maintained.

At the outbreak of the First World War, Frank was called up as Controller of the Army and Navy Canteen Board, leaving Arthur in sole charge. Although Frank was to rejoin the Midland Railway when hostilities ended, he resigned soon afterwards to take up the post of Managing Director of Gordon Hotels. Arthur remained at the helm until 1917 when he was appointed Director at the Ministry of Food, later receiving a CBE for his war services. Between 1919 and 1920 he acted as Controller of Hotels for the post-war Peace Conference in Paris.

Returning to the Midland Railway in 1920, Arthur became Manager of its Hotels and Catering Services and five years later was made Controller of Hotels, Refreshment Rooms and Restaurant Car Services of the newly created London Midland and Scottish Railway, a post he held for nearly twenty years. Like his father before him, Arthur was resolved that any new hotels built by the Railway Company should be at the forefront of design, incorporating the latest in construction technology. William Towle had set the trend with the Midland Hotel, Manchester (1903) and Liverpool's Adelphi Hotel (1914) and Arthur continued it when he oversaw the completion of the LMS's first post-war hotel at Gleneagles in Scotland (1924). Continuing its commitment to architectural excellence, the LMS employed Sir Edwin Lutyens to design an annex for the Midland Hotel, Manchester in 1930, a project that was never realised due to the economic depression of the time.

While Lutyens' plan for Manchester's Midland Hotel was relatively traditional, the same could not be said of that proposed for the LMS's new hotel at Morecambe two years later. Once Arthur Towle had persuaded the Railway Company that the resort's old Victorian hotel needed replacing, he was determined that the new building would enhance the standing of the LMS and to this end was largely instrumental in the appointment of Oliver Hill as architect.

Later in the 1930s, he guided the construction of the Queen's Hotel in Leeds and, but for the Second World War, would have implemented plans for a new hotel at Euston. Arthur Towle continued to serve the LMS as Controller of Hotels until 1944. Sadly, he enjoyed only a brief retirement before passing away at his London home on 26 August 1948, a few days after his 70th birthday.

Arthur Towle in 1925.
(The Railway Gazette)

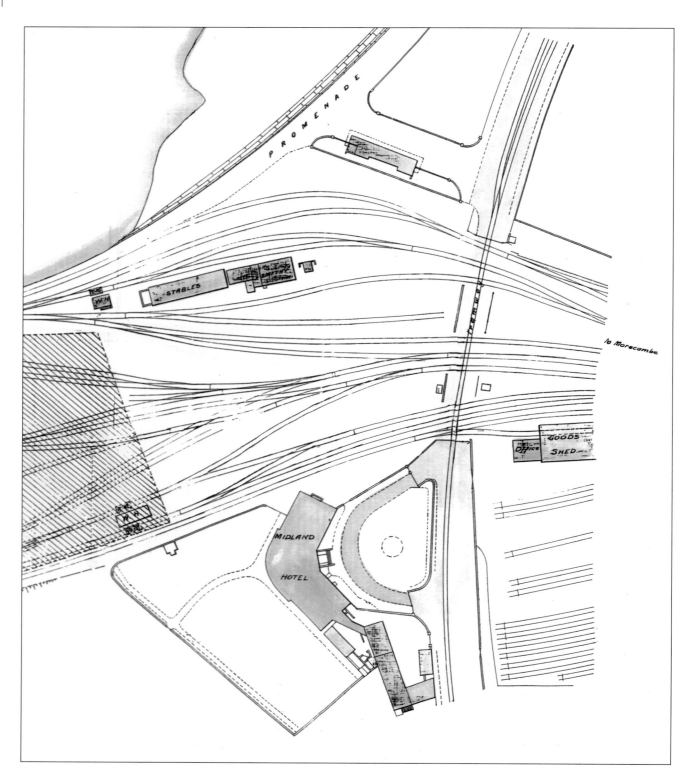

Map showing The Midland Hotel in 1905. Nine sets of railway lines once crossed Marine Road, constantly disrupting traffic. After negotiations with Morecambe Corporation, the Midland Railway agreed to remove all but one line,. with movement of goods being controlled by level crossing gates. (Lancaster Maritime Museum)

As it transpired, the LMS's Executive Committee decided to leave the matter in abeyance until discussions had been concluded with Morecambe Corporation regarding the purchase of the old harbour site. These were likely to take some time as the Corporation first had to gain authorisation from the Government to borrow the required money. When this was achieved in August 1928 with the passing of the Morecambe Corporation Act, the way was clear for the deal to be finalised. The railway company agreed to sell the site for £34,000 but only when it was satisfied that the Corporation was in a position to proceed with the construction of a promenade and other seafront improvements. This took a further three years, during which time Towle managed to convince the Executive Committee that a new hotel on more modest lines and costing about £60,000 would be a viable proposition. As it would take up less space than the earlier design, the surplus land could be sold to Morecambe Corporation and the money used to help fund the rebuilding.

Accepting this proposal, the Executive Committee recommended that the land be offered to the Corporation for £23,000 with the proviso that it 'may only erect pleasure gardens or other buildings which will not interfere with the amenities of the hotel'. Obtaining this additional money would be crucial as the projected cost of the new hotel had risen to £70,000 even though the number of bedrooms had been reduced from 80 to between 45 and 50. If Morecambe Corporation agreed to purchase the land for the price stated, and paid £34,000 for the old harbour site, the LMS would receive a total of £57,000, sufficient to enable it to go ahead with the project.

At the meeting of the Hotels and Catering Committee on 16 December 1931, Arthur Towle was able to report that the signing of the sale contract between the LMS and Morecambe Corporation was imminent and work on the new hotel could start once the protective sea wall had been completed. Committee members were then shown an outline plan for the hotel drawn up by Mr Adam the company architect. While they felt it to be generally acceptable, their approval was less than enthusiastic. Sensing their reservations, Towle proposed that an outside architect of his acquaintance might be approached for an alternative design. He suggested that

> Mr Oliver Hill, a young and promising architect, should be consulted, not only in regard to the façade, but also in connection with the internal decoration.

The committee agreed, on the understanding that his estimate should not exceed the £57,000 expected from the sale of railway company land to Morecambe Corporation. Towle undertook to contact Oliver Hill and ask him to prepare plans for the next meeting of the committee.

This took place on 27 January 1932 and proved to be pivotal. Acting on Towle's advice, Hill had spent several days in Morecambe looking at the site before finalising his plans for the hotel. During this time he had met the Borough Surveyor and studied the Corporation's scheme for the new promenade which was being laid out in a wide sweeping curve. Hill concluded that the line of the building should conform to the same curve, with its long flank facing the sea enabling as many rooms as possible to have a sea view. For its design, he proposed a hotel in the modern style, one whose 'treatment generally, both inside and out, would be simplified and without unnecessary detail, relying upon its lines, proportion and the massing of light and shade for effect'. Hill entreated the committee to be bold.

> I have made it my business to keep in touch with the best Continental work of this kind, both in France, Germany, Austria and Scandinavia, etc., and I feel that you have here an unique opportunity of building the first really modern hotel in this country.

As to cost, Hill confirmed that, including all fees, the hotel could be built within the authorised budget of £57,000. Towle pointed out that the committee should be aware that this figure was exclusive of furnishing and that a further £12,000 would be required to equip the hotel and the café. Also, it might be desirable to strengthen the foundations and steelwork to enable another storey to be built if the need arose in the future. He calculated this would add about £2,000 to the total.

After a lengthy discussion, the committee decided to recommend that the proposed scheme be approved at an estimated cost of £71,992, made up as follows:

Hotel building	£51,000
Strengthening foundations and extra steelwork for additional storey if necessary	2,000
Hard tennis court, surrounding walls, gardens, etc	2,000
Architect's fees	3,227
Contingencies	1,000
Quantity Surveyor's fees	665
Furniture	6,000
Allocation to be reported subsequently	£65,992
Additional furniture (cost to be debited to Hotel Renewal Fund)	6,000
	£71,992

The committee also endorsed the appointment of Oliver Hill as architect for the building. While stating that this decision was in no sense a criticism of the plans submitted by Mr Adam, in their view

> it was desirable to take advantage of the present opportunity and make a new departure, based to some extent on the experience of other countries. It was felt that Mr. Oliver Hill, who had international experience in regard to modern hotel building practice and construction, would enable the Committee to carry out their ideas in the most favourable circumstances.

Chapter Two

BUILDING FOR MODERN TIMES

At the time, the choice of Oliver Hill as architect for the new Midland Hotel must have raised a few eyebrows. Trained in the Arts and Crafts tradition, he had only recently been converted to Modernism following a trip to the Stockholm Exhibition in 1930. Moreover, he had no previous experience of hotel construction. True, he had travelled widely in Europe but it could be said that his knowledge of 'modern hotel building practice' was largely derived from staying in such hotels during his continental excursions!

Prior to his appointment by the LMS, Hill's only venture into the modern style had been the design of a private house called Joldwyn's at Holmbury St Mary in Surrey (1930–2) which, while visually impressive, was plagued by damp and, according to the owners, impractical to live in. Joldwyn's was in marked contrast to Hill's earlier work which consisted mainly of private houses, for wealthy clients, in mock Tudor and neo-Georgian styles – more Lutyens than Le Corbusier. This was not entirely surprising as Hill had grown up under the influence of Sir Edwin Lutyens, a family friend and early inspiration.

Hill's privileged upbringing and influential connections may have helped him obtain the Midland Hotel commission by bringing him into contact with Arthur Towle. Both came from public school backgrounds, were members of London clubs and probably moved in similar social circles. Towle knew Lutyens through his designs for the extension to the LMS's Midland Hotel in Manchester and it is not unreasonable to conjecture that Lutyens might have recommended Hill as architect for the railway company's proposed hotel in Morecambe.

His visit to Sweden had convinced Hill that architecture and the decorative arts should reflect 'our new way of life' and that 'directness, fitness and economy are the paramount requisites' with designers 'free to rely on proportion, line form and rhythm, and the selection of material for their effect'. As well as allowing him to design

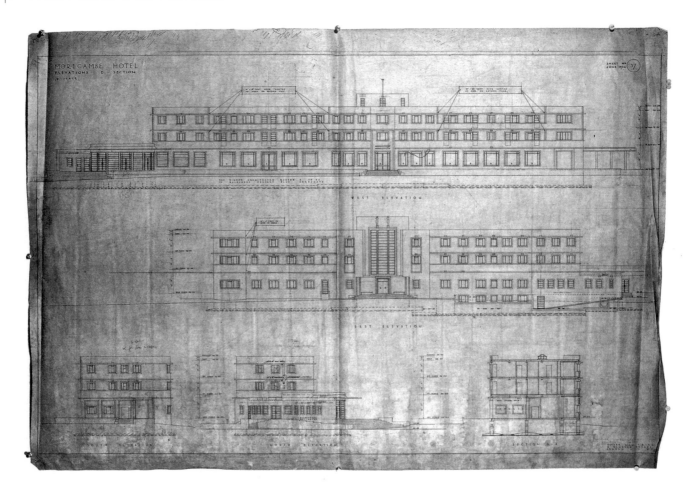

a substantial building in the new style he had embraced with enthusiasm, the Midland Hotel gave Hill the opportunity to put into practice his vision of unity in architecture and decoration. It was his belief that a building's external appearance should be intimately linked to its internal décor, furniture and upholstery – a philosophy he likened to 'the French ensemblier system of architect, sculptor, decorative painter and other craftsmen … collaborating to one end and ideal'. It was this holistic concept that Hill brought to the Midland Hotel, one that would see him take complete control of all aspects of the project, from the building's exterior design to its colour scheme, works of art, decoration and furnishings – even down to the waitresses' outfits, the colour of the hand towels and the shape of the door handles!

Hill's design was for a three-storey curved structure which followed the sweep of the new municipal promenade, with its convex side towards the sea enabling 'all the public rooms, the private sitting rooms, and as many bedroom suites as possible to have the sea view'. The concave side facing the railway station was divided by a glazed tower containing the main entrance and spiral staircase. A rounded bastion with an open loggia finished off the south end of the building while the north end widened out into a circular café and terrace. The hotel was to be constructed around a steel framework with concrete/hollow tile slab floors and brick walls resting on shallow foundations which would spread the load across the sandy surface of the site. Its external façade would be finished in a white render called 'Snowcrete' composed of cement and carborundum and electrically polished to produce a surface resembling marble. This would be relieved by treating the architraves of the windows with a mixture of carborundum and minute particles of crushed blue-green glass, and coating the soffits, loggia ceiling and the undersides of the balconies with a verdigris-coloured cement glaze.

Inside, the impression would be one of space – from the airy, light-filled entrance lounge to the open staircase with its cantilevered steps ascending to the first and second floors. Here, the bedrooms would be the latest word in luxury while higher still, on the flat roof, guests would be able to enjoy sunbathing in total seclusion.

Annotated rough sketch by Oliver Hill of the Entrance Lounge and Staircase. (RIBA Drawings Collection)

Oliver Hill

Oliver Hill was born in London on 15 June 1887, the youngest of seven children. His father was a prosperous businessman and the family lived in comfortable circumstances in Knightsbridge, sufficiently well off to own another property in the Bedfordshire countryside.

Schooldays were spent in Reigate and at Uppingham where his housemaster encouraged the young Oliver's growing interest in architecture, a career he was intent on pursuing after leaving school. Following the advice of the architect Edwin Lutyens, a family friend and early influence, he spent eighteen months working in a builder's yard, a training which helped to develop his understanding of materials and techniques. In 1907 he became the pupil of Scottish architect William Flockhart, furthering his studies by attending evening classes at the Architectural Association where he gained a reputation as a talented draughtsman.

Through good connections he was able to set up in practice at the early age of 23, his first major commission being the restoration, in baroque style, of the gardens at Moor Close in Berkshire. However, his career had hardly begun when it was interrupted by the First World War. Joining the London Scottish Regiment he served with distinction in the trenches of northern France, rising in rank from private to captain.

When the war ended, Hill returned to architecture, gradually building up a portfolio of wealthy clients. Still very much influenced by Lutyens and his own Arts and Crafts background, Hill designed country houses in traditional styles using stone, timber and thatch with great skill. He also built solid, neo-Georgian town houses in London, taking responsibility for their internal decorations as well as their outward appearance – early signs of the holistic approach to architecture he would later bring to the Midland Hotel.

In the late 1920s Hill made frequent trips to the continent where he became exposed to architectural developments which had yet to make their mark in England. Visits to Scandinavia brought him into contact with the work of architects such as Alvar Aalto and Gunnar Asplund and the possibilities offered by the use of new materials. Asplund's buildings at the Stockholm Exhibition of 1930 demonstrated to Hill how glass and steel could be used expressively to achieve a great lightness of effect.

While many of his contemporaries in England were a little wary of adopting 'the new architecture', Hill embraced it with enthusiasm and embarked on the design and construction of a number of buildings in the continental style, beginning with a house called Joldwynds in Holmbury St Mary, Surrey for the barrister Wilfred

Greene. Its curved front divided by a glazed staircase tower became something of a leitmotif for a Hill building of the early 1930s, reappearing on another house, Holthanger in Wentworth, Surrey and, on a larger scale, at the Midland Hotel in Morecambe.

While his design for the Midland Hotel might have been radical for an English seaside resort, it was relatively conservative when compared with the coolly geometrical, almost abstract, style favoured by many of his continental counterparts. Hill's interpretation of Modernism was warmer and curvier, more human – and, like the Finnish architect Alvar Aalto, he saw his buildings as inseparable from their surroundings, both aesthetically and functionally.

With its seaside location, light and airy rooms and rooftop solarium, the Midland Hotel could be seen as a shrine to sunshine, fresh air and healthy recreation – very much in keeping with the philosophy of the time, and with Hill's own rather unconventional outlook on life. Seldom seen without a cigarette he was, nevertheless, a great believer in the beneficial effects of healthy outdoor activities – sunbathing, swimming, hiking, etc, – preferably (as he was a keen naturist) unencumbered by any form of clothing!

Perhaps because he had none of his own, Hill loved the company of children. A good friend of the muralist Mary Bone (nee Adshead) he became something of an unofficial uncle to her three children when they were growing up in the 1930s. Sylvester Bone remembers Hill playing games with them on the beach, taking them dinghy sailing on the Solent and for hair-raising rides in his pale green Rolls-Royce.

Oliver Hill pictured with two favourite companions – a cigarette and pet monkey called George. (RIBA Photographs Collection)

Oliver Hill in his office with Maria Callas. Hill could be very charming with clients but at times would use his slight deafness as an excuse for obstinacy when wanting to get his own way with projects. (RIBA Photographs Collection)

We had lots of fun with Oliver. The first memory is of him bringing his monkey in to see my brother and myself in the bath … we thought it would bite us. Oliver was extremely mischievous. At a little railway station in Wales he pinched the stationmaster's hat and flag and signalled the train to start. In a Christchurch tearoom he balanced the table on his knees and bounced it up and down singing "Little Brown Jug" at the top of his voice. When they asked him to leave he turned to the other customers with a profuse apology in his best public school manner, offering to pay for their tea if he had unintentionally spoiled their afternoon.

Following his success with the Midland Hotel, Hill became involved with two other seaside projects. He was invited by Earl de la Warr to enter the competition for a new pavilion in the Sussex resort of Bexhill (eventually won by Erich Mendelsohn and Serge Chermayeff) and was chosen to design a community in the Modernist style at Frinton-on-Sea in Essex, only a few houses of which were completed due to financial problems. Undeterred, Hill worked tirelessly to promote Modernism in all its aspects. He was particularly gifted at organising exhibitions and played a major part in the Exhibition of British Industrial Art at Dorland Hall in 1933. Four years later he was appointed to oversee the British Pavilion at the Paris Exhibition of Arts and Crafts in Modern Life. As well as helping to select exhibits, he was also responsible for employing several well-known artists – Eric Ravilious, Edward Bawden and Mary Adshead among others – to design various stands reflecting the theme of outdoor life and English country traditions.

During the 1930s he developed an interest in social architecture and became involved in a number of school projects, often waiving his design fees. Only one was actually built, the impressive Whitwood Mere Infant School at Castleford in Yorkshire, which was finished just before the outbreak of World War Two. Too old to enlist, Hill spent the war years finishing off existing jobs, doing conversions and taking up painting. The war effectively ended his career and few new commissions came his way. Out of fashion, he drifted into semi-retirement in the Cotswolds, buying a rambling old property called Daneway and immersing himself in his house, garden and menagerie of exotic animals and birds.

In 1953, when he was 66, he married Margaret Beverley, the daughter of an architect and little more than a third his age. Despite some initial parental opposition, Hill and his young wife, who he called Titania, enjoyed fifteen happy years together until his death on 29 April 1968, a few weeks short of his eighty-first birthday.

Although Oliver Hill was attracted by the continental style, he was no fanatical Modernist and throughout the 1930s continued to build traditional houses in whatever style his clients fancied. As his biographer Alan Powers observed, Hill slipped in and out of Modernism with a chameleon-like talent – a trait which brought him criticism from younger, more dogmatic practitioners. Hill, however, saw no reason why both interests could not be combined, especially as not all modern architecture met with his approval. 'Much of what passes for "modern" has very little to be said in its favour, mainly perhaps owing to its lack of grace.' To Hill, grace was 'the supreme desirability in fine architecture' and could be found as much in traditional houses as in their modern counterparts.

Hill was also a realist. As a practising architect in difficult economic times he was unwilling to reject commissions on a point of principle. If critics wished to describe him as a commercially inclined dilettante then so be it. At least he was working. While some reproached him for not being 'committed' to Modernism, others regarded this as a strength rather than a weakness. Roderick Gradidge considered Hill to be 'one of the most interesting and versatile architects of the interwar period working in any country … a man who never allowed his natural wit nor his great talent as a designer to be distorted by doctrinaire attitudes from whatever source they came'.

Perhaps architectural historian Ken Powell summed up Oliver Hill's contribution best when he wrote

> Alongside the revolutionary dynamics of the Thirties, an older tradition of craftsmanship persisted. Oliver Hill was, almost uniquely, able to bridge the divide between modernism and tradition. His work, hedonistic and even self-indulgent, may lack the purity and progressive zeal – and the breadth of imagination – of a Lubetkin or a Mendelsohn, yet Hill was a keen populariser of modern architecture, selling it to clients who were not interested in social revolution.

Oliver Hill's architecture, like that of his inspiration Alvar Aalto, was on a human scale and exuded the warmth lacking in many of the soulless machine-like constructions which gave Modernism a bad name.

On 23 February 1932, Hill submitted detailed plans to the Morecambe Hotel Rebuilding Committee, a sub-committee established specifically to oversee the project and which included the Controller of Hotels, Arthur Towle as one of its members. In addition to the hotel's public rooms, Hill envisaged 15 double bedrooms, 26 single bedrooms, 16 bathrooms, 3 private sitting rooms and 16 staff and service rooms. Following a lengthy discussion, the plans were approved and a decision taken to put the building out to tender.

Although pleased with Hill's design for the hotel, Towle had reservations concerning the architect's plans for its fixtures and fittings. During the 1920s, Hill had acquired a reputation not only for well-built houses but also for extravagant interiors, using glass, chrome, marble, vitrolite, mosaics and exotic woods to achieve the required effect. For the Midland Hotel, Hill saw the use of such materials and a carefully chosen colour scheme as softer counterpoints to the relative austerity of the building's architecture. He was also keen to incorporate works of art by leading painters and sculptors of the day. Such ideas troubled the more conventional Towle who wrote to Hill cautioning him not to be 'too much influenced by what is done in what I may call the more artistic circles of London. Do not let us get too "precious"'. Considering his integrity questioned, Hill retorted:

As far as I am concerned, there is no chance of the hotel or its furnishings being 'precious' … we have a unique opportunity of providing something worthy, without being in the least meretricious or precious.

The Rebuilding Committee's April meeting was largely taken up with deciding which methods of heating, lighting and cooking to choose for the hotel. Towle favoured an all-electric service but felt he could not recommend it as the cost was prohibitive. Coal, in his opinion, should be avoided at all costs. After much deliberation, the committee opted for coke boilers for heating and hot water, and gas for cooking. It considered that the proposed charge for electric current for lighting was excessive and would try to secure a reduction in terms from Morecambe Corporation (the electricity suppliers), a representation which proved successful.

Organising the tendering process was the Quantity Surveyor appointed for the project, Mr F. Clive Grimwade of Bedford Row, London. Working from Hill's drawings, Grimwade's initial task was to prepare a 'bill of quantities' setting out in exact detail the amount of materials, labour, etc, required to erect the hotel, and to provide an accurate guide to the costs involved. Key elements of the building – its steelwork, windows, heating system, etc, – were then offered for tender, with specialist contractors invited to submit a price for the work based on the architect's drawings and an unpriced 'bill of quantities'.

By the end of June, Grimwade had received enquiries from nearly twenty firms interested in bidding for the main building contract. From these a shortlist of eight was drawn up by Arthur Towle and invited to deliver their tenders in sealed envelopes to Oliver Hill by mid-day on Monday 25 July. Only one local firm, Edmondson Brothers, builders of Morecambe's new Town Hall, made it onto the shortlist. However, its estimate turned out to be nearly £2,000 more than the lowest tender, that of Messrs Humphreys of Knightsbridge, London, who quoted a sum of £48,678 and were duly awarded the contract.

While the tenders were being considered, Oliver Hill had been making modifications to the accommodation layout of the hotel – increasing the number of double bedrooms from 14 to 19, reducing the number of single bedrooms from 26 to 22 and improving the staff rooms. Although Humphreys' original tender had been accepted, the committee realised that Hill's amendments would result in additional costs and approved the firm's revised figure of £51,517. After allowing £4,150 for the gardens and surrounding walls, and taking into account Oliver Hill's fees, the expenditure on the new hotel (excluding furniture) would amount to £59,004 which compared favourably with the sum of £59,992 budgeted for by the Hotels and Catering Committee in January.

It was agreed that Humphreys should be ready to begin by mid-August, a stipulation of the contract being that 'the whole of the works were to be completed and the building left fit for occupation within a period of nine months of the date on which Humphreys received possession of the first portion of the site' – a surprisingly short time considering that the contract involved the demolition of the existing hotel as well as the construction of its replacement.

Preliminary site investigations had already been carried out by Mr B. L. Hurst, the Structural Engineer employed by the LMS Railway. He was anxious to discover how the ground would stand up to the weight of the steelwork and had been conducting trial borings to determine the level and thickness of the substrate. The results showed a sand layer of varying depth lying over a base of thick clay. In a letter to Morecambe's Borough Engineer requesting him to drill additional holes, Hurst outlined his concern.

> I have told the architect that, if practicable, we should like to spread our foundations upon the surface of the sand, but that we shall have to prove that the sand exists over the whole of the site and that its thickness is in all parts sufficient to distribute the load; if this is not so, we shall have to carry out loading tests on the clay in the bottom of the new trial holes.

In the event, such tests proved unnecessary as the extra borings confirmed a sufficient depth of sand to be present across the site. Hurst contacted Oliver Hill with the news that he would be able 'to float the building at a low pressure upon the top of the surface of the sand at about 3' 0'' below existing ground level'.

(N.B. At the shoreline in Morecambe the water table is very near the surface. Following heavy rain or high tides the underlying soil water has been known to rise high enough to cause floors to lift in buildings close to the sea. When constructing the new hotel it was important that the weight of the foundations was sufficient to counteract this pressure from below.)

With his principal contractor in place and a start date decided, Oliver Hill approached Arthur Towle for permission to engage Mr B. H. Goulding as Clerk of Works for the project. In Hill's opinion, Goulding 'was somewhat outstanding in his suitability for the position' having acted in the same capacity for the recent extension to Claridge's Hotel in London. After a brief interview Goulding was appointed to the post, his contract to commence on 15 August. As the 'man on site' his job would be to ensure the satisfactory progress of the building work by liaising with the architect, the quantity surveyor, the structural engineer, the main contractor, and numerous sub-contractors spread over the length and breadth of Britain, as well as Morecambe Corporation who were constructing the adjacent promenade. In recognition of this responsible position he was to receive a salary of £10 per week with a bonus of £25 'on the conclusion of the work, if satisfactory'.

A late revision of the plans for the hotel's drainage system caused the start date to be delayed by two weeks, work finally getting underway on 29 August with the demolition of an old wall and some buildings on the south side of the site. At this time the Corporation was in the process of laying out its promenade of red and white squares, including a special large white square designed to line up with the hotel's rear entrance. Once the precise position of the new hotel had been set out, excavations for its foundations began in earnest and by the end of September were sufficiently advanced for concreting to begin.

To ensure that construction would not be hampered by T. W. Ward's shipbreaking activities on the adjacent stone jetty, the firm was given until 2 April 1933 to vacate the land it leased from the LMS Railway. Despite this deadline, Ward's calculated there was enough time to make a start on breaking up a naval training ship which had arrived on 2 September. However, its iron structure proved more robust than anticipated and, as

Morecambe seafront, photographed at the beginning of November 1932. The steel framework of the new hotel's north wing rises behind the existing hotel. To the right, workmen remove the last of Morecambe Motors' garage and showroom and the Harbour Pavilion. Behind can be seen the buildings of shipbreakers T. W. Ward, accessed by rail through the level crossing gates. (Morecambe Visitor) pressure to clear the site mounted, Ward's were forced to tow the partly dismantled hulk round the coast to its yard at Preston. There still remained a substantial amount of scrap metal, some 11,000 tons, to be removed over the coming months and it was by no means certain this could be achieved in time, given the recent slump in prices for scrap.

After a few weeks on site, Goulding had begun to realise that his position did not automatically guarantee him ideal working conditions. A letter written to Oliver Hill suggested that he (Goulding) might benefit from 'an office with benches, drawers and suitable windows' as well as somewhere simply to store cement and hoardings. Even at this early stage there were niggling hold-ups. The quantity surveyor had failed to send a list of the sub-contractors for the next phase of the work, Carnforth Quarry could not supply a good enough aggregate and the steel rods for the reinforced concrete had not arrived – all symptomatic of the problems that were to beset construction over the ensuing months.

In late October the *Visitor* newspaper was able to inform its curious readers that

> Behind the concealing boarding … the seaward side of the present hotel looked as if preparations were being made for war. What used to be the lawn has been dug into pits and trenches in which the foundations are being laid. Forty or fifty men are at work on laying the foundations, which are already well advanced and the Clerk of Works, Mr B. H. Goulding, stated that as much local labour as possible is being employed … and rapid progress is being made.

This reassuring assessment did not quite match that of the structural engineer who was in Morecambe at the same time. Writing to Oliver Hill on 29 October, Hurst was

> somewhat perturbed at the slow progress made to date; I believe that some nine or ten weeks of the nine months total contract time have elapsed and only about one third of the foundations are completed, whilst the steel erection is only just being commenced. I raised this point with Messrs Humphreys' representative who told me that they will be proceeding very rapidly from now onwards and should have the whole of the concrete foundations in the northern half of the building ready for steel by the end of next week. Even assuming this, and allowing say seven weeks for complete erection of the steel and floors, about half the contract time will have gone before much of the brickwork can be started.

Acting on Hurst's concerns, Goulding decided that the only way to speed up progress was to have binding agreements with Humphreys and all the sub-contractors to complete specific sections of the work by certain definite dates. As he pointed out to Humphreys, 'If I have this information [re sub-contractors] I can greatly assist you by continually worrying them.' This seemed to have the desired effect and within a short time Goulding was able to report to Hill that 'we shall soon be starting brickwork to the boiler house and kitchen section' – only to add later that the calorifiers of the boilers were too big to go through the proposed boilerhouse doorway which hurriedly had to be enlarged! However, the steelwork was rising rapidly behind the old hotel and Bolton & Hayes had made a start on the hollow tile flooring.

Towards the end of November the weather, which until then had been generally good, took a turn for the worse. Strong winds and heavy rain battered the site resulting in several suspensions of work and a consequent loss of time. Despite the hold-ups, Hurst was able to relay some positive news to Oliver Hill following a site visit in mid-December.

> With regard to progress, the steelwork appears to be up to scheduled time. The tile floors are about 25 per cent behind schedule time, but I understand from Mr Bolton that they are concentrating on a greater output from now onwards. The whole of the ground floor in the north block is in and about half of the ground floor in the south block. Practically the whole of the north block is in and about one third of the second floor in the north block.

This emphasis on completing the north block of the hotel ahead of the rest was the result of a decision taken long before work began. Incredibly, as its replacement was looming behind it, the old hotel was still open 'as normal'. Hill's original plan had been to complete part of the new hotel by the beginning of February 1933 and then to transfer the business from the existing building. He thought that 'a temporary hoarding fixed to the scaffolding on the old hotel side … would not be too unsightly' and would suffice to shield guests from the noise and dust of the construction work. Sadly, no record remains of the guests' impressions of this arrangement! Unfortunately, one consideration which had not been taken into account was the close proximity of the old hotel to the proposed entrance steps of its replacement which could not be constructed until the existing building was demolished.

Approaching Christmas, work was running some three weeks behind schedule and it seemed very unlikely that the north wing of the new hotel would be ready for occupation by the intended date. Hurst was in no doubt where the blame lay. On 19 December he wrote in veiled threatening terms to Bolton & Hayes.

> I regret to note … that you are getting seriously behind with your work, and that brickwork, asphalting and other trades are being held back. I have to point out that the progress of your work is at present the sole factor affecting completion of the building, and that unless you can show some very considerable improvement from now onwards, you will be largely responsible for non-completion to date and for such penalties as the main contractor may be called upon to pay.

For reasons he kept to himself, Oliver Hill preferred to gloss over any delays or problems when reporting to the Rebuilding Committee. At its December meeting he was more concerned to obtain approval for the artworks and decorations he had conceived for the hotel. This, he knew, would not be easy.

At the beginning of the month Grimwade had asked Arthur Towle's permission to place various contracts, including one with H.T. Jenkins & Son to supply blocks of Portland stone for two statues over the hotel entrance and for a panel in the Lounge to be carved by the sculptor Eric Gill. Towle had refused to sanction the order and, in a letter relaying this decision, Grimwade alerted Oliver Hill to the fact that

> as regards the statues over the staircase window and the stone panel in the lounge, he (Towle) does not personally like the idea of these items and that he will require your designs in these circumstances to be referred to the Directors for their approval.

Forewarned, and realising that he needed inside help on the Rebuilding Committee, Hill approached Major Ralph Glynn M.P. to try to solicit his backing. Of the five members of the committee, Glynn – whose day job was Parliamentary Private Secretary to the Prime Minister, James Ramsay MacDonald – was regarded by Hill as the least conservative in outlook and the one most in sympathy with his vision for the hotel. In the week before the meeting he wrote to Glynn with a request.

> As it may be difficult for me to make clear to the meeting the nature and necessity for this part of the work, may I have the opportunity of explaining the drawings and design to you beforehand, so that I may have your support.

In the event, Hill's powers of persuasion met with only limited success. The statues' design failed to gain approval and the committee requested him to submit an alternative. While agreeing to the idea of a stone panel for the Lounge, it recommended that the subject should be 'an allegorical one representing mermaids'. Hill's proposed use of terrazzo tiles inlaid with mosaics for the Lounge floor also met opposition. Might he not consider wood or parquet flooring instead? However, the committee did accept his plans for the Dining Room and the Café (with a mural by the artist Eric Ravilious), and left him to agree with Arthur Towle the décor of the other rooms.

Unlike the rest of the hotel which was unashamedly elitist, the Café was conceived with the casual visitor in mind. Holidaymakers strolling along the promenade would be able to call in for a cup of tea (or something stronger in the adjacent bar) and either sit inside or enjoy the view from the terrace. While accepting that the Café should be very modern, Towle argued that the bar should be quite plain as its clientele would largely be 'members of the working class on holiday in Morecambe … and we must not confuse them with the class of people who will be using the hotel'. 'We must', he said, 'walk with kings in the hotel but not lose the common touch in the bar, thus the decorations must not be too exotic'. Hill, probably smiling to himself, promised to 'keep the bar very sober'.

As the north wing of the hotel takes shape, the railway running across Marine Road to the shipbreaking yard on the Stone Jetty still remains in operation. (Beverley Hicks)

On the seaward side of the hotel the skeleton of the circular café is in place while brickwork is well advanced on the second floor of the main building. (Beverley Hicks)

Scaffolding encloses the loggia at the south end of the building, only the ground floor of which has been completed. Part of the old hotel can be seen in the background. (Beverley Hicks)

Inside the hotel, the framework for the cantilevered spiral staircase has reached the first floor. Rising behind are the latticed steel columns which will provide the reinforcement for the staircase tower's concrete supports. (Beverley Hicks)

The photographs, above and left, were taken in early 1933 by G.A.W. Hicks who was Superintendent of Works (Building Manager) for Humphreys of Knightsbridge, the main contractors for the Midland Hotel.

George Hicks was 36 when he arrived in Morecambe to oversee work at the Midland, living in a flat on Sandylands Promenade with his wife and young son. Two of his brothers – a carpenter and a bricklayer – were also employed on the building. One eventually married a local girl while the other was, for a time, a boyfriend of Thora Hird.

After completion of the Midland, George Hicks worked on several projects, both at home and in the Middle East, before leaving Humphreys and joining the firm of Richard Costain Limited. In 1949 Costains were awarded the contract for the South Bank Exhibition Site of the Festival of Britain. With a reputation for bringing jobs in on time and within budget, George Hicks was given responsibility for the construction of several key buildings, including the Dome of Discovery (1951's equivalent of the Millennium Dome) and the iconic Skylon. In recognition of his work on the site he received the British Empire Medal.

The New Year opened with some optimism. Goulding was able to report that the brickwork and main staircase were up to the first floor, sufficiently advanced for F. Tibbenham Ltd to take measurements for the panelling in the Dining Room and the Billiard Room. In the basement, electricians were busy installing tubing for the wiring and sockets, while the three solid fuel boilers had arrived and were being assembled. The hollow tile floors, which should have been completed by the end of December, were now almost finished (Bolton & Hayes' men had worked through the Christmas holidays to make up time), plastering was soon to begin on the first floor and doors and windows were going in.

To the annoyance of the Quantity Surveyor the contract for the metal window frames had been awarded to Henry Hope & Sons. Hope's initial tender had been 30% higher that its rivals, a result, the company claimed, of the special zinc finish used 'which is superior to that of any other firm in its resistance to the action of the salt in the sea air' and which came with a guarantee 'to be free of corrosion for a period of 10 years'. Towle advised Hope's to send in a revised (i.e. lower) estimate. In response, Hope's bypassed Towle and appealed directly to Sir Josiah Stamp, Chairman of the LMS Railway, arguing that it had won previous contracts 'upon the quality of our work, although we were not the lowest price'. Unmoved by this representation, Grimwade recommended that Towle accept the lowest tender, that of Messrs Williams & Williams, advice which Towle chose to ignore, preferring instead to employ the Crittall Manufacturing Co. at a higher cost. However, on learning the following day that Hope's were willing to match Crittall's price, he changed his mind and offered Hope's the contract – perhaps swayed by the quality of its product, perhaps by a word from the Chairman. Not only did Grimwade consider that the LMS would now be paying more than necessary for the windows, he was also upset to see his contingency fund, already dangerously low, being eroded still further.

Meanwhile, Oliver Hill had managed to get his way with the Lounge floor. This was to be of 'Biancola' terrazzo (a composite of marble chippings set in a cement matrix and then polished) with a seahorse mosaic designed by Marion Dorn as its central feature. The Lounge walls would be sprayed with 'Marb-L-cote' plaster, vertically combed and painted a pinky-beige colour, the use of which would extend up the staircase as far as the walls of the corridors.

The Rebuilding Committee had approved a seahorse design for the statues above the main entrance. It confirmed that these would be carved by Eric Gill who had also been commissioned to create a ceiling medallion above the stairwell, a map of North West England in the Children's Room and to carve the stone panel in the Lounge. In Gill's sketch for the panel, however, the mermaids advocated by the committee were nowhere to be seen. Instead, several naked youths were portrayed cavorting in a watery landscape, a composition the committee deemed too risqué for the delicate sensibilities of LMS hotel guests. It asked Gill to produce a toned down version.

(Hill had also persuaded the committee that Marion Dorn's seahorse design should be adopted as the emblem for the new hotel. It would appear etched into the ends of the staircase handrails and feature extensively on crockery, glassware and table linen – even on the hotel flag which had been designed personally by Hill. His instructions to flagmakers Piggott Bros. of Bishopsgate, London were unequivocal: 'Herewith full size details of Flag, both sides to be similar. The ground azure blue, the wave bands in white, and the seahorse in silver, also one half of the eye in vermilion, the other half white, and the bristles in vermilion.')

With the seahorse statues approved, Goulding asked Jenkins & Son to deliver the Portland stone blocks as soon as possible so they could be built into the concrete wall over the main entrance. He also wanted to arrange a date for F.Bradford & Co. to make a start on the external rendering 'as this work will take a good time as there is much to do'.

By the beginning of February the optimism of the previous month had started to evaporate. Severe frost had brought work to a virtual standstill and the Clerk of Works was getting worried. A conscientious man, Goulding was becoming increasingly frustrated as schedules started to slip further behind. There were insufficient plumbers, doors and lifts were missing and it seemed impossible to instil any sense of urgency into many suppliers. He urged Humphreys to 'push forward' particularly with the flooring, glazing the windows and making the roof watertight, reminding them that 'there is a lot to be done and the time is going on'.

Particular sub-contractors were singled out for Goulding's admonishment. He rebuked Tibbenham's for their casual approach.

> I have heard, with surprise, that you do not expect to start fixing joinery before the beginning of April next and must point out to you that you must considerably improve on this date, especially with the Dining Room.

… and berated Hope's over non-deliveries.

> I wish to point out that you are seriously delaying progress of the work. We shall be ready for the staircase windows in the course of a few days and trust, therefore, that you will endeavour to give us better and quicker deliveries. We are also waiting for, and require urgently, the composite frames to openings on the balconies – the plasterer cannot get on until these frames are fitted.

As for Doulton's, who had not replied to Goulding's request for particulars of the sinks they were supplying, 'They want waking up.'

With February drawing to a close, it was obvious that the north wing of the new building would not be finished for some time and the decision was taken to start demolishing the old hotel on 27 March and not recommence business until the official opening of the new hotel by Lord Derby which had been provisionally fixed for Friday 7 July.

None of the above difficulties seemed to impinge on Hill's progress reports to the members of the Rebuilding Committee, who were told at their March meeting that 142 men were currently employed on site and that 'the various works were proceeding satisfactorily'. In part this was true but to Goulding it seemed as if only the steelwork was 'proceeding satisfactorily'. This was the one bright spot in his life, so much so that he was later moved to write a letter of commendation to Oliver Hill.

> I have to report that Messrs Banister, Walton & Co. completed the steelwork erection … and that the work has been carried out in a very satisfactory manner. Great credit is due to the Foreman and the erectors who, at all times, gave great care to detail throughout the whole of the job. A first class job has been made.

The same could not be said of J. D. Robertson & Co. whose workers were applying the plaster coating to the interior walls — although obviously not at a rate to Goulding's satisfaction.

> The progress of your work is not good enough, and I should be obliged if you would kindly get more men on the job without delay. You have had good scope for the last two weeks to make good progress and notwithstanding that I have repeatedly asked your man to get help, no notice has been taken.

Goulding's blood pressure could not have been improved by news of a strike at Hope's factory in Birmingham. Fortunately, most of their windows had been delivered but not the special handles which the firm had recently been instructed to make. In the event, the stoppage did not last long and disruption was minimal.

In spite of all the various setbacks, the hotel was steadily taking shape. Brickwork was complete, the floors were in and the asphalting of the roof virtually finished. Inside, screeding for the 'Biancola' paving was underway, the room partitions were in place and electricians were fitting the latest tube lights to the staircase window. The water storage tanks, each capable of holding 2,000 gallons, had been delivered and hoisted to the roof, while pipe fitting to the boilers and cold water services was in progress. A start had been made on installing sanitary ware in the lavatories.

Outside the hotel, preparatory work had begun on the gardens with advice and plants from Mr G. Alexander of the LMS's Gleneagles Hotel. The sandy soil presented serious problems for anything other than grass and, although he recommended the addition of '10 to 12 cuts of good soil for spreading round the roots when planting', Alexander's choice of trees and shrubs seemed wholly inappropriate both in numbers and species. Where he envisaged locating 18 spruce, 12 pine and 24 yew — trees which could reach between 20 and 60 metres in height — is difficult to imagine, and while privet and holly were suitable for hedging, the rampant rhododendron would soon have created a problem in the hotel's relatively restricted surroundings. In the event, common sense prevailed. The trees were abandoned and the grounds eventually laid down to grass interspersed with a few clumps of low-growing shrubs.

In the last week of March work began on the demolition of the old hotel. First to go was the adjoining stable block which for many years had been occupied by Fahy's Garage. By the middle of April the roof had been stripped and much of brickwork knocked down but a further three weeks would be required for the job to be finished. The addition of several demolition men to the hotel workforce helped make the second week of April the busiest of the entire construction programme with 172 workmen from eighteen different firms employed on site.

April also saw the vacation of the adjacent office of T. W. Ward so that its demolition could take place and the Café's terrace and steps built – but, as the office building was half on LMS owned land and half on Corporation land, nobody was quite sure who was responsible for pulling it down. The nearby weighbridge also needed dismantling but was still required as a considerable amount of scrap metal had yet to be removed. With the rail lines onto the stone jetty about to be lifted, Ward's finally managed to clear the site by using its own coaster to transport the remainder of the scrap by sea to other depots.

Back in the new hotel the heating system had been switched on and appeared to be functioning satisfactorily. Ventilation fans had been installed in the kitchen, good progress was being made with the tile flooring, glazing of the windows was nearly complete as was asphalting of the roof, and a start had been made on polishing the external render. Engineers from Marryat & Scott were fixing the passenger lift.

However, things were not going well in the Café. Eric Ravilious and his wife had arrived but were unable to make a start on the mural as the base paint on the walls had blistered and peeled. Goulding believed the problem was caused by the paint being applied too hurriedly with insufficient time elapsing between each coat. He ordered the walls to be stripped and underpainted with an insulator. This appeared to solve the problem but before Ravilious had finished sketching the outline, heavy rain found its way through the Café roof, soaking the ceiling and walls. Despite the use of a

By mid-March 1933 demolition of the old hotel is well under way, gradually revealing its replacement behind. The roof has been stripped of slates and workmen are busy dismantling the rafters.
(Morecambe Visitor)

portable heater, the plaster took several days to dry thoroughly. There were no such problems for the sculptor Eric Gill and his assistant, Donald Potter, who were finishing carving the seahorses high above the hotel's main entrance and were nearly ready to begin work on the stone panel in the Lounge which was being fixed to the wall by workmen from Jenkins & Son.

As April slipped into May and the days lengthened, Goulding took stock of the position. On the positive side the structural work was essentially complete. The boilers were in and working; windows were glazed; the terrazzo flooring was laid and ready for polishing; plastering was well advanced; Tibbenham's had begun panelling although progress was slow; carpenters were hanging doors and fixing wardrobes; James Gibbons' men were assembling the staircase balustrade; Eric Ravilious had at last managed to make a start on the mural and Eric Gill was busy carving both the Lounge panel and the ceiling medallion. On the negative side Haden's were having problems with the pipe-work (Goulding blamed an incompetent foreman who was later sacked) while Bradford's – despite doubling their workforce – were a week behind schedule with the polishing of the render. The continued presence of their scaffolding was hampering other jobs, such as the laying of outside paving, and was a major worry for Goulding. The timescale was tight. With only two months to opening day it would be touch and go.

Meanwhile, Oliver Hill had calculated that the bulk of the furniture, curtains, linen, crockery and glassware needed to be delivered to the hotel in the third week of June by which time the building should be secure – a date which seemed rather optimistic considering he was still making changes to the configuration of the rooms and much of the furniture, especially the beds, had yet to be manufactured. This in itself appeared a somewhat odd process, with examples of box-mattresses being sent from LMS stores in Derby to Tibbenham's so that they could make the bedsteads, examples of which would then be sent back to Derby for the appropriate mattresses to be made!

Hill continued to concern himself with every minute detail of the new hotel, from the design of the clocks to the front door mats, from the shape of the hooks in the bedrooms to the letter rack in Reception. He was very particular about the number of cushions allowed in each room – 'four per sitting room in smooth silk material' – and the colour of the bedroom curtains which were to be 'mostly blue, some beige, all with buff linings', while a special 'Morecambe blue' was to be used for the waste and linen baskets and the pear-shaped bell-push. He also specified the number and type of all the different chairs to be supplied throughout the hotel, although Arthur Towle, still suspicious of some of Hill's ideas, insisted he be sent a chair to try personally as soon as one was available as he 'must be satisfied that all the easy chairs for the sitting rooms, bedrooms, lounges, etc are of the most comfortable type'.

On 23 May, Hill reported to the Rebuilding Committee that

the structure, grounds (including the new entrance drive) and the boundary walls were now generally complete and that all the finishing trades, that is to say, those

Two similar views, taken from the Winter Gardens but some 25 years apart.

Tram lines curve towards the original Midland Hotel with its many chimneys and shuttered windows. The adjacent building, once the hotel's stables, is occupied by Fahy's Garage. Part of the Winter Gardens' fairground can be seen bottom left while next to the road are a few stalls, probably serving refreshments. (Lancaster City Museum)

A gleaming new Midland Hotel dominates the seafront. Motor cars have replaced the horse-drawn carriages and a line of purpose-built kiosks (one selling postcards) has taken over from the ad-hoc arrangement of stalls. (Barry Guise)

engaged in painting, panelling, the erection of bedroom fittings, wall finishes, floor specialists, lift constructors, were well advanced and … there were generally no delays on the work.

By the beginning of June, according to the original contract, the hotel should have been nearing completion but much still needed to be done. Hill arrived on site to check on progress and issue instructions for some of the finishing touches. His attention to detail had not waned. Humphreys, for example, were not only notified precisely what colours and shades of paint to buy but also where to purchase them!

I have selected "Duresco" cream white, shade No 422 for the walls and ceilings of all Guest Bedrooms, Lobbies and the three Private Sitting Rooms. Will you please place your order for this with Messrs. John Line & Sons, 214, Tottenham Court Road, W.I.

… and …

I have approved the pattern of Japonette No 103 for the colour finish of the walls and ceilings to Lounge, Staircase, Ground, First and Second Floor Corridors, Walls and Ceilings. Please place your order with Messrs. Blundell, Spence & Co. of 9, Upper Thames Street, E.C.4.

Anything not to his satisfaction had to be re-done. Tibbenham's earned his displeasure for 'the yellow colour you have put on the Dining Room panelling, the walls, dado and walnut mouldings. I have instructed your polisher to strip it all off with acids if necessary. This finish is not the finish of the pattern I gave you originally and would have completely wrecked the effect of the Dining Room.'

They had very little time to comply as Towle wanted the public rooms, a bedroom and a sitting room finished by the end of June. The LMS required photos for its brochure which had to be printed in time for the opening day.

(These were taken on 4 July by Dell & Wainwright, official photographers to the *Architectural Review*, who had set new standards in architectural photography through their expressive camera angles and dramatic use of light and shadow. Oliver Hill was one of the first architects to recognise that high quality photographs reproduced in architectural journals could be of great value in promoting his work.)

Even at this late stage, some jobs were still lagging behind and overtime was being worked by most firms. Goulding was urging Bradford's workmen to 'take some quick and serious action' in finishing the outside walls so the scaffolding could be dismantled – furniture and carpets were arriving soon and he didn't want any dust getting into the hotel. Elliot & Sons were encouraged to 'expedite delivery and fixing of the revolving door, as it is very important that we get the building shut up without delay'.

By mid-June Eric Gill had finished the Lounge panel and the ceiling medallion (leaving its painting to his son-in-law Denis Tegetmeier) and had begun carving the North West England map in the Children's Room. The staff quarters, including the manageress' rooms, were ready for occupation and the kitchen had been handed over. Most of the carpets were down and furniture for the first floor bedrooms was being delivered. Against all the odds, Ravilious and his wife had nearly finished the mural, despite having to cope with the inconvenience of workmen laying the Café's wooden floor at the same time!

Nevertheless, for Goulding an element of desperation was creeping in. Would he be blamed if the building was not finished on time? Would everything be ready for the opening ceremony? To his relief, this had been put back to 12 July at Lord Derby's request, giving him a few more precious days. The last two weeks passed in a whirlwind of painters, plumbers, electricians, carpet fitters, curtain hangers, etc, – all trying to complete innumerable small tasks while the hotel staff weaved their way between them as they were put through their paces in preparation for the big day.

The morning of Wednesday 12 July was dry and warm with a gentle breeze off the sea. On the promenade holidaymakers were enjoying the summer sunshine and, together with many residents, were looking forward to the official opening of the resort's gleaming new hotel. Also anticipating the event was the town's newspaper. Under the headline 'Morecambe's White Hope' the *Visitor* enthused about the Midland Hotel's 'unique design' and 'striking appearance' and praised the LMS Railway Company for having the courage 'to select Morecambe as a resort worthy of erecting one of the best and most attractive hotels in the country'.

The hotel was scheduled to be opened by Lord Derby at a luncheon in the presence of leading officials of the LMS Railway, civic dignitaries and representatives from the local, regional and national press. Rather surprisingly, given the significance of the building to both the town and the Railway Company, there was to be no open-air ceremony to mark the event, the proceedings being confined to an informal reception, tour of the hotel and then luncheon.

Although the *Visitor* had stated there would not be a public opening, by 1 o'clock a crowd of around 500 people had assembled in front of the hotel – but there was nothing for them to see. Inside, the assembled guests had drunk their aperitifs and were sitting down to a meal of Morecambe Bay shrimps or iced melon, cold soup, a main course of salmon or lamb followed by strawberries and ice cream and coffee – all served on the hotel's specially commissioned tableware. The lack of any sort of public opening ceremony was a big disappointment to many, especially as the *Visitor*'s editor had declared that 'The coming of the new Midland Hotel has fired everyone with enthusiasm' and asserted that 'from Easter onwards every visitor has gazed in wonderment for hours upon the unique white building until they have scarcely been able to believe they were in the Borough of Morecambe'. He was convinced that 'Those who may not have visited our shores before will be moved to say "So this is Morecambe – the Golden Gate of the West"'.

PLAN OF TABLES

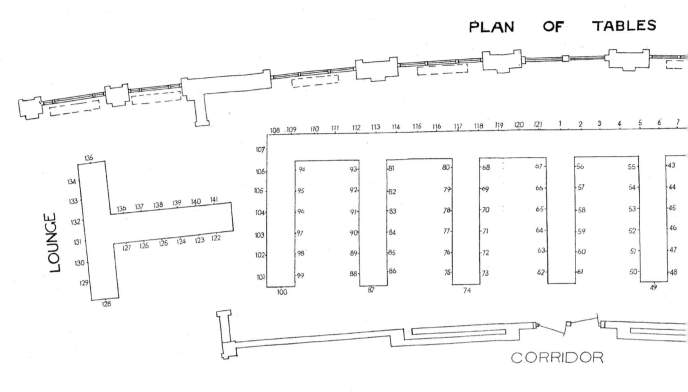

LOUNGE

CORRIDOR

MIDLAND HOTEL

MORECAMBE

	Seat No.
F	
Fahy, Councillor, J.P.	107
Fahy, Miss	110
Fielden, E. B., M.P.	6
Follows, J. H., C.V.O., C.B.E.	56
Follows, Mrs.	66
G	
Gates, Councillor A., J.P., Lord Mayor of Liverpool	4
Gardner, Councillor W., J.P., Mayor of Morecambe and Heysham	121
Gardner, Mrs.	7
Gill, Eric	55
" Glasgow Herald "	111
Glyn, Major Ralph, M.C., M.P.	20
Gourlay, W.	63
Gray, A. C., " Press Association "	93
Grimwade, Clive, F.S.I., F.F.A.S.	137
H	23
Harris, D. J.	116
Hartley, Sir Harold, C.B.E., F.R.S.	130
Helme, Mrs. A. E., Mayor of Lancaster	68
Helsbey, J. B., " Topical Press "	22
Hill, Oliver, F.R.I.B.A.	9
Hirst, Stuart	119
Hirst, Mrs.	5
Hichens, W. L.	81
Hichens, Mrs.	77
Holt, H. E.	30
" Hotel and Catering Weekly," Quarry, W. E.	
Hurst, B. L.	34
I	
Inwood, F. M., London Editor, " Starmer Newspapers "	26
J	
Jackson, H., " Thos. Cook & Son, Ltd."	21
James, S. H., " Pickfords, Ltd."	124
Johnstone, J.	126
Jones, E. W.	8
K	79
Knutsford, Rt. Hon. Viscount	
Kay, J. A., " Railway Gazette "	

	Seat No.
L	59
" Lancaster Guardian "	53
" Lancaster Observer," A. J. Gibson, Editor	38
Leigh, Col. F. A. Cortez	46
Leigh, Mrs. Cortez	96
" Liverpool Express "	106
" Liverpool Post & Echo "	10
Longley, Alderman J. W., Lord Mayor of Bradford	13
Longley, Mrs. J. W.	
M	122
	64
Mackay, C. A.	104
" Manchester Daily Dispatch "	101
" Manchester Evening News "	85
" Manchester Guardian "	37
Milligan, J. A.	76
Middleton, R. M., Town Clerk, Morecambe and Heysham	72
" Morecambe Boro' Advertiser ", F. P. Broom	92
" Morecambe and Heysham Visitor "	140
" Morning Post "	88
Morse, A.	84
Morse, Esmond	49
Morse, Mrs.	43
Mosley, H. V.	11
Muggeridge, Major C. E.	91
Muggeridge, Mrs.	33
N	
" News Chronicle "	
" Northern Daily Telegraph "	61
O	
Oxenford, Miss P. M.	136
P	117
Pittolo, C.	
Price, E. Cox, Editor, " Hotel Review "	77
Pullar, A. E.	80
Q	69
Quarry, W. E.	
Quirey, J., C.B.E.	79
Quirey, Mrs.	31
R	
" Railway Gazette," J. A. Kay	
Ravilious, E.	

	Seat No.
A	
Allen, G. H. Loftus	
" Allied Newspapers," Manchester Editor	40
" Autocar," Editor, H. C. Lafone	51
B	52
Baker, T. H.	
Banks, Alderman E., J.P.	
Bates, Councillor Capt., M.C., C.C.	127
Beale, H. K.	58
Booth, Charles	35
" Bradford Telegraph," W. Fleming	27
Brook, J. F.	14
Brudenell, W.	102
Burleigh, S. W.	127
Burleigh, Mrs.	129
	45
C	54
Cadwallader, J., " Dean & Dawson, Ltd."	
Capper, Bentley, Editor, " The Caterer "	
Carlisle, Rhoda Countess of	25
Chamberlain, W.	78
Church, R. F.	47
Clay, W. H. C., " Central News "	120
Clay, Mrs.	99
Clegg, P.	60
Coleman, F. C., " Modern Transport "	29
Cooling, F. G.	18
Cowell, F. H.	75
	70
D	139
" Daily Express "	138
" Daily Herald," B. Wilson	
" Daily Mail "	
" Daily Sketch "	39
" Daily Telegraph "	47
Davies, Ashton, O.B.E.	32
Davies, Mrs.	48
Derby, Rt. Hon. Lord, K.G.	83
Derham, Alderman Dr. T. C. H., Mayor of Preston	87
Derham, Mrs.	89
	2
E	12
Entwistle, T., Town Clerk, Morecambe and Heysham	114
Etherton, Sir George, O.B.E.	50
	112

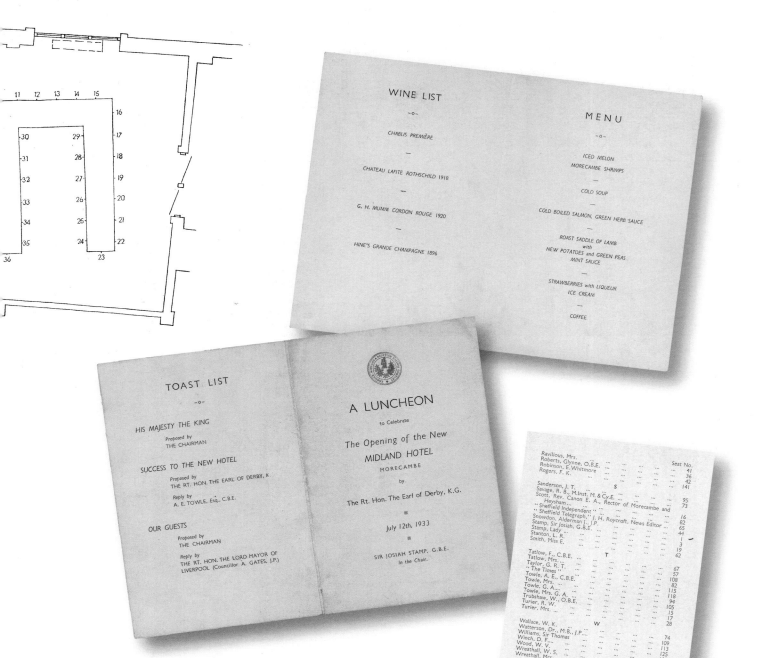

WINE LIST
-o-

CHABLIS PREMIÈRE
—
CHATEAU LAFITE ROTHSCHILD 1918
—
G. H. MUMM CORDON ROUGE 1920
—
HINE'S GRANDE CHAMPAGNE 1896

MENU
-o-

ICED MELON
MORECAMBE SHRIMPS
…
COLD SOUP
…
COLD BOILED SALMON, GREEN HERB SAUCE
…
ROAST SADDLE OF LAMB
with
NEW POTATOES and GREEN PEAS
MINT SAUCE
…
STRAWBERRIES with LIQUEUR
ICE CREAM
…
COFFEE

TOAST LIST
-o-

HIS MAJESTY THE KING
Proposed by
THE CHAIRMAN

SUCCESS TO THE NEW HOTEL
Proposed by
THE RT. HON. THE EARL OF DERBY, K
Reply by
A. E. TOWLE, Esq., C.B.E.

OUR GUESTS
Proposed by
THE CHAIRMAN
Reply by
THE RT. HON. THE LORD MAYOR OF
LIVERPOOL (Councillor A. GATES, J.P.)

A LUNCHEON
to Celebrate

The Opening of the New
MIDLAND HOTEL
MORECAMBE
by
The Rt. Hon. The Earl of Derby, K.G.

July 12th, 1933

SIR JOSIAH STAMP, G.B.E.
In the Chair.

		Seat No.
Ravilious, Mrs.		41
Roberts, Glynne, O.B.E.		36
Robinson, E.Whitmore		42
Rogers, F. K.		141
	S	
Sanderson, J. T.		95
Savage, R. B., M.Inst. M & Cy.E.		73
Scott, Rev. Canon E. A., Rector of Morecambe and Heysham		
" Sheffield Independent "		16
" Sheffield Telegraph," J. H. Roycroft, News Editor		82
Snowdon, Alderman J., J.P.		65
Stamp, Sir Josiah, G.B.E.		44
Stamp, Lady		1
Stanton, L. R.		3
Smith, Miss E.		19
	T	
Tatlow, F., C.B.E.		62
Tatlow, Mrs.		
Taylor, G. R. T.		67
" The Times "		57
Towle, A. E., C.B.E.		108
Towle, Mrs.		82
Towle, G. A.		115
Towle, Mrs. G. A.		118
Trubshaw, W. O.B.E.		94
Turier, R. W.		105
Turier, Mrs.		15
	W	
Wallace, W. K.		17
Watterson, Dr., M.B., J.P.		28
Williams, Sir Thomas		
Winch, D. F.		74
Wood, W. V.		109
Wreathall, W. S.		113
Wreathall, Mrs.		125
		100
	Y	90
Yates, Gordon		86
" Yorkshire Evening News," F. E. Cook		123
" Yorkshire Observer "		97
" Yorkshire Post," Finnerty, W. J.		98
		103

Seating Plan and Menu for the Luncheon to celebrate the
opening of the Midland Hotel on 12 July 1933.
(The National Archives/Anne Greenham)

Hotel staff line up in the Dining Room which has been arranged in preparation for the opening day luncheon.
(J. H. Helsby/Hulton Archive/ Getty Images)

Guests are entertained by a musical trio in the Lounge of the hotel before the official opening ceremony.
(J. H. Helsby/Hulton Archive/ Getty Images)

Aerial view of the Midland Hotel taken in the summer of 1934, a year after its opening. The recently completed Bandstand and Harbour Band Arena can be seen top right. (Bradford Museums, Galleries and Heritage)

If the speeches inside the hotel had been relayed by loudspeaker to the people outside, they would have heard Lord Derby championing the cause of British seaside resorts in more measured language. Toasting success to the new hotel, he urged the relaxation of restrictions in Britain, especially on Sundays, which militated against owners of hotels and restaurants coming into line with their continental competitors. 'It is not the slightest use asking people to come here unless you can give them the accommodation and the life which they desire.' He believed that with the opening of the Midland Hotel the LMS was not only providing a magnificent building for visitors but also setting an example for others to follow. 'May it bring people to Morecambe, may it bring profit to its proprietors, may it bring pleasure to all who come to stay in it.'

Replying to the toast, Arthur Towle, Controller of LMS Hotels, emphasised that the development of tourism in Britain was bound up with hotels. While conceding that only a small percentage of people stayed in first-class hotels like the Midland, he argued that the quality of accommodation in a town was graded down from the top and if the top was right the rest would be right.

Modernism and The Midland

Modernism is not an easy term to pin down, as it has been applied to many aspects of culture and philosophy, as well as social and political issues and was first used in the nineteenth century to mean 'something contemporary'. However, a useful definition which can be applied to architecture and particularly to the Midland Hotel comes from Christopher Wilk's introductory essay to the catalogue for the 2006 Victoria and Albert Museum's exhibition 'Modernism: Designing a New World'

> In the 1930s Modernism became a style, used to identify new and innovative design based on the abstract, rectilinear geometry and the use of industrial forms and materials

Although the Midland Hotel is commonly thought of as a luxury Art Deco hotel, it really belongs more to the International Style of architecture which had its origins earlier in the century. The clean lines and plain white surface of the building signpost a development from the earlier architectural schools of the Bauhaus in Germany and De Stijl in the Netherlands, whose ideas Oliver Hill had clearly assimilated.

Walter Gropius took over the leadership of the Weimar Academy of Fine Art in 1919 and merged it with the former School of Applied Art to form the Staatlicher Bauhaus Weimar. The Bauhaus was key to the founding of the Modernist movement and the school's educational beliefs are still influential in the teaching of design and architecture today. Under Gropius's influence art, design and architecture were united into one philosophy based on a workshop environment which used modern industrial materials and produced goods for large manufacturing companies. There was no place for any form of extraneous decoration or ornamentation, the underlying principle being that everything from a teapot to a building should be simple and functional in design. This 'corporate identity' concept was developed by Gropius and, most notably, by Gerrit

Rietveld of the De Stijl group who designed the Schroder House in Utrecht (1924) which is based on the rectangles, simple geometry and primary colours of a Mondrian painting. He designed every aspect of the living accommodation including innovative ideas for storage (IKEA still borrows from these) and his famous Red/Blue chair.

In the 1930s the relationship between technology, style and materials became increasingly important. The new ideas of practical design found their way into everyday objects as well as architecture, with decorative disguise and unnecessary detail shunned in favour of sleek modelling. While Oliver Hill readily absorbed the stylistic influences of the Bauhaus and De Stijl, he was no hard line Modernist, as can be seen in his design for the Midland Hotel which is gentler, curvier and more lyrical than those of his European counterparts. Hill was aware that the stark continental approach to modern architecture, with its emphasis on flat surfaces, sharp angles and large expanses of glass, might be viewed with suspicion by the British public and believed that his own interpretation would be more acceptable.

Even so, to the unsuspecting population of Morecambe it must have seemed as if an alien spacecraft had landed on the seafront. To build something so modern in a seaside resort whose vernacular architecture was largely Victorian and Edwardian represented a huge gamble for the LMS Railway. Perhaps it saw the streamlined new hotel as a means of revitalising the company's image in an age obsessed with travel and speed, or perhaps it wanted to make a statement that the LMS was at the cutting edge of hotel design. Ironically, while the Midland Hotel may have been radical for the time, in many ways its Modernism was only skin deep, relying more on its shape and proportions than any innovative use of modern materials or construction methods. Built of brick on a bolted steel framework and then coated with cement render, the hotel was, in fact, rather more traditional than it actually appeared.

I feel that the erection of this hotel will do a great deal of good … because quality counts. I hope that visitors are going to roll up in their thousands to patronise the hotel … and we are going to do everything to attract people here, except actually fetch them!

To much applause, Sir Josiah Stamp, President of the LMS, said he had recently seen the most up-to-date hotel accommodation in Chicago, Copenhagen and Stockholm, embodying the latest modernism, cubism and other 'isms' but the new Midland Hotel eclipsed them all. He was confident that when developments around the hotel were completed, Morecambe would have a front of great beauty and dignity which would be a tremendous attraction to the holiday-maker.

With the audience left in no doubt as to the prosperous future in store for the new hotel and Morecambe, the luncheon ended with the National Anthem, after which the guests departed – those from other towns making their way across Marine Road to the railway station where a special train awaited to transport them home.

The passing of the original Midland Hotel was not mourned by the editor of the *Visitor* who, after the opening of its replacement, wrote:

Those who saw the old structure with its limited accommodation, its old-fashioned, green-shuttered windows, and the ugliness of the ship-breaking yard with its derelict warships, massive cranes and zinc-roofed buildings, cannot but be impressed by the wonderful transformation that has been effected. Everything has been swept away. Not a brick or a sentimental piece of furniture has been left of the old hotel. It has been razed from top to bottom, and there has arisen a building the design of which may not please everyone, but it is outstanding and unique.

LMS New Hotel at Morecambe

The LMS Hotel at Morecambe, which is today officially opened by Lord Derby, is the most "up-to-the-minute" seaside hotel in the British Isles and, in fact, in Europe.

Designed by Mr Oliver Hill, RIBA, a leading architect of the modern school, the Midland Hotel, Morecambe, with its modern design and equipment, marks an entirely new phase in seaside hotel construction. It represents an effort to bring to an already prosperous and modernly designed seaside resort, the benefits of a really first-class hotel.

"Sun-trap House" would perhaps be a good designation for the new Hotel, for in its construction special regard has been had to its location so that the maximum sunshine can be obtained; large windows have also been specially incorporated to admit as much light as possible. Balconies facing the sea give a certain amount of shelter from wind and sun, without altogether excluding them.

By a great circular staircase, that rises in majestic sweeps from the Entrance Hall to the roof level, a roof solarium is reached where those who follow the cult of the sun can do so to the full. At night the staircase is illuminated by concealed lights from between double glazed windows. Floodlighting by night will render the Hotel visible for miles out to sea.

There is definitely nothing else like it in the country – a Hotel which stands out as a beacon – a landmark along the whole coast and, incidentally, a landmark in Hotel construction.

(from LMS publicity brochure)

Chapter Three

MORECAMBE'S 'LATEST AND GREATEST'

The new Midland Hotel opened to widespread critical acclaim. Newspapers and specialist journals were alike in their enthusiasm. Under the headline 'Morecambe's Latest and Greatest Landmark', the *Visitor* declared that the hotel 'is so striking in appearance as to arrest immediate attention. The more it is looked at – and it has been gazed upon by thousands and thousands during the course of its erection – the more it is admired'. *Architecture Illustrated* devoted over thirty pages to the building in its September 1933 issue, concluding that it represented 'the best available in the way of hotel design, material and workmanship' and combined 'the essential practical requirements of a modern hotel with all the necessary comfort and grace of environment for its guests'.

Writing in the *Architectural Review*, Lord Clonmore considered the hotel to be in complete harmony with its natural surroundings. 'It rises like a great white ship, gracefully curved … like a great Venus Anadyomene in white cement.' He praised its architectural excellence and simplicity of design and hoped it would have a far reaching influence. 'Good railway hotels are as fitting an ending to a railway journey as a well-attended funeral and a well-worded inscription to a respectable life.'

Country Life also evoked the nautical analogy, describing the hotel as 'a compact, white, curving hull, like a ship's, lying across the sands and looking across the bay to the blue hills of Cumbria'. It commended the LMS for having the courage to do something radically different, challenging the supposition 'that the public always wants the same old thing and will not support imaginative enterprise'. The company's decision to commission the best artists, craftsmen and designers of the day was seen as 'a gesture of faith' earning it comparison to Maecenas, wealthy patron of the arts in ancient Rome.

THE MIDLAND HOTEL

In order to appreciate the attention which the Midland Hotel attracted, some description of Oliver Hill's remarkable new building is required. Pictures can give a much better idea of its appearance than any number of words so the photographs will largely speak for themselves, with only brief explanatory notes plus further snippets from the contemporary reviews.

Approaching the hotel from Marine Road, the visitor would pass through a pair of spiralled entrance pillars topped with glass finials before proceeding towards the main entrance. On the landward side, the smooth concave curve of the building was accentuated by a series of projecting ledges, broken only by the central entrance tower. A blue-green glaze was used to pick out the architraves around Hope's metal-framed windows and the areas beneath the ledges, providing a contrast with the sparkling white façade. To maintain its sleek appearance all rainwater pipes were concealed within the structure. Rising from above the ground-level entrance, the circular central tower projected a little way above the roof; doubly-glazed windows, stretching almost its entire height, were lit from within. The only embellishments on the outside of the building were the stone seahorses, carved *in situ*, at the top of the tower.

The top of the central tower, showing a seahorse carved in Portland stone by Eric Gill and Donald Potter. Some people have claimed, rather fancifully, that the creatures were based on Morecambe Bay shrimps. Whatever their provenance, Gill himself was quite pleased with them. (Dell & Wainwright/ RIBA Photographs Collection)

This postcard by Matthews of Bradford was one of a series featuring the Midland Hotel. (Barry Guise)

THE MIDLAND HOTEL

The seaward aspect of the building followed the convex sweep of the promenade. Fortunate guests with rooms on this side were able to enjoy the use of balconies, separated from each other by obscure-glass screens.

As there was a general belief in the health-giving benefits of fresh air, the spacious flat roof was also designated as an area for sunbathing. A large number of vents had their outlets on the roof and had to be hidden by tubs of flowers. Unfortunately, the flowers could not always be relied on to mask some of the more unpleasant exhalations from the pipes.

At the southern end of the hotel was an open loggia. Its blue-green glazed ceiling was intended to reflect sunshine and water as were the undersides of the balconies. In the original plans, a portico had been envisaged leading from the south-east corner of the loggia (see frontispiece) but in the actual building it was replaced by a simple walkway and steps.

The northern part of the building was occupied by a circular café and terrace. Essentially a one-storey independent block, it was mainly for the use of the general public who could gain access from the promenade without venturing into the hotel itself. Two hundred people could be accommodated at one time, taking tea or making

Steps leading from the loggia to a grassy area originally intended for clock golf.
(Architectural Press Archive/ RIBA Photographs Collection)

The seaward façade of the Midland Hotel, rising 'like a great white ship, gracefully curved'.
(RIBA Photographs Collection)

MIDLAND HOTEL MORECAMBE   OLIVER HILL F.R.I.B.A.

use of the bar or the Australian walnut dance-floor. Furniture was modern tubular steel, the tables topped with shell-pink vitrolite, while in keeping with the hotel's nautical theme the central ceiling light combined a set of lighthouse lenses. The interior solid wall was decorated with Eric Ravilious' mural of day and night views of a fantasy seaside.

The writer of the *Country Life* article was much taken with these pictures but was 'afraid that the paintings may be a little above the heads of Lancastrian bathers. But there's no swimming till you venture out of your depth.'

Entering the hotel from Marine Road, the visitor would have mounted a short flight of shallow steps to reach a doorway at the foot of the circular tower. On either side of the solid, rectangular stone surround the words 'MIDLAND HOTEL' were picked out in projecting blue cellulosed metal in plain, simple lettering. The main verdigris-coloured copper doors would have stood open during the day, revealing a set of wood and glass revolving doors, leading directly into the Entrance Lounge.

Hotel guests were able to make use of Cox & Co's modern metal-framed chairs and tables in the loggia.
(RIBA Photographs Collection)

Liberal use of glass in the 'walls' of the Tea Room/Café afforded excellent views of the sea, promenade and site of the Super Swimming Stadium (opened in 1936). A glazed screen to protect the terrace from the prevailing wind was added later.
(RIBA Photographs Collection)

Inside the Tea Room/Café the
burr-ash veneered counter with
Birmabrite wave motifs continued
the seaside theme of
Eric Ravilious' mural.
(Dell & Wainwright/
RIBA Photographs Collection)

From the bottom of the staircase,
the seashore theme can be recognised
in the floor of the Entrance
Lounge. As well as the inset bands
of silver mosaic there is the seahorse
designed by Marion Dorn and her
ripple-effect hand-tufted rugs. The
easy chairs and sofas are covered
in string-coloured fabric and the
wooden furniture is described
as being 'weathered sycamore'.
Standard lamps by Blunts of
London were widely used on the
ground floor of the hotel.
(Dell & Wainwright/
RIBA Photographs Collection)

THE MIDLAND HOTEL

Once inside, the immediate impression was of light and space. This was achieved by the large windows overlooking the sea and the colour-scheme of the light beige walls and pale Biancola floor. Ivory, blue and silver were used for the fabrics, with the furniture having very simple lines in keeping with the room's uncluttered appearance. Oliver Hill was responsible for the design of all the furniture, including the semi-circular walnut and ebony cases for the Strohmenger pianos, played regularly for the entertainment of guests. Dominating the southern end of the room was the feature for which the Midland has become most renowned – Eric Gill's carved stone panel.

The imposing Eric Gill panel, carved in low relief in polished Portland stone, symbolises hospitality; it depicts Nausicaa welcoming Odysseus onto dry land after his shipwreck on her father's shores. (Dell & Wainwright/ RIBA Photographs Collection)

In the Dining Room the curve of the building is readily apparent. The light fittings are unusual with large oval tubular lamps recessed into the ceiling, the light being diffused by suspended glass rings. Further illumination projects upwards from the dado and window sills. When required, the carpet could be rolled back to reveal a hardwood floor suitable for dancing.
(RIBA Photographs Collection)

The Dining Room was accessed from the northern end of the Entrance Lounge, separated from it by a grille. This was formed of tubular and flat sections of polished aluminium and glazed with both clear and acid-obscured glass. It was matched at the opposite end of the room by a similar screen which hid the service doors to the kitchen. Sixty feet long, the Dining Room's western wall had the same large windows as the Lounge, looking out on to the promenade, while its eastern wall was veneered with pale burr-ash, the panels divided by stainless steel strips. A similar colour scheme to the lounge was used, with ivory satin curtains and chairs upholstered in blue and silver silk.

From the other side of the Entrance Lounge a gently curving corridor led to three smaller rooms: the Writing Room, the Residents' Lounge and the South Room. Darker wood panelling was used in the Writing Room and Lounge while the South Room's walls were coated in beige Marb-L-Cote plaster to accommodate Eric Gill's large incised pictorial map of North West England. (This was excluded from the photo-shoots when the hotel was opened because it had not been completed in time and the room is rarely mentioned in reviews.)

The Residents' Lounge with blue, silver and string-coloured furniture, warm brown and ivory carpet and small circular cocktail bar. The recent, hasty completion of the room can be deduced from the hole in wall awaiting the insertion of a clock. (Dell & Wainwright/ RIBA Photographs Collection)

One outstanding feature, which attracted universal admiration from the contemporary reviewers, was the open cantilevered staircase, spiralling upwards from the Entrance Hall. In *Country Life*'s opinion, it was

Truly both in its airy construction and colouring, a fairy staircase that one would willingly climb till it reached to Heaven.

The steps and landings were actually of reinforced concrete, with blue and white rubber strips let into the treads. Lighting for the stairwell came from the windows running almost the complete height of the tower; these consisted of two thicknesses of decorative glass with electric lights placed between them. The visitor's eye would have been drawn upwards to Gill's medallion of Triton and Neptune looking down on them from the ceiling of the top storey.

Some parts of the first and second floors were occupied by staff accommodation but most were given over to guest bedrooms. The best of these were on the seaward side with their balconies affording breath-taking views across the bay. All rooms were furnished with built-in wardrobes and drawers and simply-designed beds in Nigerian cherry wood. Some of the larger suites had sitting rooms equipped with white burr-ash furniture upholstered in string-coloured woven fabric with blue and white silk cushions.

The spirals of the staircase are echoed by mosaic semi-circles in the ground floor. The seahorse etched into the end of the handrail can just be seen [it appears more clearly in the lower photograph on page 53]. (Dell & Wainwright/ RIBA Photographs Collection)

From the seemingly unsupported staircase with its balustrade of tubular uprights and flat hand rails in polished 'anodium' there is a clear view of a Marion Dorn rug and the grille separating the Entrance Lounge from the Dining Room. (Dell & Wainwright/ RIBA Photographs Collection)

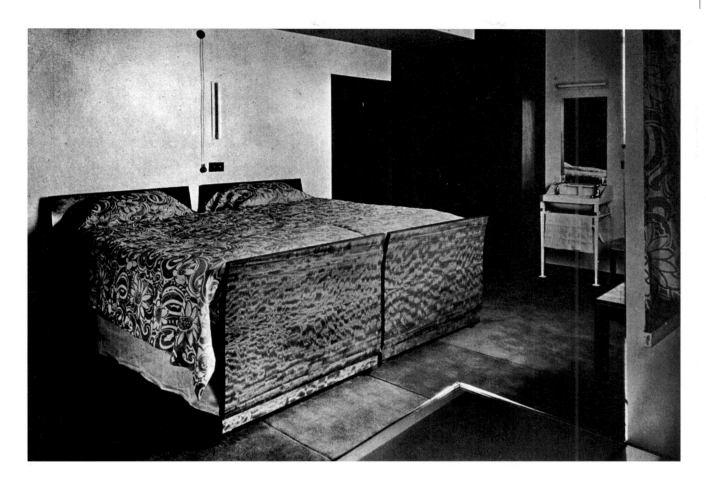

Giving 'just the reminder of the curving motif that is needed to add grace to simplicity', the bed heads and feet have a slight serpentine shape. The wash-basin is illuminated by a strip light above the mirror which is fastened to the wall on a black vitrolite splash-back. (RIBA Photographs Collection)

Having enthused over the 'stairway to Heaven', *Country Life* went into further raptures over the bedroom wash-basins.

I doubt if even Heaven has such good wash-basins … Their supreme merit is that they provide numerous surfaces for one's soap and brushes etc., that are flat and do not project them into the basin. And they provide lovely slots to stand one's tooth brushes in, and instead of a plug or stopper that makes vulgar noises, there is an adorable tethered rubber ball that, as gifted with intelligence, never rolls back into the plug-hole when the water is running out.

Impressed by their first visit, the reviewers were of one mind. *Country Life* summed up their feelings:

This building is obviously the latest thing in construction, materials and decoration. It is exquisite, with nothing cheap or shoddy about it. Everything is of the best … [The Midland Hotel is] in the opinion of many the most beautiful contemporary building in this country.

A later photograph of the staircase and the ceiling medallion. Within the first few months of the hotel opening, the management received complaints that the handrail was too low and the gap between the bottom rail and the steps was too wide. As this compromised the safety of guests, the manufacturers, James Gibbons, were asked to add a new handrail above the original one and a strip of metal at the base. (Anne Greenham)

THE MIDLAND HOTEL
Ground and First Floor Plans

On the Ground Floor the public/guest rooms were located on the seaward (convex) side while the service rooms, along with the main entrance, were on the landward (concave) side overlooking the forecourt. The arrangement of the bedrooms on the First Floor was replicated on the Second Floor.

From the very beginning there was some indecision as to the nomenclature of the principal rooms and different names appear in different publications and at different times. In an attempt to dispel confusion the main variations are given below.

Lounge = Entrance Lounge = Public Lounge = Hall = Foyer.

Writing Room = TV Room

Billiard Room = Card Room = Residents' Lounge = American Bar = Cocktail Bar.

South Room = Children's Room = McEwan Room = Eric Gill Suite.

Dining Room – remained unchanged.

Tea Room = Café = Empire Café/Bar = Seahorse Bar = Royal Lancaster Suite.

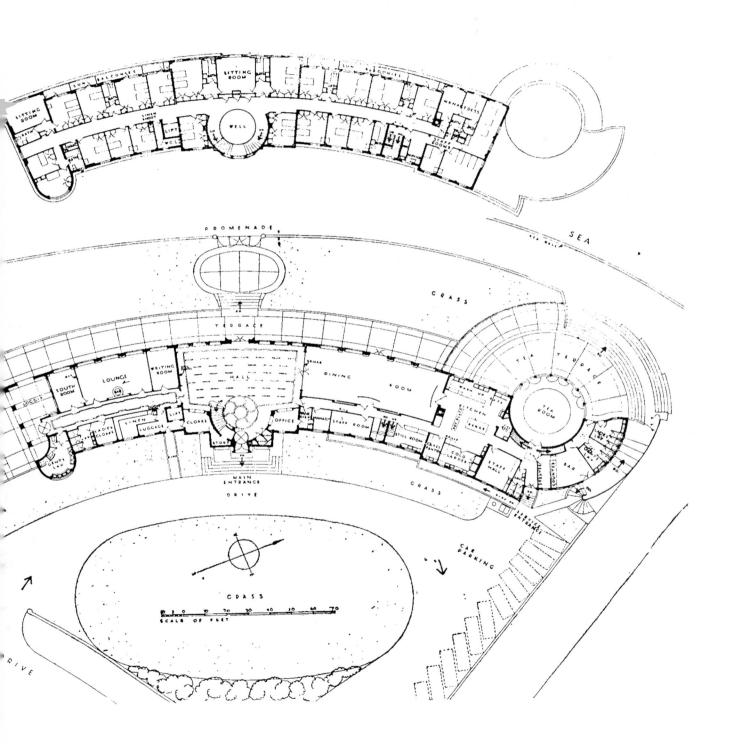

Flushed with Pride

When the Midland Hotel opened in 1933 the newspapers, magazines and specialist journals of the time were full of praise for its radical design, graceful curves and no-expense-spared fixtures and fittings. However, what virtually all the writers tended to ignore was the basic nitty-gritty of the building — the unglamorous and largely unseen elements that actually made it work. One notable exception was Mr E. Cox Price who attempted to redress the balance with an article in the *Architectural Review*, catchily entitled 'Notes on the Equipment of the Midland Hotel, Morecambe'. In it he described in loving detail the intricacies of the Boiler House Plant, Heating and Hot Water Mains, Mechanical Ventilation and Stillroom Equipment. While others were waxing lyrical about the hotel's appearance, he was enthusiastically extolling the virtues of the revolutionary Erith Syphonic Toilet System, even including a measured diagram so his readers could fully appreciate its design from different angles!

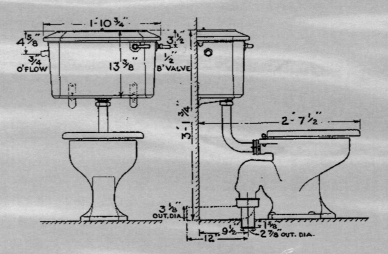

Elevation and section of the type of w.c. fitted at the Midland Hotel, Morecambe. This w.c. is known as the Erith syphonic set. It has a comparatively silent and quick flush, which is a necessary consideration for an hotel. The set is made in Doulfort Ware which is exceptionally strong. *Designers :* Doulton and Company.

Chapter Four
ART IN THE MIDLAND

Once his architectural plans for the Midland Hotel had been confirmed, Oliver Hill turned his attention to the decorative works of art he envisaged for the building. He approached a number of artists, designers and craftsmen whose style he thought might be appropriate, eventually eliminating several on the grounds of either cost or suitability.

In the early summer of 1932 Hill contacted Boris Anrep and Eric Newton, two of the country's leading mosaicists, asking them to submit designs for a fish mosaic to be set in the floor of the Midland's Entrance Lounge. He also wrote to Edward Wadsworth regarding 'a decorative panel to be carried out for a modern hotel' and corresponded with Mary Bone in a similar vein. As Mary Adshead, before her marriage to the artist Stephen Bone, she had been a prize winner for composition at the Slade School of Art in 1924. In his book *A Day in the Sun*, Timothy Wilcox notes that:

> The subject set that year was 'The Picnic'. Adshead created a setting like a seventeenth-century tapestry, showing more concern for tradition than for the contemporary resonances of her theme.

Following Hill's inquiry, she replied that she had done 'one design which I rather like' but felt her style was not really what he wanted, explaining 'I don't think it will suit you as it is more concerned with trippers on the sands, than with smart young things bathing', adding that she found it difficult to do a painting of 'bathing belles' that didn't look like an illustration from *Vogue* magazine. Hill asked her to send him the sketches but emphasised that the design should be 'modern, modest and treated lightly as a background without being too dominant'. He later requested that 'exciting people' be incorporated – but doubted that the Welsh folk where she was staying at St David's in Pembrokeshire were likely to inspire her! Hill kept her designs but chose not to use them for the hotel. Neither did he pursue his initial approach to Edward Wadsworth – who, two years later, would produce a mural with a more abstract marine theme for another Modernist seaside building, the De La Warr Pavilion at Bexhill-on-Sea in Sussex.

In July, Boris Anrep quoted a sum of £800 for the proposed mosaic, stressing that its laying would be a highly specialised job and could not be undertaken by the general contractors. Hill replied 'I fear the figure you mention is far beyond that which may be available.' As a cheaper alternative, he suggested that Anrep might consider a mosaic of six fishes which could be produced in the studio, fixed on canvas and then sent to the hotel to be laid by the flooring sub-contractors. Could he also send a quotation for 'a simplified motif in the centre of the ceiling'? It is unclear whether Hill is referring to the Lounge ceiling or if he had a mosaic in mind for the ceiling at the top of the central staircase. In the event, he obviously found Anrep too expensive and took their correspondence no further.

(The following year Boris Anrep was commissioned by the National Gallery in London for a marble mosaic entitled *The Awakening of the Muses*. This can be seen set into the floor of the first landing in the Gallery's main entrance.)

While Eric Newton's quotation for the floor and ceiling mosaics was more affordable, Hill found his designs 'too busy'. Newton thought Hill might have been misled by the drawings as they did not include the coloured cement between the individual tesserae.

> If however you consider the general type of design too fussy perhaps you would let me have the drawings back for modification. But from my experience of mosaic work, I find that the effect of the actual material is always more subdued and unified than that of the design.

This may well have been the case but Hill had definite ideas of how the decorative scheme of the hotel should appear and had already written to James Powell & Sons on the 9 August 1932 requesting that a selection of mosaic tesserae be sent to Eric Gill who had also been consulted. Newton continued to offer Hill amended patterns for the mosaics, none of which he liked, and, after putting him off for several months, Hill finally informed him that he had 'unfortunately not been able to do anything in the matter of the designs you kindly made'.

(The floor mosaic was eventually designed by Marion Dorn and became a seahorse rather than the fishes originally proposed.)

A similar correspondence took place between Hill and Edward Bawden during March and April 1933 regarding the decoration of a wall in the Children's Room. Hill had asked for a design to be painted on either a roughly combed 'Plastex' surface' over a cement and sand ground or on polished ivory 'Marplax' over a cement ground. Bawden said he preferred the latter and asked if the ground could be kept to a buff or ivory colour. Bawden's first design was not to Hill's taste while his second, based on a tent and valence scheme, caused him even more disquiet as it seemed completely out of keeping for a modern building. Hill relayed his concerns to the artist:

Firstly the curtains of zebra effect may not harmonise with the conventionally striped tent and would I fear look silly. Also the room is so small that I fear it may be easily overloaded with detail and things, but principally because the tent form suggests to me an eighteenth century character rather than one of today.

Bawden protested that he had used such a scheme in a contemporary setting and that Hill 'need have no fear of lack of harmony with the curtains: it is my job to create this, not yours'. He then complained 'Why did you choose these curtains before the decoration scheme was settled, i.e. without my advice?' Hill had no intention of taking his advice, particularly as Bawden's ideas for the internal decor seemed to have little in common with his own. Eager to be rid of Bawden, but at the same time not wishing to hurt his feelings, Hill was unexpectedly given a way to back out gracefully. On 24 March he wrote to him to break the news that the Hotel Company had decided to put a door in the wall and change the function of the room to one which would be available for 'Masonic purposes'. 'Therefore, our playful scheme is killed. I am, of course, very sorry.'

Eric Gill's invitation to work at the Midland arose from his friendship with Oliver Hill. He came to the hotel as a mature artist at the peak of his career. Sculptor, stonemason and typographer, Gill had studied at Chichester Technical and Art School and then the Central School of Art in London. Prior to his Midland commission, Gill's projects had included a series of carvings of the *Stations of the Cross* for Westminster Cathedral, a controversial war memorial for Leeds University and the figures of *Prospero and Ariel* for the front of the BBC's new headquarters in London.

The two stone seahorses seen at close quarters.
(Barry Guise)

It was while working at the BBC in June 1932 that Gill received a letter from Hill asking him if he would be interested in carving two figures for the exterior of a new hotel about to be built in Morecambe. By the end of July other items had been added — mosaic fishes for the floor of the Entrance Lounge, a ceiling mosaic depicting Neptune and a 'Dining Room Panel' in stone with 'dancing nymphs and sea monsters and flowers' — all of which would evolve through various modifications over the ensuing months.

For the external sculptures, the original intention had been to have human figures but the Directors on the Rebuilding Committee were not keen on the proposal and suggested that carvings of seahorses might be more suitable. At the end of February 1933 two blocks of Portland stone arrived from the Torquay firm of H.T. Jenkins & Son and were built into the front of the hotel's central tower, ready to be carved *in situ*.

Eric Gill's preliminary sketch for the ceiling medallion of the Midland Hotel annotated with suggested size and colours. (Velma Reed)

A later watercolour for the medallion which is very similar to the finished version. (Sheffield Art Galleries)

With a small model of a seahorse for guidance, Gill and his assistant, Donald Potter, worked on the figures during March and April. Gill was rather pleased with the finished result. In a letter to Oliver Hill on 23 April he wrote:

> They look good I think – of a kind of solidness and roundness which goes well with the round staircase tower. Of course they haven't much of a front view but that was inevitable.

The marine theme of the Midland's decorative artworks, begun by the seahorse sculptures on the outside of the hotel, was continued indoors. Gill contributed three more pieces, the first of which was a ceiling medallion depicting Neptune and Triton positioned over the circular staircase. He submitted the dimensions of the medallion on 26th February 1933 but told Hill that as he had still to finish the *Prospero and Ariel* commission for the BBC he hadn't had a chance to do anything more. The medallion was to have a diameter of 9' 4'' with colours of red, green and blue against walls of light brown. This corresponds with a preliminary sketch which depicts a bearded Neptune figure enthroned and accompanied on each side by mermaids. A more developed pencil and watercolour study, in which the figure of Triton has been added, was executed by Gill on 5 April 1933 although he inadvertently dated it 1932 – an error noticed by Judith Collins when she catalogued it for an exhibition of Gill's work held at the Barbican Gallery in 1992. Currently in the collection of Sheffield Art Galleries, it is much closer to the final version except that Triton is holding a trident rather than a horn. Another, slightly earlier, drawing is owned by Gill's biographer Fiona MacCarthy. Gill seemed unsure if the design was quite what Hill required. 'Perhaps it is too frivolous or too brightly coloured'. However, he thought that the colours needed to be bright because 'on the ceiling it won't get too much light'.

The final version of the ceiling medallion (showing slight discolouration). The figures depicted are two mermaids/sea-nymphs, an enthroned Neptune and a bearded Triton with horn.
(Pam Brook)

Hill's original idea that the ceiling medallion should be a mosaic – which he had discussed with Boris Anrep and Eric Newton, as well as Gill himself – was eventually abandoned in favour of an incised carving. On 10 April, he wrote to Humphreys asking them to arrange for a

> ten foot diameter circular panel in the centre of the circular ceiling over the Main Stairs, to be in Polished Natural Ivory colour 'Marplax' and raised a quarter of an inch below the surface of the surrounding ceiling, which is to be finished in Marb-L-Cote.

Humphreys wrote back to confirm that this would be done and the resultant piece was carved by Gill and painted by his son-in-law Denis Tegetmeier.

Eric Gill

Eric Gill, sculptor, engraver, typographer and writer, was born in Brighton on 22 February 1882, one of twelve children. Such a large family meant money was tight and his parents often found difficulties in making ends meet. Learning to live with few material possessions, plus a strict religious upbringing – his father was a Nonconformist minister – instilled in the young Eric a sense of self-discipline which was to last throughout his adult life. As a schoolboy he was good at arithmetic and grammar and loved drawing. When the family moved to Chichester in 1897 he enrolled at the local art school where he studied various crafts and, more significantly, developed an interest in lettering.

Hoping for a career as an architect, Gill left for London in 1900 to take up an apprenticeship in the practice of W. D. Caroe, specialists in ecclesiastical architecture. Over the next three years he received a basic grounding in architectural drawing and building techniques but became frustrated with the training. This led him attend evening classes in stone masonry at Westminster Technical School and calligraphy at the Central School of Arts and Crafts, skills for which he displayed a natural aptitude. Encouraged by a number of small commissions from private clients, he decided to give up his architectural studies and establish himself as a self-employed letter cutter and monumental mason.

On 4 August 1904 Gill married Ethel Moore, daughter of the sacristan at Chichester Cathedral, and set up home in Battersea. Growing increasingly left-wing in outlook Gill joined the Fabian Society, actively promoting his socialist views on craftsmanship and art through his writings and lectures. Keen on putting his radical philosophy into practice he moved to the Sussex village of Ditchling in1907 where he was to found a community of like minded artists and craftsmen. In 1913, greatly affected by a visit to a French monastery, Gill and his wife converted to Roman Catholicism, which he felt was more suited to his growing ascetic approach to life. Later that year the Gill family moved to a new home on Ditchling Common, two miles north of the village, gradually converting the outbuildings on his land into workshops which were eventually occupied by a succession of artists and craftsmen, mostly with Catholic leanings.

When war broke out in 1914, Gill was at work on a major commission – the carving of fourteen panels depicting the Stations of the Cross for Westminster Cathedral, a project which would take him four years to complete and for which he was granted exemption from military service. More commissions followed, notably a sculpture of St Michael the Archangel at Dumbarton (his only painted work) and a controversial war memorial for Leeds University based on Christ driving the money changers out of the temple.

In 1924, increasing tensions within the community at Ditchling led Gill to uproot his family and move to a former Benedictine monastery called Capel-y-ffin in the Black

Mountains of Wales. He was soon followed by some of his disciples from the village plus a virtuoso letter carver called Laurie Cribb who would become Gill's chief assistant.

Many people considered Gill eccentric, probably due in no small part to his sartorial idiosyncrasy. His friend Douglas Cleverton described him as being 'rather short in stature, with twinkly eyes behind strong glasses … he always wore a roughly-woven, knee-length tunic or smock, usually belted at the waist, with golfing stockings turned down at the knee'. All this and his grey beard lent him the appearance of a Biblical patriarch – perhaps not such a far-fetched comparison for someone who saw himself very much the head of his remote, quasi-religious community. While at Capel-y-ffin Gill engraved illustrations for the Golden Cockerel Press and was invited by the Government to produce designs for a set of postage stamps and new silver coinage. He also met Stanley Morison who asked him to design lettering for the Monotype Corporation; this resulted in the creation of Gill's famous *Perpetua* and *Sans-Serif* typefaces.

Eric Gill, in trademark beret and smock, working on a sculpture at Moorfields Eye Hospital, London in 1934.
(Fred Morley/Fox Photos/Getty Images)

After four years exile in Wales, Gill returned to England, buying a collection of red brick buildings grouped around a central farmhouse at Pigotts, near High Wycombe in the Chilterns. This would be his home for the remainder of his life. Gill was now in his mid-forties, highly regarded in several fields – and with a growing order book. Prestigious commissions came his way; the first after arriving at Pigotts was for a series of carvings for London Underground's new headquarters where he was in charge of a small team of sculptors, including a young Henry Moore. In 1930, he suffered a breakdown, possibly caused by a combination of overwork and the death of his mother. After recovering, he resumed work with a renewed energy, notably with typography. His designs for *The Four Gospels* for the Golden Cockerel Press are considered by many to be the height of his achievement in wood engraving.

Probably Gill's best known sculpture, that of *Prospero and Ariel* over the entrance to Broadcasting House in Portland Place, was begun in 1931. Working in all weathers on scaffolding in full view of passers by, Gill, in his smock, knee socks and black beret, became something of a public attraction, especially as he was reputed to work without any underwear! One day a young man climbed the scaffolding and asked for a job. Donald Potter, already an accomplished wood engraver and carver, would join Gill on his next major commission – at the Midland Hotel in Morecambe.

Gill was first approached by Oliver Hill in June 1932 to sculpt two figures on the exterior of the LMS's new hotel in Morecambe and to carve a stone relief in the Dining Room. These were executed in the spring and early summer of 1933, together with a ceiling medallion above the main staircase and a map of North West England in the Children's Room, both incised in Marplax plaster. Donald Potter helped with the carving, Laurie Cribb cut the lettering and Gill's son-in-law, Denis Tegetmeier, painted the medallion and the map.

Commissions were also coming from abroad. In 1934 Gill spent several months in Jerusalem carving reliefs for the new Archaeological Museum and the following year began work on three huge panels depicting *The Creation* for the Assembly Hall of the League of Nations building in Geneva.

By the late 1930s Gill's health was failing – he had aged visibly and had become very frail following a bout of bronchitis. Showered with awards and honorary degrees he spent the summer of 1940 writing his autobiography. In October that year he was found to have lung cancer and died on 17 November aged 58.

Following his instructions the lettering on his headstone, cut by Laurie Cribb, read simply:

PRAY FOR ME
ERIC GILL
STONE CARVER
1882 – 1940

Though much of his work was done in the 1920s and 1930s, and he had modernist associates, Eric Gill is rooted in the slightly earlier Arts and Crafts period. Like the medieval craftsmen he admired, Gill saw himself not as an artist but as a skilled workman whose business was 'to make what is wanted for those that want it'. He held strong views against machines and machine-made things and disapproved of the social and economic trends of the times, blaming industrialised commercialism for the separation of artist and workman.

Gill's interpretation of what constituted natural and normal led to some of his work being viewed as erotic even indecent, even though it was allied to a deep religious conviction. This, together with his unconventional lifestyle, has made Gill a controversial figure, his reputation as an artist tending to be overshadowed by a prurient preoccupation with his private life.

The medallion portrays Neptune wearing a crown and enthroned amongst waves with the bearded figure of Triton emerging from the water clasping his golden horn. There are two female figures in the finished picture who are believed to be mermaids. The whole medallion is encircled by text from a Wordsworth sonnet of 1807 which reads 'AND HEAR OLD TRITON BLOW HIS WREATHED HORN', a misquotation from the last line which actually reads 'Or' and not 'And'.

> The world is too much with us; late and soon,
> Getting and spending, we lay waste our powers:
> Little we see in Nature that is ours;
> We have given our hearts away, a sordid boon!
> This sea that bares her bosom to the moon;
> The winds that will be howling at all hours
> And are gathered up now like sleeping flowers;
> For this, for everything, we are out of tune;
> It moves us not – Great God! I'd rather be
> A pagan suckled in a creed outworn;
> So might I standing on this pleasant lea,
> Have glimpses that would make less forlorn;
> The sight of Proteus rising from the sea;
> **Or hear old Triton blow his wreathed horn.**

Gill's use of the sonnet connects the hotel to Wordsworth's home, the Lake District, across the sands of Morecambe Bay. He picked up this romantic theme of the Lake District as a place of innocence and natural idyll again in his incised map of the region in the Children's Room.

Wordsworth's poem refers to Proteus, an ancient sea god who assumed many shapes to evade having to tell the future. In Gill's preliminary sketch the central figure could be Proteus while the female figures at either side of him allude to the line in the sonnet where the sea bares her bosom to the moon. By the second sketch, however, the mythology implicit in the depiction is that of Neptune and Triton. Neptune is the god of the sea who, after the sack of Troy, calms the waves but not until several Trojan ships have been sunk. He stands in the midst of the waves on a chariot drawn by prancing seahorses, brandishing his trident at the winds and threatening to punish them for their audacity. Neptune is generally portrayed as old and bearded holding his trident, although this has been omitted from the Gill's final design. The female figures could represent sea-nymphs, often depicted with scaly fishtails (like mermaids). One of them may be Neptune's wife, the nereid Amphitrite, who bore their son Triton.

In his composition Gill has reversed the youth of Triton and the age of Neptune and the quotation from the final line of Wordsworth's sonnet citing 'Old Triton' engages with this reversal. This may also be explained by the hidden religious meaning incorporated into Gill's work at the Midland Hotel. The hands and feet of Neptune have marks on them which, significantly, are carved into rather than painted onto the plaster. Judith Collins, in her catalogue entry for the Barbican exhibition, relates these marks to the stigmata of the Christ figure taken down from the cross. The apparent youth of Neptune and his central position in the medallion are consistent with a comment made by Oliver Hill in a letter to Gill dated 26 June 1933 when he describes the figure as 'the seated Christ over the staircase'. The attendant mermaids could also be the two Marys at the tomb with Christ still shrouded, called back to the world by Triton's horn. In this picture Gill, like many artists of the Italian Renaissance, successfully gives themes from classical mythology a hidden religious meaning.

Gill's best known work at the Midland Hotel is his large carved stone panel or bas-relief, originally intended for the Dining Room but eventually located in the Entrance Lounge. Entitled *Odysseus Welcomed from the Sea by Nausicaa*, the panel has had a controversial and chequered history dating back well before its completion. Its fluctuating fortunes, owing largely to changes in the ownership of the hotel over the last thirty years, are described in more detail in Chapter Nine.

Oliver Hill and Eric Gill met at the Midland Hotel in August 1932 to consider the design for the panel. One wonders if their discussion revolved around the theme of 'smart young things bathing' as Hill had earlier suggested to Mary Bone. Gill sent Hill his first sketch on 16 August 1932. With the title of *High Jinks in Paradise* it showed a central female figure and two amorous looking couples (all naked) cavorting in the sea, the curling surf of the waves somewhat reminiscent of seahorse tails. 'I hope you'll like the idea and find it suitable – i.e. young things disporting themselves.'

'The King Receives His Guests', Gill's amended design which was thought too risqué for the sensibilities of the Midland's clientele. (Peter Wade)

'Odysseus Welcomed from the Sea by Nausicaa', the design eventually used in the hotel. The panel was positioned in the Lounge to give the impression that Nausicaa was greeting Odysseus as he stepped ashore from the waters of Morecambe Bay. (Peter Wade)

'High Jinks in Paradise', Eric Gill's first idea for the stone bas-relief in the Entrance Lounge. (Peter Wade)

THERE·IS·GOOD·HOPE·THAT·THOU·MAYEST·SEE·THY·FRIENDS

HOMER

Hill wrote back two days later. 'I like the idea of your young things disporting immensely and my only criticisms are that: I think the scale of your figures too large. I feel that being over life size, they would tend to be overpowering and have the effect of making the ceiling appear too low.' In the same letter Hill also asked 'is there not too much movement?'

Gill replied on the 22 August saying he was 'sorry that you think it a bit too lively' but that he would have another go and make the figures smaller in scale. It took him some time, the revised design not being completed until 19 November. In it a central bearded figure wearing a crown sits with a baby at his feet. A child reaches out to the baby. The 'king' offers his left hand, as if in assistance, to a female who, in turn, has her arm linked to a male holding on to a tree. On the left of the scene a second male, his arm also round a tree, seems to be helping another female out of the water. As in Gill's earlier sketch all the participants, apart from the 'king', are nude. In an accompanying letter Gill explained his design.

> The notion is: – The Hotelier welcomes the bathers to his hotel. On the right two of them are emerging from the water – on the left a young man already landed assists a maiden. The idea can be taken symbolically, allegorically, mystically, metaphorically and heraldically, as well as naturalistically!

Hill thought the panel design was 'perfection' and said he would do his best to get the members on the Rebuilding Committee to accept it. However, they did not share his opinion, considering the naked figures unsuitable for the hotel. Gill had previously encountered this type of censure from the governors of the BBC with regard to his *Prospero and Ariel* carvings. Disturbed by the size of Ariel's genital organs, they requested him to make them more diminutive. Although Fiona McCarthy claims Gill enjoyed such scenes immensely, she recognised that he also benefited from the publicity of 'shocking the bourgeoisie'.

(Oliver Hill was quite taken with Gill's rejected designs and asked him to carve two stone panels for the dining room he was planning for the British Industrial Exhibition at Dorland Hall in June and July 1933. Afterwards, the panels were put into storage until 1937 and then used in Oliver Hill's town house at 35, Cliveden Place, London where they remained until the early 1960s. In 1980 they were bought by the Southern Methodist University, Texas.)

Gill's third design for the stone panel, *Odysseus Welcomed from the Sea by Nausicaa*, met with the Directors' approval and is the one which was carved for the hotel. Inscribed with the text THERE IS GOOD HOPE THAT THOU MAYEST SEE THY FRIENDS plus the word HOMER in smaller capitals, the panel is based on three episodes of a story from Homer's *Odyssey*. Odysseus, having been shipwrecked, finds himself washed up on the shore of the Kingdom of Alcinous of the Phaeacians. The king's daughter Nausicaa has been visited by the goddess Athene in a dream in which she is sent to wash clothes at the river. On the following day, after completing her task

Nausicaa and her handmaidens play in the water. When Odysseus is woken by their cries and sees Nausicaa, he covers his nakedness with a leafy bough. However, the reaction of the handmaidens is to run away in fright and it is not until Nausicaa has calmed them down and made them offer Odysseus food, drink and clothing that the scene shown in the panel takes place. He recounts this later to the King at the palace where Nausicaa takes him.

> The sun was on his downward path when I awoke from my refreshing sleep to find your ladies playing on the beach. The princess herself was with them, looking like a goddess. I asked her help. And she proved what good sense she has, acquitting herself in a way you would not expect in one so young – young people are thoughtless as a rule. But she gave me bread and sparkling wine, bathed me in the river and provided me with the clothes you see.

On the surface, the scene suggests welcome and hospitality but Gill intimated further meaning in a letter written to G.K.Chesterton in May 1933. 'Incidentally it is technically what is called a "holy picture" – but the LMS don't know that.' Judith Collins suggests that the religious content might correspond to the phrase in the St Matthew's Gospel 25 vv 35–6: 'For I was hungry and you gave me food, I was thirsty and you gave me drink, I was a stranger and you made me welcome, naked and you clothed me.'

Gill carved the panel out of Perrycot Portland stone which had been supplied by H.T.Jenkins & Son and fixed to the south wall of the Entrance Lounge. Despite Gill's protestations that it was difficult to carve – 'full of holes and sand pockets' – Hill persuaded him that it would look fine once it had been polished. Gill took just over five weeks to complete the carving, leaving the lettering to his skilled assistant Laurie Cribb. Gill was loath to attempt the polishing, suggesting that 'Jenkins' people ought to do it as they know all the tricks.' However, when Hill requested Walter Jenkins to send a polisher up to Morecambe, the managing director was less than enthusiastic. Worried about the possible consequences, he replied:

> I have before me a print of Mr Eric Gill's effective work and my word, I think you are asking pretty much for us to polish this type of work in Portland Stone. Anyway I hope no harm will be done to Mr Eric Gill's work but it will be pretty much to ask us to be responsible if anything does happen.

Fortunately, the polisher was more than competent and the appearance of the finished work was all that Oliver Hill had hoped. Although initially received rather unfavourably by several critics, the panel has since undergone a reassessment and in the opinion of Fiona McCarthy is 'Gill at his best: assured, lighthearted, very supple … much in tune with the spirit of his age.'

While working on the panel, Gill received a letter from Oliver Hill with details of his next commission.

I send you the half-inch plan and elevations of the Children's Room, which is to have the incised conventionalised picture map, and have indicated on the elevation, the scope of the map as I think it should be, bringing the Lake District on the left, the conventionalised view of the Midland Hotel in the centre, Liverpool on the right, with the LMS railway and Royal Scot along the top.

In reply, Gill said that he and Denis Tegetmeier would spend a day or two going round the district noting its characteristic features. He sent Hill an outline design for the map in early June which was approved by the Rebuilding Committee, subject to some minor amendments. Covering most of one wall of the Children's Room, it depicts the Lake District and the Lancashire coast, from Whitehaven to Birkenhead, and was incised by Gill and painted by Tegetmeier. The main centres are represented by prominent landmarks: Liverpool by its two cathedrals, Blackpool by its tower and Morecambe by the Midland Hotel, complete with seahorse. Historic buildings such as Furness Abbey and Lancaster Castle are also included. Along the top of the map the Royal Scot races northwards, emitting billowing clouds of steam which merge with the industrial smoke from the factory chimneys of Liverpool and Preston. Two figures are shown next to the cathedrals — one crawling on hands and knees, the other kneeling in prayer. Across the Mersey a prosperous figure dressed in a tail coat and 'porkpie' hat gestures from his isolated position in Birkenhead — possibly a ship owner as a curving incision in the map joins him to the largest of three vessels afloat on a sea of wavy blue lines.

In contrast, Wordsworth's Lake District is more romantic and lyrical, portrayed by leafy trees, blue lakes and rounded fells. Near Haweswater, hounds chase a fox through the countryside. A couple deep in conversation enter the scene from middle left; close by, a man and a woman float towards each other with outstretched arms. Near the coast, another figure seems to be 'swimming' away from Barrow towards the Lake District.

The stylisation and form employed in the map echo Gill's other work in the hotel. Here it is used to emphasise the distinction between nature/pleasure (represented by the Lake District and the seaside) and industry/work (represented by the towns and their factories). The Lake District might be depicted as an idyllic 'Garden of Eden', but industry is never far away — identified by the smoke which drifts along the coast from the winding engine of the coal mines at Whitehaven to the shipyard cranes at Barrow.

Transferring his design onto the wall, Gill encountered difficulties with the scale of Liverpool's two cathedrals. On 30 June 1933 he wrote to Oliver Hill explaining that, although he drew them both to scale, Lutyens' (proposed) Roman Catholic cathedral appeared surprisingly larger than the Gilbert Scott's Anglican cathedral, a problem he solved by making Lutyens' building partly disappear in the industrial clouds.

(Although its foundations were laid in 1933, only the crypt of Lutyens' grandiose cathedral was ever finished. The present Roman Catholic cathedral now stands on the site.)

The finished map, with its muted colours and hint of mystery, has a unity created by the curling clouds of smoke, Gill's elegant lettering and a series of concentric circles centred on the Midland Hotel. Later enlargement of the Children's Room has enabled the map to be viewed in a proper perspective.

For his work at the Midland Hotel, Eric Gill was paid a total of £400. This comprised £165 for the two seahorses, £85 for the ceiling medallion, £100 for the stone panel and £50 for the map.

The artist Eric Ravilious also worked at the Midland Hotel. Like Eric Gill he had an interest in design and typography and the two men got on well together. According to Fiona MacCarthy:

> There was an immediate compatibility. Ravilious shared Gill's delight in curiosities, the idiosyncratic passing scene, the small-town oddities, as well as his devotion to lettering. They had a common background … of strict Nonconformist parents, and both had been brought up on the south coast.

Ravilious was first contacted by Oliver Hill in July 1932 and invited to design a mural for the circular Tea Room/Café of the new hotel. Hill had been impressed with the murals Ravilious and Edward Bawden had executed for the Refreshment Room of Morley College four years earlier and thought Ravilious' style would be ideal for the Midland. Ravilious accepted the commission and on 17 August wrote to Hill that he had been 'making some drawings for the Tea Room decoration as I had what I think is possibly a good idea', offering to bring them to Hill for his opinion.

On 21 December Hill informed Ravilious that his design for the mural had been accepted by the Rebuilding Committee and that a model of the Tea Room was available if he wished to examine it but stressed that the actual room was still to be built. In fact, it wasn't until the 23 March 1933 that Hill was able to write to Ravilious with the news that:

> The circular room will be ready for you to commence on April 4th. The total height available for your fresco is 11' 7" and it starts 6" above the floor level; there is a "Biancola" skirting round the room.

Ravilious had previously asked Hill if his artist wife Tirzah could accompany him on the project, arguing that 'if the painting is to be finished this summer I would quite certainly need an assistant'. The couple arrived on 10 April and found lodgings with Mrs Brook at her cottage in Lower Heysham. After visiting the hotel for the first time, Ravilious sent an enthusiastic letter to Hill. 'We were delighted with your tea-room at the Midland Hotel, and the seascape outside is all it should be. With any luck my painting will suit the position it is in to a T.' However, once the Raviliouses started work they immediately ran into difficulties. The Tea Room walls were still damp and

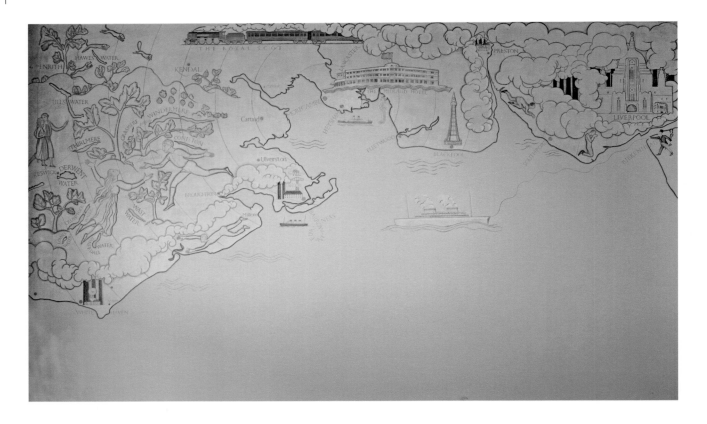

had not dried sufficiently for the paint to adhere properly – the first indication of a series of problems that were to afflict them over the coming weeks, problems which were never fully solved and led to the mural eventually being painted over. Tirzah Ravilious recorded some of the worst in her diary. On 14 April she wrote 'found walls would have to be stripped as paint isn't safe – 2 days work to come off'. Later entries include 'Roof flooded at Hotel, walls and ceiling dripping wet'; 'wall still peeling'; 'this part of wall mended for the third time'. Conditions hadn't improved greatly by the end of the following month. On 22 May she wrote, exasperatedly, 'ceiling wet again due to ventilator leak' while on the 30th the workmen laying the Tea Room's wooden floor 'hammered so hard so had to give up'. To make matters worse, cracks had started to develop in the plaster. On 5 June her diary notes 'patched one crack down left wall – another bad crack appeared right wall' – and so on, a recurring theme.

Ravilious became increasingly worried about the state of the walls but, while Hill acknowledged his concerns, the date for the mural's completion had to be kept. Somehow, against all the odds, Eric and Tirzah managed to finish it in time for the official opening of the hotel on 12 July – but it had been a close run thing. For their efforts they received the sum of £150.

Eric Gill's Map of North West England in the Children's Room. (Anna Goddard)

Contemporary photographs of the completed mural show day and night scenes at an idealised seaside with diving platforms, pavilions, jetties, obelisks, lighthouses etc. Variously referred to as *Morning, Noon and Night* or *Day and Night* or, because it is sometimes seen as two separate works, *Day* and *Night*, the mural's subject matter has a certain ambiguity. No one is quite sure what it represents and whether or not it is a complete fantasy. While not actually depicting Morecambe (hardly surprising since Ravilious had not visited the resort prior to undertaking the Midland commission) it does seem to have several local references woven into the design. The old lighthouse on the stone jetty appears in reworked guise and there are allusions to the Super Swimming Stadium soon to be opened on a site adjacent to the Midland.

In *Day* the architectural forms are decked with triangular flags while biplanes fly in the sky above, all lit by a luminous sun. Three figures float through the air – a naked youth wrapped in a ragged garment holds a trumpet (a reference to Triton's horn perhaps); a female figure, adorned with flags and whose garment tails off into feathers, arrows across the sky; another, almost naked female, partially enclosed in a shell-like cloak, rises above the sea at the point at which the day scene meets the night scene. *Night* shows an explosion of fireworks and a full moon shining on the edge of a platform stretching out to the sea. Both works have an intriguing *trompe l'oeil* effect when seen in relationship to the furniture used in the room. The distinction between the tubular legs of the Bauhaus-like chairs and tables and the architectural forms in the mural appears to blur, drawing the viewer more fully into the scenes as if into the outdoor seascape. Alan Powers sees the aeroplanes and angel-like figures as ancient and modern metaphors for liberation from gravity and earth – like the diver's solitary flight through space – while the fireworks in the night scene suggest subliminally the arousing atmosphere of beaches, sun and hotel encounters. In its open-work forms an angular planes (first used at Morley College), the mural reflects the influence on Ravilious of the artists he had studied during his time in Italy.

Two studies for the Midland Hotel mural are extant. One, entitled *Fireworks*, became the night scene with little alteration, while the other, called *Flags*, was developed into the day scene. In the study for the latter, descending parachutes and a hot-air balloon appear instead of biplanes; there is also the figure of a young boy flying a kite which does not appear in the realised work although many of the quasi-architectural features do. As no colours photographs of the mural exist, it is difficult to determine whether the palette of the studies bears any resemblance to that of the final version. However, there seems no reason why this should not be so. In some ways, the mural is interesting not for what it contains but for what it excludes. At Ravilious' seaside there is no place for people. Instead, he created an abstract interplay of light and dark in a composition where design, not the holiday-maker, is celebrated.

Eric Ravilious

Considered by some art historians to be among the greatest watercolour painters of the twentieth century, Eric Ravilious was born in Acton, London on 22 July 1903, the youngest of four children. While he was still a small child the family moved to Eastbourne in Sussex where his father acquired an antiques shop. Brought up in a strict Non-Conformist household, the young Ravilious showed a talent for drawing at an early age and from his secondary school gained a scholarship to Eastbourne School of Art. After three years hard work another scholarship followed, this time to the Royal College of Art in London where he arrived in the autumn of 1922. Easy-going and charming, if a little shy, Ravilious was a popular student and before long had formed what was to be a long-lasting friendship with two other gifted young artists, Eric Bawden and Douglas Percy Bliss.

Encouraged by his tutor Paul Nash, Ravilious experimented with various media during his course, eventually choosing mural painting for his RCA Diploma examination. He passed with distinction and was awarded the Design School Travelling Scholarship, which he used to visit Florence and Siena where he assimilated the work of the fresco painters of the Italian Renaissance. On his return to England Ravilious found himself caught up in the new enthusiasm for wood-engraving and soon became one of the finest and most original exponents of the art. After leaving college he gained commissions from a number of publishers including the prestigious Golden Cockerel Press. His book decorations and illustrations made striking use of bold tonal contrasts and patterning and set new standards for the medium.

To support himself financially Ravilious took up the offer of a part-time teaching post back at the Eastbourne School of Art which provided him with a small but steady income and the time to do freelance work. It was here in 1926 that he met an attractive and talented art student called Tirzah Garwood who would later become his wife. In 1928 Ravilious and Edward Bawden were selected to decorate the walls of the Refreshment Room at Morley College, an adult education institution in Lambeth. Painted directly onto the plaster walls, the murals took nearly two years to complete and depicted scenes from Elizabethan and Jacobean Dramas, Miracle Plays and Pantomime. They received unanimous praise when the Refreshment Room was officially opened in February 1930 by the Leader of the Conservative Party, Stanley Baldwin. His Parliamentary Private Secretary, Sir Geoffrey Fry, was so impressed he commissioned Ravilious to paint three door panels for the Music Room of his London flat. That summer Eric and Tirzah were married and after two years in London moved to Great Bardfield in Essex where they rented a house with Edward Bawden and his wife before finding a permanent home in the nearby village of Castle Hedingham.

The success of the Morley College murals (sadly destroyed by German bombs in 1940) led to further commissions, one of which was from Oliver Hill, architect of a new railway hotel being built at Morecambe. Ravilious was invited to design and paint a mural for the hotel's circular café, the theme to be the seaside by day and night. Unfortunately, its execution

Eric Ravilious and his wife Tirzah at work on the mural in the Midland Hotel's circular Tea Room/Café. (Towner Art Gallery)

was beset with problems not least the fact that the hotel was being finished in a great hurry. As a result, the plaster of the café walls was not drying properly and cracks were appearing. Ravilious and his wife managed to finish the mural in time for the hotel's official opening but it continued to require constant patching. By 1934 underlying damp problems had caused the paint to peel off so badly that a year later the mural was considered to be beyond repair and was painted over.

In November 1933 Ravilious held his first one-man exhibition of paintings at the Zwemmer Gallery in Litchfield Street, London. Twenty of the watercolours on show were sold, including two sketches for the Midland Hotel mural, entitled *Flags* and *Fireworks*, at 15 guineas each. Both were bought by Sir Geoffrey Fry. By this time Ravilious was now teaching in the Design School of the RCA and spending an increasing amount of time exploring the countryside in search of suitable locations for his growing passion of landscape painting. However, this was not entirely to the exclusion of other activities; he also designed furniture, glass and textiles, produced lithographs, and worked frequently for the Wedgwood pottery factory designing, among other things, a commemorative mug for the intended coronation of Edward VIII. A major publishing project was the illustration of a book on shops called 'High Street' with his friend J. M. Richards supplying the text. He also drew the emblem for the cover of Wisden's *Cricketers' Almanack* which still continues to grace each edition.

In 1937 Ravilious again crossed paths with Oliver Hill who had been appointed to organise the British Pavilion at the Paris International Exhibition. Hill asked him to produce an exhibit typifying tennis (one of Ravilious's favourite games) for the Sports Section. Ravilious also engraved the front and back covers of the official catalogue.

Two more successful shows of his work took place in 1936 and 1939, both receiving excellent reviews. Since his first exhibition, Ravilious' painting style had gradually matured, the earlier muted tones having gained in strength and the subjects approached with a greater confidence.

When war broke out Ravilious joined the local Observer Corps and in January 1940 was appointed as an official war artist with the rank of Honorary Captain in the Royal Marines. Stimulated by the sights and sensations of war, Ravilious produced some of his best pictures in this capacity. After working mainly in Britain for two and a half years he was posted to a Royal Air Force base in Iceland. On 2 September 1942 he went out with the crew of a Coastal Command aircraft intending to sketch a rescue operation. The plane failed to return and after an exhaustive search all hope was given up of finding anyone alive. Eric Ravilious was 39.

'Day'

Eric Ravilious' mural for the
Midland Hotel' Tearoom/Café.
(Dell & Wainwright/
RIBA Photograhs Collection)

Ravilious' friend J. M. Richards
described the mural as 'one of
Eric's gaily ingenious designs,
composed of stylised recreational
scenes, with a background of sea
and sky, fluttering flags and
fireworks.'

'Night'

In the weeks that followed the hotel's opening the mural continued to crack and require patching. Visiting Morecambe in December, Eric Gill was dismayed to see how badly it had deteriorated. He wrote to Ravilious saying he was 'terribly sorry about the Tea Room – I wish I knew what to suggest. The proper thing of course would be for the Railway Company to pay you handsomely to renovate it … but I suppose there is not the least chance of that. It seems a frightful shame to even talk of whitewashing it out, but can you possibly leave it as it is?'

The following March, Eric and Tirzah Ravilious had one more go at the wall which was now dry enough to be repaired but they were fighting a losing battle. As the damp returned and the paint began to peel, Oliver Hill contacted Leonard Barton, a former teacher of Eric Ravilious, who was then head of the School of Arts and Crafts in Lancaster, seeking a solution.

Studies for the Midland Hotel mural. 'Flags' which became 'Day'. 'Fireworks' which became 'Night'. The pictures were shown and sold at Ravilious' first one man exhibition held at the Zwemmer Gallery in London in November 1936.
(Simon Craven)

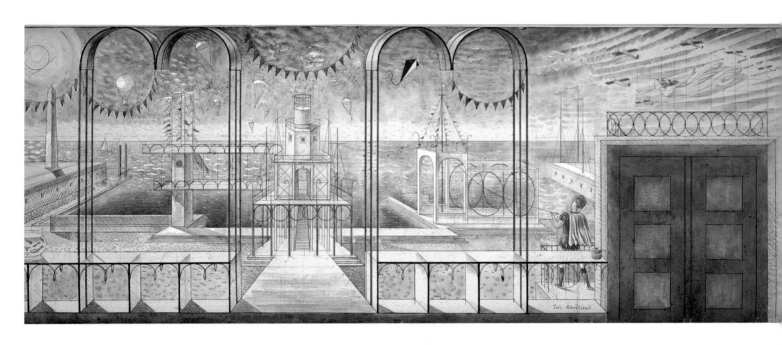

Marion Dorn

Marion Dorn is widely regarded as one of the most imaginative textile designers of her generation. Born into a wealthy San Francisco family on Christmas Day 1896, she studied fine art at Stanford University in California, graduating with a degree in Graphic Arts in 1916. After a short-lived marriage to one of her former tutors she arrived in Paris in 1923 where she met the American artist and graphic designer Edward McKnight Kauffer. Later that year they settled in London, living together for 27 years before eventually marrying in 1950.

During her time in Paris Dorn had developed an interest in textiles and began her career in England as a batik artist. By the mid-1920s she had also started to design rugs and in 1928 began to work with the Wilton Royal Carpet Factory. In 1929 she held a successful joint exhibition with Kauffer at the Arthur Tooth Gallery in New Bond Street which led to a number of significant commissions, notably from prestigious London hotels such as Claridges and The Savoy. Dorn's striking circular carpet for the lobby of Claridges anticipated the interlocking pattern she would employ in her rugs for the LMS's Midland Hotel in Morecambe.

It was probably the favourable publicity she received for her hotel work that brought her to the attention of Oliver Hill. Dorn's designs, essentially abstract in nature, were particularly attractive to modern architects. Most consisted of twisted coils, spirals, zig-zags and geometric patterns, although figurative elements such as stylized animals, plant motifs and shells frequently appeared. Her colours tended to be sombre with the emphasis on cream, brown, beige and grey.

Marion Dorn saw her floor coverings as integral features of a modern interior and wherever possible attempted to create them for specific spaces. This she achieved at the Midland Hotel where she took into account its location and architecture when designing carpets and wave-patterned rugs for its public rooms. She was also responsible for the seahorse which became the emblem of the hotel.

By this time she had become the most influential designer of rugs and carpets for the modern interior and was dubbed 'the architect of floors' by the journalist Dorothy Todd. After the Midland Hotel commission Dorn and Hill became great friends and, in addition to employing her where possible, the architect did all he could to promote her work. He asked her to design the curtains for the staircase windows of Holthanger, a Modernist house in Wentworth, Surrey (1935) and the rugs for Landfall, another of his commissions, at Poole in Dorset (1938). He also encouraged her to show her work at important exhibitions such as that for Contemporary Industrial Art held at Dorland Hall in 1934.

Marion Dorn by Eric c.1941. Eric (Carl Erickson) was an illustrator on Vogue magazine. (Christine Boydell)

In addition to her hotel work, Marion Dorn also contributed to the interior design of a number of ocean liners. Her first commission came from the Orient Line in 1935 where her rugs for the passenger liner *Orion* were used in the public areas of the ship and in the special state room. Two years later she worked on the *Orion*'s sister ship, *Orcades II*. Dorn also produced rugs and fabrics for the Cunard Company's luxury liner *Queen Mary* which made her maiden transatlantic voyage in June 1936.

In 1934 she set up her own company, Marion Dorn Limited, offering her clients a wide range of textile services. Her versatility was illustrated in 1936 when she designed the complete interior of a flat – rugs, fabrics, wallpaper, furniture, graphics, etc. – for the actress Diana Wynyard. The result was praised by *The Studio* as demonstrating 'all the qualities which have made Miss Dorn's work so outstanding in the past. Each room displays a brilliant use of line and colour, the grouping of the furniture is practical and harmonious, and there is an effective combination of contrasted weaves and textures.'

Towards the end of the decade Dorn was responsible for a number of designs for moquette seating fabrics for London Passenger Transport and worked again for the LMS Railway Company, designing a carpet for the saloon of the Royal Train (now in the National Railway Museum, York).

Soon after war was declared in 1939, the American Embassy advised all its nationals to leave England and Dorn and Kauffer reluctantly returned to the USA, settling in New York. After an initial struggle to re-establish her reputation, Dorn began a long-lasting collaboration with the rug manufacturer Edward Fields, running the design department of the firm from 1951 to 1962. She also sold patterns to wallpaper companies and printed and woven fabric manufacturers. The high point of her career came in 1960 when she was invited to design a carpet for the Diplomatic Reception Room of the White House in Washington.

In 1962, after suffering a heart attack, she retired to Morocco where she spent most of her time drawing and painting. The following year she was diagnosed with cancer and died in Tangiers on 28 January 1964, aged 67.

I feel there is much too little good contemporary mural work about, to allow this one to be lost without straining every effort to retain it, and if you can suggest anything before it is too late, I should be grateful indeed.

But Barton could not help and in 1935 Arthur Towle took the inevitable decision that what remained of Ravilious' seaside scenes should be painted over. In a letter of April 1939, written to an old college friend, Ravilious commented on the demise of the mural.

It – the painting – doesn't exist any more; the restaurant was an outside building put up in a wet Lancashire winter and the resulting action on the cement was fatal. When I saw it (and mended the painting) there were brown spots all over the wall like dung thrown liberally at it, and very distressing it all was. I mended the painting but the spots came back worse than ever.

(In 1990 a version of the original mural was reconstructed in the hotel by set designers from London Weekend Television, the Midland having been used as a location for an episode of *Agatha Christie's Poirot*.)

By the time Oliver Hill approached Marion Dorn to provide carpets and rugs for the Midland Hotel, she had already built a reputation as an innovative designer of Modernist interiors. Her patterns were based on simple but strong motifs with an emphasis on colour and texture to harmonize with the objects and furniture of a room. Dorn had a considerable knowledge of production techniques and had already established a strong liaison with companies such as Wilton Royal, H. M. Southwell, Old Bleach Linen and Edinburgh Weavers who produced her designs. As her biographer Christine Boydell pointed out, Dorn's willingness

Sketch showing the interlocking wave pattern of Marion Dorn's design for the circular rugs in the Entrance Lounge.
(Peter Wade)

to work closely with customers helped her acquire more business. In her designs for Oliver Hill's Midland Hotel, Morecambe for example, she worked closely with the architect, taking into account the seaside location of the building, the architectural materials, the colour scheme of the rooms in which her carpets and rugs were to be positioned, as well as the interior fixtures and fittings.

Marion Dorn's partner, the graphic artist Edward McKnight Kauffer, was asked by Hill if he would be interested in doing two posters for the Midland Hotel. Kauffer agreed but advised Hill that before going ahead he ought to arrange a price. 'I will do the two Quad Royal and Double Royal for 150 guineas. In the event the designs are not accepted I shall ask 15 guineas for submitting the "roughs".' Hill must have declined his offer, perhaps put off by the price, as no posters of the hotel by Kauffer have since come to light.

Mosaic seahorse designed by Marion Dorn and set in the centre of the floor of the Entrance Lounge.
(Anna Goddard)

Hill commissioned Dorn for various carpets, rugs and fabric and also the mosaic seahorse that was inset in the terrazzo floor of the Entrance Lounge. It was here that Dorn's most impressive pieces were positioned – two large circular rugs which she described as 'the best rugs I have ever done – for some funny reason'. These were hand tufted by H.M.Southwell of Bridgenorth after Wilton Royal were unable to give a definite confirmation of the order. Each measured 15' 6" in diameter and echoed the marine theme of the hotel with broad bands of wave-like patterns culminating in a curve that strongly related to that at the base of the seahorse tail. Choosing the colours from her personal tuft box she used brown, ivory and brick red to complement the colours of the room. The rugs were positioned in front of Eric Gill's carved stone panel and seen from the Dining Room the curvilinear effect of their bold design offers a contrast to the rectangles of the glazed grille and the ribbon mosaics of the floor.

Marion Dorn was also responsible for the machine-made carpets in the Dining Room and the Residents' Lounge. These had repeat patterns to reflect the colours, shapes and textures of the individual spaces. She was paid 15 guineas for the designs for these carpets and 10 guineas for the rugs. The rugs were lost when the hotel was converted into a hospital during the Second World War and its contents removed and put into storage. In 1990, hand-tufted replicas were made to the same dimensions by Atelier Interiors, Halifax. The colours were changed to Deep Brown/Donkey and Orange/Beige and were more subtle in appearance than the original's strong contrasts.

On 7 March 1933 Hill wrote to Dorn enclosing a half inch plan of the lounge floor and asking her 'to consider the design for the seahorse motif to be inlaid in the centre … using Messrs James Powell's glass mosaics, in silver and "undersea" colours.' She had sent him a design in November 1932 which Hill had liked and he had persuaded the Rebuilding Committee that her seahorse should be adopted as the overall motif for the hotel. Set in the middle of the floor of the Entrance Lounge, the mosaic seahorse broadly follows an S-shaped curve and has a blue and green body partly edged in silver with its eye and 'bristles' in vermilion. Arthur Towle paid Marion Dorn a fee of £20 for the seahorse design, suggesting to Oliver Hill that this amount should cover all its uses in the hotel.

I notice … it is stated this covers the advertising, glass and crockery, but as I also understood it was to be used for carpets, I think it would be better if it were stated that the £20 was an inclusive fee for the use of the design on any equipment of the hotel.

The artists and designers employed by Oliver Hill at the Midland Hotel demonstrated versatility unusual in today's preference for specialism. Eric Gill's combined skills of sculpture and typography, the range of skills provided by Eric and Tirzah Ravilious, and Marion Dorn's skills as a textile designer and mosaicist allowed for a cohesion of style, theme and motif. This resulted in unity in the decorative scheme of the hotel. The work of Gill, Ravilious and Dorn combined stylistically without any loss of individual identity, resulting in an unusual and consequently important landmark of British 1930s decorative style.

One of the rugs is clearly visible through the open doors of the grille separating the Dining Room from the Entrance Lounge.
(Dell & Wainwright/
RIBA Photograhs Collection)

Chapter Five

THE GOLDEN YEARS?

While the appearance of the Midland received unanimous praise, not everyone was impressed with the practicalities of the hotel's design. After training at the Queen's Hotel in Leeds, Noel Jeffrey was appointed Kitchen Clerk and Buyer at the Midland. In his opinion the layout from an internal service point of view was 'quite barmy'. He listed its deficiencies: 'No beer cellar for the Empire Bar. No wine cellar. No dry goods store. No changing room for "outdoor" staff. All had to be excavated alongside the boiler house – originally the only department with interior foundations.' During the hotel's construction there had been no intention of using the basement for services – its purpose was simply to provide a foundation for the floors above – and only later was it appropriated for general service and storage accommodation. Consequently, it contained no damp-proofing, heating or proper ventilation. Three days after opening, following heavy rain, the basement was inundated by backwash from the Corporation sewer. Dry goods floated around on several inches of floodwater, mixing with raw sewage which had risen up through the WC pans in the staff toilets. 'A very nasty and unsanitary state of affairs' observed the Clerk of Works. It was obvious that the drainage system was inadequate to cope with excessive run-off, and while two open gullies were designed to remove surplus water, there was a need to fit the drains with one-way valves to prevent any backwash returning. Despite remedial work, the basement continued to be susceptible to flooding, particularly at times of high spring tides.

In his speech at the opening ceremony, Sir Josiah Stamp had paid special tribute to the main contractors 'for the swift and efficient manner in which they had carried out their work'. The fact that the hotel had been completed 'in marvellously quick time' undoubtedly contributed to the range of problems, both internal and external, which began to emerge over the ensuing weeks and months. There was no doubt that jobs had been rushed and corners cut to meet the 12 July deadline.

After its completion the building was put on a 'maintenance period' for one year during which time the main contractors, Messrs Humphreys, would be responsible

Beauty Surrounds, Health Abounds

When the adjacent seaside resorts of Morecambe and Heysham amalgamated in 1928, one of the outcomes was a new civic crest and the motto 'Beauty Surrounds, Health Abounds'. Whether by accident or design these four words succinctly captured the zeitgeist of the late 1920s and 1930s, a time when the seaside was seen not just as a place for leisure and enjoyment but also as beneficial to health and well-being. Salt water bathing was advocated for its 'restorative' qualities while sunshine and fresh air – especially sea air – were deemed to be good for the 'vital energies'.

This strong belief in sunshine, exercise and outdoor activity as a means of improving one's health can be traced back to the influenza pandemic of 1918–19 (said to have cost more lives than the First World War) and the malnutrition, tuberculosis and unhygienic living conditions prevalent in industrial towns and cities. By the late 1920s the British government had become convinced that improvements in the physical fitness of the nation would not only aid its productivity but its military capacity as well, a view shared by many of its European neighbours. Timothy Wilcox in his essay 'A Day in the Sun' quotes Prime Minister Stanley Baldwin as recognising the need not only to provide jobs, but also leisure.

In Britain, the 'Big Four' railway companies were not slow in recognising this new trend and using it to their advantage. The Great Western Railway installed 'Vita' glass on its Cornish Riviera Express, claiming that it admitted 'health-giving' ultra violet rays and that 'passengers by these new trains will literally commence their sunlight treatment en route to the holiday destination'.

References to outdoor pursuits in the beneficial environs of the seaside also began to appear on railway posters. In common with the other companies, the London, Midland and Scottish Railway

THE NEW LUXURY SWIMMING POOL

MORECAMBE AND HEYSHAM

BRITAIN'S MOST MODERN AND PROGRESSIVE RESORT

EXPRESS SERVICES AND CHEAP TICKETS BY L M S

OFFICIAL HOLIDAY GUIDE FROM ADVERTISING MANAGER, TOWN HALL, MORECAMBE.

The civic crest of the newly amalgamated Borough of Morecambe and Heysham, complete with Lancashire roses and Morecambe Bay fishing boat. (Lancashire County Library)

Drawn by Frank Sherwin, the poster shows Morecambe's Super Swimming Stadium' which was completed in 1936 and which echoed the Modernist style of the Midland Hotel. (NRM/Science & Society Picture Library)

had long used this medium to advertise those holiday destinations it served. As travel to coastal resorts became more common and competition between rival companies heightened, the quality of the design and artwork of the railway poster rose dramatically, reaching its peak in the mid-1930s. LMS poster art, although generally reliant on portrayals of some of the outstanding countryside through which the railway passed, responded to the changing times by adopting the aesthetically pleasing modern woman in fashionable swimwear for some of its depictions of the seaside. Of particular note is its poster illustrating Morecambe and Heysham's 'new luxury swimming pool'. The principal figure in the foreground is portrayed sunbathing under a parasol, with arms and shoulders exposed. Her high vantage point overlooking the pool suggests, given a degree of artistic licence, that she is sitting at the edge of the roof of the Midland Hotel. The overall image is stylised using the flat colouration typical of railway posters during the 1930s while being representational in its depiction of Morecambe's coastline.

The notion of the slimmer, fitter and tanned physique had developed in the 1920s and had transformed the ideals of Edwardian Britain, particularly with regard to women's bodies. As Christopher Wilk commented:

> It was, of course, the woman's body that was seen and revealed as never before in daily life and, significantly, in magazines and films. Widespread participation in sport (whether Olympic or in a public park) and exercise saw men, and even more so women, dressing both in practical clothing for sport and in fashionable sportswear which drew attention to their bodies,

This is clearly apparent in the LMS poster for New Brighton and Wallasey which shows a woman in a very sporty looking bathing suit on the diving board high above a large outdoor swimming pool. The image is again highly representational and almost photographic in appearance.

*Model of the Super Swimming Stadium.
(Lancaster City Museum)*

In the 1930s the concept of health, happiness and 'fitness for all' was an important part of Modernist thinking. It is significant that not only were swimming stadiums and lidos built in the Modernist style of architecture but so too were 'open air schools' for children and sanatoriums for the treatment of tuberculosis. Such buildings, with their large windows, balconies and terraces, made extensive use of sunshine and fresh air – the main cure for TB at that time. Architects believed these buildings would help counter the effects of poverty and deprivation.

The seaside, as 'a particular kind of desirable environment, exploiting the perceived health giving properties and scenic beauties of sea, beach and coastline' (John Walton), provided the ideal location for this type of architecture. The De La Warr Pavilion at Bexhill-on-Sea in East Sussex and Morecambe's Super Swimming Stadium are just two expressions of Modernist seaside buildings which supported the leisure requirements of the working classes. Other buildings in similar style catered for an entirely different class of visitor. As the poster on page 95 (top) shows, the Midland Hotel is certainly Modernist – seen by the artist as a series of architectural forms dropped into an empty seascape with no adjacent railway station or people in evidence – but it was a building primarily for an elite clientele.

Designed to be light and airy, with furnishings of a minimalist nature, the Midland Hotel was, at the same time, both luxurious and comfortable. Its balconies and loggia were open to sunshine and sea breezes while the roof area, accessed from the top of the circular staircase, was originally intended as a solarium. Phyllis Goodwin, then Miss Busby, the daughter of a wealthy Liverpool businessman, recalled how, in later years she sat in the lounge looking at the staircase and thinking how she "used to fly up it to sunbathe". The hotel's position almost on the beach enhanced the perception of the health-giving benefits of a vacation there, notwithstanding the beauty of the location.

GUIDE BOOK
ON
APPLICATION
TO
TOWN CLERK
WALLASEY

NEW BRIGHTON
& WALLASEY
SERVED BY LMS

FOR PARTICULARS
OF CHEAP FARES &
TRAIN SERVICES
APPLY
ANY LMS
STATION
OR AGENCY

In this Septimus Scott poster the woman's sensible bathing cap and her use of the high diving board suggest swimming as a serious pursuit.
(NRM/Science & Society Picture Library)

Frank Sherwin's poster of the Midland Hotel emphasises the health-giving aspects of the seaside, with people of all ages enjoying the fresh air and sunshine.
(Barry Guise)

The artist for this poster of the Midland Hotel is unknown but the image is based on a photograph which appeared in the September 1933 issue of Architecture Illustrated. (NRM/Science & Society Picture Library)

for putting right any defects discovered. Humphreys were to be very busy indeed. Following a detailed inspection of the hotel on 15 September the Clerk of Works compiled a list of problems which ran to an astonishing 27 pages. Admittedly, some of the faults were minor, some had already been addressed and many were repeated as the report detailed them according to their position on or in the building and then ascribed the blame for them to individual contractors. Few firms escaped censure and several received severe criticism.

Cracks were appearing everywhere, inside and out, some serious enough to allow water to collect and possibly penetrate the building. One fissure, where the café joined the main building, was particularly noticeable. On the roof, the coating of white insulating paint on top of the asphalt was perishing a mere four months after its application; as it turned to powder it was causing the underlying asphalt to craze and crack. Painting generally had suffered from lack of time and certain outside areas had been insufficiently painted or not painted at all, simply because the scaffolding had been taken down before the jobs had been finished. The plastering too had been hastily completed, leaving areas where it was lumpy or loose. Insufficient time had been left for the plaster to dry properly before further work had been carried out and the dampness had caused rusting of metal and shrinkage and warping of wood. This in turn had led to a request being made to Tibbenham's to replace 31 room doors and 34 wardrobe doors; they did agree to do adjustments where necessary but were not prepared to supply any new doors, laying the blame squarely on the dampness of the hotel and its unsuitable state at the time of their original installation. In the café, dampness was still affecting Eric Ravilious's mural which was spotting badly and beginning to deteriorate. The artist returned in the autumn to attempt remedial work but must have realised he was fighting a losing battle. Less than two years later it would be beyond repair and painted over. All was not well with the other art works. Gill's ceiling medallion had discoloured near the centre where alkaline salts had seeped from wet cement used to fill a hole (had a light fitting once been intended?). By mid-September the map in the Children's Room remained unfinished, awaiting the return of Denis Tegetmeier to complete its painting.

The catalogue of faults continued, no detail too small to be excluded. They ranged through unfinished floor tiling, leaking pipes, unfixed radiators, cold towel rails, scratched glass and mirrors, non-drying putty, fading paints and glazes, unsatisfactory curtain tracks, noisy lifts and ventilators, lights that were too big (necessitating cutting of the plaster to fit them in the Dining Room), wobbly lights in the Lounge, wrongly positioned locks and bolts, loose door handles, stiff door handles, missing handles, handles which fell off, broken perimeter chains possibly caused by bad welding but definitely due to 'people swinging on them', 'foreign matter' in the beer pumps and a totally inadequate ice-cream machine. Perhaps this last, which had been worked to well beyond its capacity, is some indication of the popularity of the new hotel in the warm, sunny months after its opening.

Sadly for Mr Goulding he would not be at the Midland to see all the repairs completed, having been informed by the Controller of Hotels that his services would no longer be required after the 25 November. Writing to Oliver Hill on the last day of his contract, Goulding, obviously upset, said that he had suggested to Arthur Towle that 'it would have been in the interest of the Company if I could have seen this through, but as he has replied that he must dispense with my services on the 25th, which is today, I have finished up. I am therefore out of a job for the first time in my life and do not feel very happy about it as I hate idleness.' To rub salt into the wound, Goulding's request for two weeks holiday in lieu of having 'worked very long hours including Saturdays, Sundays and Holidays, for which I have claimed no extra recompense' was turned down on the grounds that it was against the rules of the company. 'Personally, I think it rather mean.'

By the end of the maintenance year most of the minor faults had been put right and Oliver Hill, following an inspection on the 10 July 1934, considered the general condition of the hotel to be 'highly satisfactory'. 'The structure is, in my opinion, perfectly secure and such minor fractures as have appeared are due solely to the exposed position of the hotel and the consequent slight and inevitable movements which take place in the steel framework on account of expansion and contraction. I do not regard any of these fractures as important.'

As if to deny Hill's assertions, the cracks in the rendering steadily worsened over the next eighteen months and the café began to experience some lateral slippage, possibly because no movement joints had been incorporated during construction. In addition, the adjacent terrace had sunk, a result of having been constructed on made up ground. There were also problems with the flat roof where the asphalt had crazed, threatening to let in rainwater. Rain was already getting into several of the bedrooms via the ventilators in the outside wall, all of which would have to be replaced.

Mr Wallace, the company's chief engineer, estimated that it would cost between £2,000 and £2,500 to effect all the necessary repairs. The Hotels and Catering Committee authorised the finance for securing the café wall, renewing the terrace on the seaward side of the hotel and fitting new ventilators in the bedrooms. Although Oliver Hill wanted the defective parts of the façade to be made good in the original render, Wallace believed the problem would just recur and advocated the removal of the faulty areas and their replacement with a coating of smooth cement. Arthur Towle argued that there was no need to spend much on the roof as it was practically never used by guests, and considered it would be sufficient to fill up the cracks in the asphalt from time to time and provide proper insulation from the sun.

The faults may have loomed large in the minds of the engineers and accountants but, for the most part, none of them mattered to the paying public. Not only was the new hotel well-received by the architectural press, it was also a success financially – at least initially. In the first week business was greater than anticipated with receipts totalling £995 of which around 80% came from catering. Unfortunately, the stress of the job and the attendant publicity proved too much for the manageress, Miss Thompson. One of the few women at this level in the LMS, she had successfully run the company's Holyhead Hotel on Anglesey before being appointed to the Midland a few weeks prior to its completion. Unable to cope with the pressure of her new post she had broken down within 48 hours of the opening ceremony and asked to be relieved as soon as possible. On hearing the news Arthur Towle acted swiftly, bringing in the Restaurant Manager of the Adelphi Hotel, Liverpool on a temporary basis. At the next meeting of the Hotels and Catering Committee Towle recommended leaving him there as acting manager, especially as his wife was also trained in hotel work. The committee had no objection and agreed 'to enter him on the weekly pay sheets at £8 per week to include, if found desirable, the services of his wife'.

'Acting' must eventually have become permanent as he was still the Midland's manager three years later when sixteen year old Harry Adams arrived for interview for the job of page boy.

> I had to see the manager Mr August, a Swiss gentleman. He and his wife and child lived in the Midland. He asked me where I'd worked – I was at the Battery Hotel at the time – and whether I thought I'd like the job. I said "I'd like to work here." He told me all the ins and outs of the job – be smart and clean and keep my eyes open in case anybody wanted anything. My uniform was a blue jacket with brass buttons and a peaked cap with Midland Hotel on, and a bow-tie, of course. The head porter was Harry Haycock. He came from the Adelphi Hotel at Liverpool. Nearly all the staff were Liverpool people apart from the waitresses and chambermaids who were local girls.

> I used to go on duty about seven-thirty in the morning till maybe two in the afternoon. If the night porter had a night off or was sick one of the two page boys had to stand in. Apart from the jobs in the hotel we had to go over the road to collect luggage from the trains and we used to take all the dirty linen over to the laundry which was behind the Promenade Station. On Sunday afternoon we used to make many a pound because both page boys would be on duty and one would be sent out onto the car park to help people in and out of their cars. The other went into the gent's toilet with brushes and a comb. When the gentlemen had washed their hands he used to brush their jackets down and get a couple of bob in the hand. The tips you got had to be put in a box called a *tronc* – a French word – and that was opened at the weekend. Of course, the head porter got the lion's share, then the junior porter got his, and the page boys got the least of the lot!

> Most people arrived in cars although some came by train. Sir Josiah Stamp used to come by train, two or three times a year. He was the chairman of the railway and a big, impressive looking man – you had to look up to him in every respect. We had to go across to the station with a trolley and pick up his luggage. Everyone was on their toes

Two elegant ladies pose outside the
newly opened Midland Hotel.
(RIBA Photographs Collection)

when he was there. He would maybe only stay for two or three days and then be off to another hotel – Gleneagles or Turnberry or the Adelphi in Liverpool.

Apart from the porters and page boys quite a crowd of people worked at the hotel. There were four or five reception staff, not all in there at once, of course. Guido Agosti was the head waiter, Gus Elvin was the wine waiter and there would also be waiters and commis waiters – probably about twenty altogether. Then there were about ten or twelve kitchen staff. Mr Massey was the head chef, only a small chap but did he control the kitchen! The meals were first class – even the staff used to eat well.

The Midland was a beautiful place then. At the front were plants, flowers and lawn – everything well kept. Either the commissionaire or head porter would be at the door to welcome guests. The front door itself was a green door which was locked at night and anybody who wanted to come in had to ring the bell for the night porter. A couple of paces inside was a revolving door which actually folded up and went back to the wall. From the foyer there was a glass entrance to the dining room. The other way was what they called the cocktail bar – the American bar at that time. Then there was the writing room with pens and ink and writing paper. At the bottom end was a small

L M S
LONDON MIDLAND AND SCOTTISH RAILWAY
SUMMER RESIDENTIAL EXPRESSES
WEEK-DAYS
MORECAMBE, BRADFORD and LEEDS.

MORNING SERVICE

MORECAMBE	...	...	...	dep. 7 42
BRADFORD	...	...	...	arr. 9 15
LEEDS	...	...	...	arr. 9 28

EVENING SERVICE

LEEDS	...	...	...	dep. 4 55
BRADFORD	...	...	...	dep. 5 10
MORECAMBE	...	...	...	arr. 6 40

This service ran, virtually unchanged, on weekdays from mid-July to mid-September from 1910 to 1966. It was obviously meant for the executive or proprietorial classes who did not have to be in their offices until 9.30am or later and who could leave before 5.00pm.

lounge with a mural on the wall showing the coastline of the North-West. The round building at the far end was the Empire bar, for people coming in off the promenade. The staff could go in there from the corridor and have a drink. One day some chaps came into the hotel, on a day trip from somewhere in Lancashire or Yorkshire. They sat down in the main lounge and kept their caps and hats on. The head porter said to me "walk across there and ask that gentleman to remove his hat". So I went over and said "would you mind removing your hat please." "What for?" I said "well, you're in the residents' lounge and it's custom to take your hat off." "Eh? Bloody Hell! A bloody funny place it is to take your hat off for a pint." Well, we didn't serve pints there so I directed him round to the public bar.

I was surprised when I found out there were only some forty bedrooms because the hotel looked much bigger. Apart from the suites the bedrooms were either double or single, quite tidy and presentable but not very big. A number of staff had quarters in the hotel which looked out over the public bar and the bandstand – there were four rooms on the first floor for the men and another four upstairs for the females.

When the Midland Hotel opened it rapidly became *the* place to stay, attracting the wealthy middle classes and bright young things from across the north of England – continental chic only a train ride away from the big cities, and just across the road from the station. Prosperous Yorkshire mill-owners and businessmen took whole suites for the summer, catching the morning Pullman train to Leeds and Bradford and returning to Morecambe in time for dinner. Socialites came from even further afield in pursuit of luxurious escapism. One such was Phyllis Goodwin, the daughter of a successful Liverpool businessman. When in her twenties, she used to spend every summer weekend with friends in Morecambe – or rather at the Midland, as they seldom, if ever, ventured into the town. The furthest they would go would be the stone jetty. 'We used to walk down there at night and swim and come back at two or three in the morning. We had our own little cliquey set.' Wealthy families would often take over the whole of the first or second floor and throw extravagant parties for specially invited guests. Joan Nantais, whose father worked in the dining room at the time, remembers seeing a plane circle round the bay and land on the beach in front of the Midland, bringing a newly-married couple who had booked in for their honeymoon – just one indication of the class of guest the hotel attracted.

As well as the wool magnates, jewellers, company directors, etc, – what Harry Adams termed 'the higher echelons' – the Midland also played host to theatre stars performing at the town's Winter Gardens. These were the days of Variety and the 'Big Bands'. Artistes such as George Formby, Robb Wilton and Billy Bennett. Harry Roy, Geraldo, Joe Loss, Ambrose, Jack Payne and Henry Hall (once the LMS's musical director) were among the bandleaders who stayed at the Midland in the pre-war years. If he was on night duty at the hotel Harry Adams used to be kept very busy. 'These artistes used to come in from the Winter Gardens after a show and there would be about a dozen hangers-on with them. They would order coffee and sandwiches and, as you were on your own, it was a hell of a job for one man. At that time the bar was closed but the office behind the reception was also a 'dispensary' – where the spirits and beer were kept for the residents after hours – so nobody went thirsty!'

One amusing cameo overheard involved Jack Payne (who had a reputation for being mean) asking Billy Bennett for some change to phone a pal, saying 'I don't want to change a ten-bob note.' Billy replied 'Here's tuppence, Jack, phone the bloody lot!'

Rumours still abound of famous people said to have passed through the Midland's doors in the 1930s – Edward VIII and Wallis Simpson, Winston Churchill, Oswald Mosley, Noel Coward, Gloria Vanderbilt and Coco Chanel among others. Most are probably little more than embroidered myths and any supporting documentation, such as pre-war visitors' books, has long since disappeared.

What was true was that only those of a certain income could afford to stay in the hotel. Even the weekly dinner dances, which were also open to non-

Advertisement in the 'Visitor' 3 August 1933.

MIDLAND HOTEL, MORECAMBE.

Dinner Dances Every Saturday.

Dinner served from 7 p.m.
Dancing from 8 to 11-30 p.m.
Inclusive Charge - - - 10/6
ORLANDO'S BAND.

Telephone: Morecambe 770.

residents, were priced to 'keep the company select'. Anyone who came in would have to pay 10/6 whether they had dinner or not, and it would cost just the same even if they only wanted to dance! Guests were assured that the hotel staff 'would see to it that there was no danger of undesirable people creeping in', a policy which successfully excluded a certain uncouth element although not completely foolproof. The well-dressed Lancaster doctor, Buck Ruxton, was a regular habitué of such functions but appearances can be deceptive – in 1936 he was tried and hanged for the gruesome murders of his wife and maid.

For the casual visitor or those who could not afford the dinner dances there was always the American Bar which became the place to be seen for those locals wishing to make an impression – while the Empire Café would serve anyone with a pot of tea or an ice cream.

A stylish couple walk their borzoi in the promenade gardens next to the Midland Hotel.
(Barry Guise)

As the Midland Hotel's reputation spread, it began to be featured in various travel guides. This advertisement appeared in the first edition of a hotel guide called 'Signpost' (still published today) in 1935. Its author obviously liked the Midland although he was surprised to find such a hotel in Morecambe, 'a place chiefly famed for its shrimps and sand'. The advertisement continued to be included unchanged in the guide until 1939.
(Priory Publications Ltd)

Midland Hotel, Morecambe

ON MORECAMBE BAY, LANCASHIRE
27 Miles from Preston and 65 miles from Carlisle.
(For position see map on page 8, square D.2).

Probably England's most modern hotel—Decoration, lighting and design reminiscent of the super luxury palace of the films.

TO find an expensive, super luxury and ultra modern hotel in Morecambe, a place chiefly famed for its shrimps and sand, is certainly a welcome surprise especially if you are making your way to or from Scotland or the Lakes via the West Coast route. For you only have to deflect your way west a few miles from the main road in order to enjoy the pleasure of feeding and resting at this amazing place. The glittering white building built in a wide curve to conform to the line of the promenade is illuminated by concealed flood lights at night and dominates the whole of the sea front. Inside you will look up in wonder at its magnificent circular stair case and then gaze at the lighting effects, striking colour schemes and decorations of the hall, dining room, cocktail bar and lounge. The wall of the last named is adorned by an amusing and impressionistic map of the district and its activities while the walls of the cocktail bar are panelled most attractively in new empire woods which produce a rich and novel effect. The bedrooms are fitted with every luxury convenience, the furnishing of the place having been entrusted to some of the most famous artists and craftsmen. Terms: Bed and breakfast from 13/-.

64

The autumn of 1939 would mark the end of the heyday of the Midland. Only six years after the hotel opened, its so-called 'golden age' would be brought to a close by circumstances beyond its control. A few months before the Midland welcomed its first guests, Adolf Hitler had become Chancellor of Germany and begun preparations for his country's relentless march across Europe, a campaign that would eventually draw Britain into World War Two. Visitors to the Midland Hotel in the summer of 1939, while aware of events unfolding on the continent, still harboured hope that a conflict might be avoided. Any lingering doubts were dispelled on 1 September when Nazi troops invaded Poland and war became inevitable.

The Midland Hotel forms the backdrop to a display of aircraft, including a captured Messerschmitt Bf 109, assembled on the promenade as part of War Weapons Week in December 1940. War Weapons Week was one of a series of financial drives to boost the nation's savings by encouraging people to invest their money in National War Bonds, Defence Bonds or Savings Certificates. "Here is your chance to help bring victory nearer!" exhorted the campaign publicity. "Help now to beat the Nazis by lending as much as you can to your country." Morecambe's response far exceeded expectations. Originally intended to raise £100,000 in War Savings investments (enough to pay for five bombers), the week's events generated over three times the target figure.
(Lancaster Guardian)

Chapter Six

FROM HOTEL
TO HOSPITAL

The official announcement on Sunday 3 September 1939 that Britain was at war with Germany came as no real surprise to the inhabitants of Morecambe. Though regretting that war had broken out, most people felt a sense of relief that the uncertainty was at last over. Throughout the summer the impending conflict had occupied the minds of residents and holidaymakers alike. Both could not have failed to notice how Air Raid Precaution work had been stepped up as the authorities started to put their contingency plans into operation. In many respects, though, the holiday atmosphere in the town masked the looming crisis. Crowds thronged the promenade and the glorious weather of late August helped take people's minds off thoughts of war, not everyone appreciating the irony of the Astoria Cinema's choice of film that month – George Formby in *Trouble Brewing*.

When the declaration came, many visitors cut short their holiday, urged to go home by loudspeaker vans which toured the town's streets. Others ignored the pleas to leave, determined to enjoy what might be their last holiday for the foreseeable future. For some, however, there was no choice. Within two days of the outbreak of war many of Morecambe's larger hotels, including the Midland, had been requisitioned for alternative uses. In anticipation that London would be the first target for German bombing raids, the Government had drawn up plans to transfer many of its essential departments to safer parts of the country. North-western seaside resorts were seen as ideal locations, being well away from the capital and having the facilities to accommodate large numbers of people. Guests were given 24 hours notice to depart in readiness for the hotels' conversion into offices. Even the well-heeled patrons of the Midland Hotel were not exempt, most packing up and departing within a few hours of the directive. The Music Hall star Florrie Ford and the eminent conductor Sir Henry Wood were said to be among the last to leave as the insurance men moved in to organise the removal and storage of the hotel's contents.

In the event, the expected aerial attacks on London did not materialise and, as a result, it was to be several weeks before the first civil servants were relocated to Morecambe during which time the requisitioned hotels remained unoccupied, much to the annoyance of those hoteliers whose livelihood had been affected. Their criticism was not against the scheme *per se* but at the abruptness of its implementation and the damage it had done to the holiday industry, especially to those hotel workers who had lost their jobs.

After this initial hiatus, large numbers of civil servants began to arrive in the weeks leading up to Christmas. Most were employed in the better seafront hotels along Marine Road East such as the Broadway, Strathmore, Headway and Empress which had been converted into offices for the Money Order Department (part of the Post Office). Nearby, the Registrar of Friendly Societies took up residence in the Grand Hotel while, just off the front, the Elms Hotel became the base for the Charity Commission. Eventually, some 5,000 civil servants found a temporary wartime home in the resort, earning Morecambe the informal epithet 'Whitehall-on-Sea'.

At the other end of the promenade a different story was unfolding. In common with many other seaside resorts, particularly those far removed from potentially threatened areas of the country, Morecambe became a basic training station for the Royal Air Force with its headquarters at the Clarendon Hotel in the West End. In early December, Wing Commander R. S. Thompson was sent to Morecambe to find suitable headquarters and training facilities for a unit which was to consist of 350 staff and 3,600 recruits, all to be billeted with subsistence. He was joined by Wing Commander G. H. Russell who was charged with the requisitioning of buildings which could be used for technical training purposes. RAF Morecambe came into being on 12 December under the temporary command of Group Captain Cox, OBE, AFC. The station comprised No. 7 Recruits Centre and No. 9 School of Technical Training, both eventually to be made up of two Wings divided into eight Squadrons.

The first batch of recruits arrived a month later and from then on the town turned blue as a conveyor belt of newly enlisted airmen spent their first six weeks of military life square-bashing behind the Winter Gardens or along the promenade, bayoneting dummy Germans at Middleton Towers and practising rifle shooting on White Lund. Afterwards, some stayed on to train as flight mechanics, flight riggers and, from 1942, M.T. (Mechanical Transport) drivers but most were posted to other units for specialist training.

The numbers involved were staggering, with tens of thousands of RAF personnel passing through Morecambe during the course of the war. Incoming drafts of recruits were divided into flights, provided with blankets (at the now requisitioned Astoria Cinema) and then billeted in small hotels, guesthouses, apartments and private houses.

Dorothy Coombs' parents owned two adjacent hotels in West End Road and she remembers civil servants and airmen staying there during the war. As a teenager in the late 1930s, Dorothy worked in the LMS laundry next to the Promenade Station.

> The railway was very busy then with the ferries that went across from Heysham to Belfast every night. We had to wash and iron the bed linen from the boats, the dining car linen from the trains and all the laundry from the Midland Hotel. The hotel had top class linen – ecru damask with a seahorse crest. In the summer I worked from 8am to 8pm, and I got ten shillings a week, less twopence for my stamp.

After war broke out Dorothy gave up her job to help her parents, their two hotels illustrating the different billeting criteria in operation at the time.

> Each hotel had 16 bedrooms. One had just been modernised with new furniture and washbasins in every room. This made it suitable for the civil servants who required single room occupancy. We called them Guinea Pigs because they paid 21 shillings a week. Most stayed the whole war and we got to know them really well. They looked after themselves; we just provided the accommodation. The RAF came after Christmas and they went in the other hotel. We had no choice but were glad because you'd got to have some income. Mind you, it was very poor but at least it was turnover and it was all the year round. We had 36 airmen in the 16 rooms, with four single beds in the big rooms. They all had to share one bathroom! We fed them three meals a day – breakfast, dinner and tea. Later in the war we took in WAAFs and then airmen who had come back from overseas service in Africa and other places.

Organising the billeting arrangements for the weekly arrival of new recruits was the responsibility of clerical staff based in the Clarendon Hotel, one of whom was an up-and-coming young actress named Thora Hird. As well as the Clarendon, other West End hotels had been taken over by the RAF. A short distance along the front the Clifton Hotel had become the Officers' Mess, while across Marine Road West the Midland Hotel, in keeping with its clinical whiteness, had been transformed into the Station Hospital. Equipped with 80 beds on the first and second floors, the hospital opened on 17 February 1940. Wing Commander R. C. L. Fisher was appointed Senior Medical Officer, overseeing nine doctors, eight sisters and three staff nurses. By April, three dentists had been added to the staff and one of the senior sisters promoted to the post of matron.

Any pre-war guest returning to the Midland after February 1940 would have found the interior barely recognisable. In the weeks since its requisition all traces of the building's previous life had been eliminated. The changes began at the entrance where the revolving doors had been removed to facilitate the passage of stretchers. Once inside there was no sign of the easy chairs and Marion Dorn rugs that once graced the foyer, nor the Eric Gill bas-relief. Instead, they would be met with all the trappings of a military hospital. The wartime layout of the Midland is still clear to John Wilson who worked there as a NCO ward-master after returning from the Middle East in 1943.

As you went in the building the left-hand side rooms were used as administrative offices by the RAF. The mural in the entrance lounge was covered up during the war. The right-hand side (the dining room) was a large ward. I can't quite remember how many beds there were, probably something like forty on each floor. There were two Nissen huts, also wards, on the grass outside [added in 1943]. They faced out to sea, end on to the hotel. The kitchens were used just the same as they are now. The far end of the building, the round part, was the physiotherapy department. On the first floor, over the top of the main entrance, four of the bedrooms had been turned into two operating theatres. All the other bedrooms were used for individual patients, the number depending on the size of the room. We had X-ray facilities, dental facilities and there was also a dispensary.

Much of the work carried out at the hospital was of a somewhat mundane nature, as was illustrated in an article which appeared in the June 1941 issue of *Morecambe Wings*, the RAF Station's magazine.

The Royal Air Force took over the Midland Hotel on 17/2/40. Since then 3,700 patients have been admitted, some very sick, some sick and some with no definite disease except what *Punch* describes as 'the sight of a job of work sets them all of a tremble'. 160 major operations and 400 minor operations have been performed. The daily attendance at the Massage Dept. averages 33, now declining with the end of the football season. The daily out-patient attendance, excluding the Medical Inspection Rooms, is very large, and if 1/- had been charged for each visit there is no doubt that a Hospital 'Spitfire' could already have been supplied. Over 1,000 airmen alone have been examined and fitted with spectacles. Most airmen will be painfully aware of another Hospital activity. Since the Station started, upwards of 100,000 have been inoculated and vaccinated.

Patients reacted to their stay in the hospital in different ways. Having undergone a minor operation and spent three weeks recuperating, one airman, identified only by his initials R.T.H., was moved to describe his experience in verse (see opposite).

R.T.H.'s hernia operation was typical of the day-to-day medical procedures carried out by RAF doctors at the Station hospital. Although a basement room had been converted into a small mortuary, deaths at the hospital were few and far between. Serious cases tended to be transferred to Lancaster where specialist treatment facilities were available. However, there was the occasionally fatality, usually the result of an accident in the blackout. In addition to these, one WAAF died from acute tonsillitis in April 1942 and another from Lymphatic Leukaemia in February 1943, while John Wilson remembers an airman succumbing to cancer just before the hospital closed. In August 1944 a New Zealand pilot on a training flight from Cark aerodrome crashed on Middleton Sands near Heysham. Badly injured, he was brought to the hospital but died two days later and is now interred in Torrisholme cemetery, a long way from home.

On the Front stands a building, so stately and white,
Where you enter all wrong, but come out all right.
You look round with awe as you enter the portal,
For 'tis the Midland Hotel to the average mortal.

As a hotel it's good, as a hospital better,
They've everything there to the very last letter.
The first thing they do is take name, rank and number,
Then relieve you of things they think may encumber.

Then one floor above, to a cute little suite,
Not even dreamed of by the man in the street.
Two nice cosy cots, with counterpanes white,
They're ours for three weeks, the A/c's delight.

So off with your RAF suits, and on with the new,
A wonderful outfit of red, white and blue.
Then into those cots with sheets gleaming white,
And right off to sleep for the very first night.

Then the very next morn comes Sister quite chic,
To give you an injection with a hypodermic.
"You won't feel a thing!" she smiles with disarm,
As she presses the needle, slowly into your arm.

You don't sing or shout, or wish to go out,
It's the nearest I know to a perfect blackout.
You're placed on a trolley, all covered in white,
Then to the theatre under lovely bright light.

The surgeon waits there, with knives in the pickle,
He's itching to start under your ribs to tickle.
Then off comes the shroud, they crowd round with glee,
All anxious to know what is wrong with me.

"Now! Stand back!" he cries, "for this is no joke,
I think I'm the chap who deserves the first poke."
So in goes the knife, he lays back the flesh,
Then puts in his hand, and tugs at the mesh.

He mutters a prayer, and hisses "I'll learn yer!"
As he pulls on my innards to replace my hernia.
Then stitch, stitch, stitch, the job is done,
The fight against nature once more has been won.

Away goes the trolley with me still on board,
As they dash down the passage, back into the ward.
So opening my eyes, I then looked around,
To see all those faces I'm sure I just frowned.

And now I am happy, the job has been done,
But three weeks in bed will not be much fun.
The Sisters watch o'er us, though well out of sight,
In case we should need them, by day or by night.

So God bless our Sisters, our Orderlies too,
With His aid and their's we'll see this war through.
And when it's all over then thanks be to you,
That we are still under the Red, White and Blue.

R.T.H.

A departure from this normally uneventful routine occurred one day in late February 1941 when patients in the hospital received an unexpected visitor in the person of Princess Mary, the Princess Royal. Accompanied by Air Vice-Marshall W. Tyrell, she was shown round by Group Captain W.V. Strugnell, Commanding Officer of RAF Morecambe, and Wing Commander E. Hillman-Gray, who had succeeded R.C.L. Fisher as Senior Medical Officer the previous August. According to the *Visitor*, the princess 'went from bedside to bedside stopping occasionally to exchange a few words, irrespective of rank. In addition to visiting the sick wards, she was shown the dispensaries and X-ray rooms. She expressed admiration for the efficiency of the hospital and complimented the matron on the charm, beauty and ability of the sisters.'

While the influx of RAF personnel and civil servants provided many hoteliers and landladies with a year-round income and gave a boost to the town's wartime economy, it had not meant the end of Morecambe as a holiday resort. If anything, the opposite was true. Not all hotels and boarding houses had been requisitioned and once the initial crisis of the first few months had passed, holidaymakers slowly started to return, despite a national "stay at home" campaign by the Government. Helped by its relatively safe geographical location – and with the south and east coast resorts effectively out of commission – Morecambe enjoyed a series of successful summer seasons, drawing increasing numbers of visitors from outside its traditional hinterland. People were keen to escape, if only for a few days, from the strain of living in darkened towns and cities with limited opportunities for relaxation and entertainment. In the opinion of Morecambe's 1940 Holiday Guide 'today's holidays are a greater necessity than ever and we feel that by continuing to cater for the health and pleasure of the nation we are fulfilling a duty of the greatest importance', a patriotic assertion which did not completely disguise an underlying element of self interest.

Strangely, one of the first acts of the Government when war broke out was to close down all places of entertainment. Few people could understand the reason for this decision and once the Government began to realise the negative effect

Officers and Sisters photographed inside the Station Hospital (Midland Hotel) after the visit of the Princess Royal on 26 February 1941.
(Morecambe Wings)

HARBOUR GARDENS AND MIDLAND HOTEL, MORECAMBE.   G.5208

Postcard sent to Shefford,
Bedfordshire on 30 July 1942.
"We are having a lovely time here.
The weather is not too bad. It is
a grand place, crowds of folks, you
wouldn't think there was a war on.
Plenty of food. Time is going too
quickly. Love …"
(Barry Guise)

it was having on morale it moved quickly to rescind the order. The re-opening of its theatres and cinemas marked the beginning of a period of unprecedented prosperity for Morecambe's entertainment industry with venues full to capacity thanks to a resident 'captive' audience of civil servants and RAF personnel, bolstered by holidaymakers in the summer months. On offer were seven cinemas (some with programmes changing twice a week), dancing on the Central Pier and at the Floral Hall, a new play every week at the Royalty Theatre, and big name Variety Shows at the Winter Gardens.

Much needed laughter was provided by comedians such as 'Big-hearted' Arthur Askey, Jimmy James, Tommy 'You Lucky People' Trinder, Max Miller the 'Cheeky Chappie' and Lancashire's very own 'Ambassador of Mirth' Norman Evans. Flanagan and Allen came 'direct from the London Palladium', while Lupino Lane brought with him the full West End cast of the popular musical *Me and My Girl*. Ivor Novello had a successful run with *The Dancing Years* as did Austrian tenor Richard Tauber in Franz Lehar's romantic operetta *Land of Smiles*. George Formby, probably the biggest star of the day, was a frequent performer, as were bandleaders Joe Loss, Henry Hall, Geraldo and Harry Roy. More cultured tastes were catered for by the Royal Ballet, Manchester's Halle Orchestra and the D'Oyly Carte Opera Company.

Local ENSA representatives ensured that patients in the Station Hospital did not miss out on all this entertainment. As a Christmas treat in 1940 they made arrangements for the artistes appearing at the Winter Gardens that week to do a one-off performance at the hospital. Volunteers fitted up the ground floor (dining room) ward with footlights and seating and patients sat or lay back, as circumstances allowed, to enjoy the show. Artistes who slipped across from the theatre with greasepaint still fresh were Elsie and Doris Waters (Radio's Gert and Daisy), Les Allen (Canada's Golden Voice of Melody) and comedians George Bolton and Freddie 'Laughs at the Piano' Bamburger, while ventriloquist David Poole brought along Little Johnny Green to tell patients what a hard life a doll leads.

For many visitors another source of entertainment, one that was completely free, could be found every day on the promenade. Here, RAF instructors had the unenviable task of trying to instil the discipline of drill into raw recruits with little or no sense of co-ordination nor timing. Roars of laughter would greet some poor innocent who had inadvertently confused left with right and set off marching in the opposite direction from the rest of the group. Even the WAAFs did not escape the indignity of being the butt of the public's (usually) light-hearted banter. As one airwoman later put it: 'There on the prom the stage was set for a free comedy show for all to enjoy except we, the victims.' Sometimes, however, the public did not always stop at commentary. On one occasion an old lady, objecting to a RAF Corporal's raucous commands, marched up to him and, digging him in the ribs with her umbrella, said: 'Don't you talk so rough to these girls, young man, I won't have it!'

No. 3 WAAF Depot had been established in Morecambe in October 1941, replacing No. 7 Recruits Centre which had relocated to RAF Bridgnorth, Shropshire. The depot, soon re-titled No. 31 WAAF Recruits Centre, was organised on the basis of four Wings each having three Squadrons with an estimated intake and output of 450 recruits daily. An unstinting welcome to the RAF's 'Sister Service' was afforded by the editor of *Morecambe Wings* in the valedictory edition of the magazine.

> We heartily congratulate you on your determined spirit, your zeal, and the part you are playing to overthrow Hitlerism. We are proud of you for helping to make a better world for your children. May your stay [in Morecambe], even though brief, be a happy one. 'Go to it, Girls, and Good Luck'.

Drafts of new WAAF recruits, often a hundred or more in number, arrived daily by train. Before being checked and billeted they were marshalled on the yard outside Promenade Station, an event which never failed to draw an audience of curious locals and holidaymakers. One particular intake, that of 17 April 1942, stuck in the memory of Squadron Officer A. M. Thompson who was WAAF Commanding Officer at the time.

> About an hour before the train was due in I received a message that nearly the whole draft was sick with diarrhoea, etc. I at once informed the Senior Medical Officer [Wing

RAF hospital staff outside the Midland Hotel 1942. In the centre of the front row is the Senior Medical Officer, Wing Commander George Paton – 'a shy man with a great sense of humour'. (Valerie Andrews. Her father, Corporal William Teale, was a medical orderly at the hospital.)

Commander G. Paton] who told me that he was clearing the hospital of every WAAF who was up and returning them to their billets. Any of the new recruits not yet ill would be sent, under supervision, to the 'services café' where tea would be laid on. All worked well, the ambulances were taken right onto the platform and the sick WAAFs carried out and into the hospital. There was one lighter touch. A taxi driver, wishing to help, picked up a WAAF and carried her across the road and into the hospital. But once through the door his nailed boots slipped on the polished marble of the hall and he slid, WAAF uppermost, right across the floor! Luckily, neither was hurt. Over seventy were admitted to hospital. Bad sausages for breakfast were suspected.

Unlike their male counterparts, WAAF recruits undertook a basic training that lasted only three weeks, missing out on rifle shooting and bayonet practice but receiving more lectures, usually delivered in whatever large spaces were available – cinemas, church halls, garages and even the swimming stadium. This meant that passing-out parades, held on the band arena next to the Midland Hotel, were a much more frequent occurrence, sometimes as many as five a week. During her fifteen months in charge at Morecambe, Squadron Officer Thompson calculated that she had passed out over 83,000 airwomen, including Sarah Churchill, daughter of the Prime Minister. However, by the time she relinquished command in January 1943, arrangements were already in place to transfer No. 31 WAAF Recruits Centre to RAF Wilmslow in Cheshire, a move that was completed by the middle of March.

With the WAAF departed, RAF Morecambe continued to function as a Personnel Dispatch Centre, a seemingly endless stream of draft airmen and ex-trainees receiving medical checks, eyesight tests and inoculations before being posted overseas. In July 1943, a typical month, the total was 3,762, comprising 165 officers, 14 civilians, 31 aircrew and 3,552 other ranks. Often their stay in Morecambe was brief, many leaving within 48 hours. According to John Wilson, in the last two years of the war most of the hospital's patients were from the PDC intake.

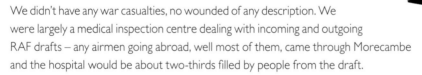

> We didn't have any war casualties, no wounded of any description. We were largely a medical inspection centre dealing with incoming and outgoing RAF drafts – any airmen going abroad, well most of them, came through Morecambe and the hospital would be about two-thirds filled by people from the draft.

As the war progressed, groups of recuperating servicemen began to be admitted to the Station Hospital on a regular basis, so much so that by late 1944 the building was operating more as a convalescent home than a hospital. As a result of this changing function it was decided to close down the Midland's surgical department. Staff and equipment were transferred and the space vacated was reorganised to accommodate facilities based elsewhere in the town – sick quarters from the Memorial Hall, inspection centres from Burtons Buildings and the Temple of Light – thus consolidating all medical activities on one site.

Following the surrender of Germany on 8 May 1945, Morecambe adjusted quickly to the post-war environment. Having emerged virtually unscathed from the conflict it was well placed to take advantage of the approaching holiday season and people's desire to escape to the seaside to celebrate the end of the war. Relieved of their billeting responsibilities, most of the resort's hotels and boarding houses were once again free to offer accommodation to visitors – and they came in their thousands in this first summer of peace, including demobbed servicemen with gratuities to spend and large numbers of airmen and WAAFs who had trained in Morecambe during the war and were returning with their families.

As the first peacetime holiday season drew to a close, fourteen of Morecambe's largest hotels, including the Midland, still remained in Government hands, much to the

An interpretation of the Midland Hotel during World War Two. (David Goard)

"The central image is part of the Midland Hotel but compressed into a Tardis-like structure. This 'impossible' architecture is surrounded by planes and crosses – reference to the hotel's role as a RAF hospital."

chagrin of the local council. Frustrated by what he perceived as a lack of urgency to vacate the properties, Town Clerk, Roger Rose, pointed out that the hotels provided potential accommodation for about 2,000 visitors and their continued occupation was likely to have a detrimental effect on the resort's ability to attract holidaymakers for the following season. Despite his complaints, the civil servants were destined to remain in Morecambe for several more months while awaiting the completion of new offices under construction in Nottingham. There was better news regarding the RAF. Plans to transfer the Station to Heaton Park in Manchester were well advanced and it was expected that by the end of October it would be possible to return all properties – several hotels, the Savoy Restaurant, Arcadian Café, garages and other buildings – to their owners. However, an objection by Manchester City Council caused the move to be delayed by a further two months and it was not until the first week of January 1946 that the RAF finally departed the resort.

Gradually, those buildings once occupied by the RAF began to be derequisitioned and on 16 February 1946 the Midland Hotel's six year life as a military hospital officially ended and it was handed back to the London, Midland and Scottish Railway Company – and an uncertain future.

Lines of people stretch back from the Super Swimming Stadium almost to the Midland Hotel, patiently queuing for admittance to the first ever final of the Miss Great Britain Bathing Beauty Contest. Weekly heats had been held during the summer of 1945, culminating in the final on 20 August. The winner, chosen by film actor Michael Rennie and his fellow judges, was local civil service typist Lydia Reid. For her prize she received seven guineas, a new swimsuit and a basket of fruit. At the time, the Midland Hotel was still in RAF hands and a number of servicemen can be seen among the waiting crowd.
(Lancaster City Museum)

Children enjoying a pony ride on the beach in front of the Midland Hotel. When the photograph was taken (1949) the hotel had not long re-opened after serving as a hospital during World War Two.
(Lancaster City Museum)

Chapter Seven

POST-WAR RENOVATION

After an absence of six years, mostly spent in the Far East, one-time page boy Harry Adams returned to a Midland Hotel very different from the one he had worked in before the war – and to a very different job.

> When I was demobbed I went to ask about my old job back and they said would I take over as caretaker, myself and a chap called Alec Burgman who used to be the cellarman previous to the war. The building was in a dilapidated condition. All the interior had been stripped – there was nothing, no furniture or anything like. A lot of stuff was stored in the cellar but nothing of any value. We each used to do 12-hour shifts. At first it was a bit eerie being alone in a big empty place like that, but you got used to it. We looked after it for about twelve months.

Following the hotel's derequisition, it had been the intention of the LMS Railway Company to re-open the Midland 'within the not too distant future' but when directors inspected the building they found it to be in a far worse state of repair than anticipated. To restore it to its pre-war condition would require a great deal of expense, a situation which prompted the Company's Hotels and Catering Committee to think seriously about the Midland's future. Even before the war, in the so-called 'Golden Age', business had not been particularly good and the hotel was seldom filled to capacity. Profits were never very satisfactory and in 1937 a trading loss had even been recorded. One committee member asked 'Why do we run a hotel at Morecambe? We don't have hotels at Blackpool and similar seaside towns.' Another argued 'We would be better off without it.'

In December 1946 F.G. Hole, who had succeeded Arthur Towle as Chief Hotels Superintendent, submitted a report to the Company's Executive Committee questioning whether the Midland Hotel 'filled a want in the locality' and if it was in the Company's interest to continue to operate the hotel. He added that British Holiday

Estates might be willing to buy the hotel, while enquiries had also been received from other interested parties. However, the Acting President of LMS, G. L. Darbyshire, was not convinced and, in his opinion, it would be difficult to justify a case for disposing of the hotel on the above grounds 'without first considering whether the Company could run it on appropriate lines to meet the demands'.

Further deliberations dragged on through the early months of 1947 and, although essential repairs were authorised to safeguard the structure, the prospects of the hotel re-opening for the summer season gradually receded. A suggestion that the building be leased to the Ministry of Works to accommodate Post Office staff still occupying hotel property in the resort fell through over disagreement concerning the length of tenancy. By autumn, pressure was mounting from Morecambe Corporation for a decision regarding the future of the hotel.

Meanwhile, the high cost involved in renovating the Midland had persuaded Darbyshire to change his mind about retaining the hotel. In October he wrote to Sir Cyril Hurcomb, Chairman of the British Transport Commission, proposing that 'it might be more advantageous if the property could be disposed of, possibly for conversion into an hotel more in keeping with the type of business at this Lancashire seaside resort'. Mindful of the effect such a course of action might have on relations with Morecambe Corporation, and aware that the Corporation had discussed the possibility of requisitioning the Midland for housing purposes, the Commission decided against the sale, recommending instead that 'the LMS Company proceed with the rehabilitation of the building and equipment, on the assumption that it will be re-opened to the public next summer'.

By April 1948 nothing had happened, partly because of organisational changes following nationalisation of the railways but mainly the result of confusion over the application for the necessary Ministry of Transport building licence, without which work could not begin. Time was running out if the hotel was to be renovated before the summer season. Concerned about the lack of progress, Miles Beevor, Chief Secretary of the BTC, contacted Lord Inman, who had been appointed Chairman of the newly created Hotels Executive, asking for his views on the future of the hotel. In reply, Lord Inman suggested he make a personal inspection of the building and review its prospects as a commercial proposition. This he did at the end of May, after which he submitted a very positive report.

> My first impressions, on inspecting the hotel, were very favourable. It is an imposing building occupying an excellent position in the centre of the promenade, and I discovered that some of the structural rehabilitation had already been completed at a cost of £2,000. This work consisted broadly of repairs to the roof, restoration of parapet walls, removal of hospital out-buildings and repairs to the external facing. In addition to this work, there will be the necessary internal rehabilitation including re-decoration, re-furnishing and re-equipment. There is also the important question of staff accommodation.

Before the war, eight of the Midland's 49 bedrooms had been allocated to key members of staff, the hotel's other workers finding their own lodgings in the resort. There were plans in hand for a purpose-built staff house but this would not be ready in time for the coming season. As a short-term solution, Lord Inman proposed that a small number of guest bedrooms could be utilised in addition to the existing eight staff bedrooms. While this would reduce the accommodation available for visitors, the hotel could be made ready for at least a part of the coming season and thus would provide an opportunity to ascertain whether the business could be conducted on a profitable basis. It would also keep faith with Morecambe Corporation which had been assured of the Company's intention to re-open the hotel.

To restore the hotel to LMS standards would cost an estimated £27,000, comprising £16,800 for structural repairs, £8,000 to replace internal furnishings such as curtains and carpets and £2,200 for the renovation of wiring and lighting. To offset some of this expense a claim for wartime dilapidations of £10,000 had been lodged with the Government. Under provisions of the Compensation (Defence) Act of 1939 the Railway Company was entitled to compensation for loss of earnings resulting from the requisition of its hotels, the actual amounts being based on net annual profits.

Having obtained the requisite building licence, work commenced on Monday 14 June using both local labour and LMS employees, with re-opening pencilled in for the middle of July.

Peter Johnson was one of the contract plumbers brought in to repair the hotel pipework. He didn't think much of the original system.

> The internal pipes had screw joints sealed with soldered metal rings, many of which had corroded over time and developed leaks. In the bedrooms the pipes had been encased in wooden frames, covered with wire mesh and then plastered over. Access to them involved opening up the wall and making good afterwards — a messy and time-consuming job.

Other pipework presented different problems.

> The original metal pipes which served the bar pumps from the cellar barrels had been disconnected and dumped in the cellar. These pipes still had beer in them and dried 'scum' on the inner walls. We had to pump gallon upon gallon of cleaning salts through them and even then I wasn't sure if they were thoroughly clean. When the hotel re-opened I went into the bar with a friend of mine and told him 'Don't drink anything from the pump.' But he ignored my warning, declaring afterwards that it was 'a damn good pint!'

He recalled teams of men and girls descending on the hotel from the LMS workshops at Derby and setting up in different bedrooms, 'the men to repair and French polish the furnishings — wardrobes, doors, etc., and the girls to make curtains and sew on the 'ring and eye' fittings for the carpets'. Even the hotel's original artwork did not escape 'refurbishment'.

> Blands of Morecambe were engaged as painters and one of their men, while retouching the Neptune scene on the central tower ceiling, painted Neptune with his 'natural features' openly, not decorously covered. This caused endless amusement, not least among the various females passing beneath – that is until the lady inspector arrived to view the ongoing work. This lady [probably Miss P.M. Oxenford, Chief Officer for Domestic Services] must have been very well trained in hotel stewardship – she did not miss a thing. You can imagine the explosion re Neptune! The guilty painter was told in no uncertain terms to immediately remove the offending addition to Neptune's anatomy.

After five weeks of intensive renovation work and almost nine years since its last paying guests departed, the Midland Hotel finally re-opened for business on Thursday 22 July 1948 with Mr A.V. Gill appointed as Resident Manager. For some reason the event was completely ignored by the *Visitor*, a puzzling omission considering the number of pages it had devoted to the hotel's original opening. In the *Morecambe Guardian* the news merited only a tiny paragraph, easily overlooked, on one of the inside pages.

> Residents and visitors in large crowds stopped in their tracks, halted by the spectacular effect of the reflected light from the grand entrance hall of the Midland Hotel, which was re-opened on Thursday. Blacked out during the war years when it was used as a hospital, the glass fronted reception hall, extending almost from ground level to the roof, glowed like an emerald in its newly redecorated setting. It was visible from the high ground over a wide area.

While the description of the hotel emitting a green glow may have been questionable, there is no doubt that the lights in the central staircase tower would have been considerably brighter than before the war, the old bulbs in the windows of the tower having been replaced by the latest neon tubing.

(While the *Morecambe Guardian* might have enthused about the Midland Hotel's new lighting when it re-opened, the *Visitor* was less than complimentary about its contribution to the town's Illuminations which had been revived in 1949. 'What an outstanding display the British Railways could have made on the Midland with its commanding position but, as in pre-war days, their indifference was reflected by a dozen anaemic floodlights.' Such bad publicity did not go down well with the Chief Hotels Superintendent who asked the hotel's manager for an explanation. Gill, somewhat piqued, claimed the display was no different from pre-war days and that several guests had remarked how nice the hotel appeared when floodlit. Determined not to be similarly castigated the following year, Hole agreed to spend £110 on the hire of nine floodlights with amber coloured screens, a decision which dismayed Miss Oxenford. She appealed to Hole. 'I would beg that we should not sink to amber floodlighting, not even at Morecambe.')

In spite of a lack of local publicity, the Midland was relatively successful in attracting custom during its first season. Many of its pre-war guests returned, possibly for reasons of nostalgia or simply out of curiosity. They were joined by a new clientele seeking a touch of luxury in the austerity of post-war Britain but only those who could afford the prices – daily inclusive terms from 33/- per person, bedroom with private bathroom from 42/- per person, breakfast 4/-, luncheon 5/-, afternoon tea 2/6 and dinner 6/6.

As winter approached, Gill took stock of the hotel's first summer season and wrote to the Hotels Executive suggesting a number of changes which he felt would be beneficial for the following year. These included: moving the American Bar to the old Children's Room (then used as an office) and possibly incorporating part of the sun loggia to make a larger space; changing the Café into a Lounge Bar with access for the general public; and restoring the bedrooms occupied by hotel staff to visitor use. While sympathising with Gill's request, Hole was wary of committing any more money for the time being.

> Having regard to our pre-war experience and to the fact that it would be unwise to decide on any major change in the light of only one season's business, I have decided that these proposals should not be developed at the moment and that the hotel should be operated in its present form until the end of next summer so that we may then consider what the future policy is going to be.

Hole's reservations were confirmed when the hotel's accounts for the first year's business were published. Although the number of visitors was slightly up on the average pre-war figure and total receipts had almost doubled, any potential profit had been eaten away by increases in expenditure, most noticeably a quadrupling of salaries and wages. When general overhead expenses were taken into account, the Midland Hotel, in its first year since re-opening, had actually incurred a trading loss of £3,300. In addition, bookings were down for the coming winter months, a situation which led the Hotels Executive to contemplate closing the hotel at the end of November and re-opening again the following Easter. This possibility troubled E. R. Cottet, Area Superintendent of the BTC, who outlined his concerns to the Hotels Executive. Acknowledging

Advertisement for the re-opened Midland Hotel in the 1949 Morecambe and Heysham Holiday Guide. (Morecambe Library)

MIDLAND HOTEL

MORECAMBE

Telephone : Morecambe 2591

An outstanding example of modern architecture, furnishing and decoration. The Hotel is on the shores of Morecambe Bay, opposite Promenade Station

Summer Terms: Inclusive rates from 33/- per day

Enquiries for accommodation will receive the prompt and personal attention of the Resident Manager

The Hotels Executive British Transport London, N.W.1.

Midland Crockery

During its lifetime the LMS Railway was a significant purchaser of pottery items from the Stoke-on-Trent area. Plates of all sizes, cups and saucers, cream jugs, gravy boats, etc, were all required to enable its hotels, refreshment rooms, dining cars, sleeping cars and staff canteens to operate. Each piece carried the company's identity letters, partly as a safeguard against theft, but also to serve as a reminder of the LMS name to those using the items. The LMS was particularly keen on exclusive patterns of crockery and plate for its flagship hotels, a trait inherited from the Midland Railway, one of its predecessors. The Gleneagles Hotel in Scotland and the Welcombe Hotel at Stratford-on-Avon were two such hotels, as was the Midland Hotel in Morecambe. This bespoke hotel ware was often of a superior quality to that used elsewhere in the company's catering operations.

While there were a number of suppliers in the Potteries, the principal source of crockery for the LMS appears to have been the Cauldon Works at Shelton, near Hanley. Started by Job Ridgway on the banks of the Cauldon Canal in 1802, the factory manufactured earthenware and porcelain goods. Over the next hundred years the company prospered and grew to be the largest in the area. At the beginning of the twentieth century the pottery industry entered a period of depression owing to growing competition from abroad, a situation exacerbated by problems resulting from the First World War. Nevertheless, the Cauldon factory continued to produce a wide range of earthenware and fine china, including some attractive gilded tableware for railway companies such as the London & North Western and the Caledonian, both later to become part of the LMS. In 1920 the company amalgamated with four other potteries to become 'Cauldon Potteries Limited' and in 1925 was granted the Royal Warrant enabling it to use the imprint 'Royal Cauldon' on its products.

Following further reorganisation a new company emerged in February 1933, just in time to start making the tableware for the Midland Hotel, then under construction. A 'Seahorse' design, similar to the Marion Dorn mosaic in the hotel's foyer, was chosen for both crockery and table linen. In the manufacturing process the blue seahorse motif was transfer printed onto a range of off-white earthenware and then fixed by the application of a surface glaze. It is difficult to estimate how many pieces

Backstamp of Royal Cauldon.

A selection of
Midland Hotel
crockery.
(Barry Guise)

of crockery were made for the Midland as few records survive but, for various reasons, it is unlikely that any was supplied to the hotel after 1939.

Cauldon continued to be dogged by financial difficulties and in 1935 was taken over by Crescent Potteries which transferred the business to its own factory. Two years later the Cauldon site was closed and the buildings demolished. Midland Hotel crockery with the 'Royal Cauldon' backmark continued to be produced at Crescent Potteries until the outbreak of the Second World War when Government restrictions curtailed the manufacture of coloured wares for the home market. When the hotel was requisitioned for use as a hospital by the RAF its contents, including the crockery, were put into storage for the duration of the conflict. However, when the building resumed as a hotel in 1948 the production of pottery was still severely restricted so no new 'Seahorse' pieces would have been available to supplement the existing stock. It was not until 1952 that the Government allowed some decorated pottery to be sold on the home market and by this date the nationalised British Railways had decided to sell the Midland and transferred what remained of the crockery to its Kyle of Lochalsh Hotel in Scotland.

Seahorse
motif.

the Midland was unlikely to have a successful winter, he nevertheless believed that closing the hotel during this period could lead to a loss of goodwill and perhaps jeopardise the subsequent summer season. Cottet's appraisal must have convinced the Hotels Executive as it agreed to keep the hotel open for a further twelve months.

By the end of 1950 the Midland's trading balance had moved into a small surplus and, buoyed by this improvement, Hole finally consented to the relocation of the American Bar but continued to veto the provision of a bar in the café. Just two and a half years since its re-opening the Midland had started to look rather tired and shabby, due mainly to reluctance on the part of the Hotels Executive to spend money on the building, even on general maintenance. Following numerous complaints from visitors, Miss Oxenford inspected the hotel the following summer and concluded that certain remedial work was essential, namely the renewal of bathroom, toilet and service flooring; the redecoration of most of the bedrooms; and the cleaning of the building's exterior. In addition, she recommended that corridors be carpeted to reduce noise levels and that Venetian blinds be fitted to the dining room windows to prevent discomfort to guests from sun glare.

Once again, Hole decided that the work should be deferred, aware of moves that were taking place behind the scenes. Although the Midland was now making a modest profit, this was deemed insufficient to satisfy the members of the Hotels Executive who were in the process of evaluating the financial viability of the Company's hotels with a view to 'eliminating unremunerative establishments'. With the debate rekindled, voices advocating the disposal of the Midland became louder and more persuasive. On 12 July 1951, Sir Harry Methven, who had succeeded Lord Inman as Chairman of the Hotels Executive, wrote to Lord Hurcomb requesting the BTC's permission to sell five of the Company's hotels, including the Midland at Morecambe, pointing out that

> while in some cases there has been an improvement in the trading position, I do not believe that it will be possible to put them on an economic footing.

At its next committee meeting the BTC agreed in principle that the sale of the Midland Hotel could go ahead, subject to a satisfactory price being obtained.

As part of its original contract with Morecambe Corporation signed in March 1932, the Railway Company had a legal obligation to give the Corporation first refusal

MIDLAND HOTEL MORECAMBE
Trading Account

	22 July 1948 – 14 July 1949	Average Base Year (1935–1937)
Number of Nightly Visitors	8,901	7,944
INCOME (£)		
Receipts for Food	12,274	9,934
Cost of Food	7,623	5,817
Profit on Food	4,651	4,117
Receipts for Wines	20,332	7,143
Cost of Wines	11,532	3,315
Profit on Wines	8,800	3,828
Gross Profit on Food and Wines	13,451	7,945
Receipts for Apartments	8,917	7,945
Receipts for Surcharges	815	-
Receipts for Sundries	468	319
Total Receipts	42,806	22,419
Total Gross Profit	23,651	13,287
EXPENDITURE (£)		
Salaries and Wages	14,702	3,367
Repairs and Maintenance	4,000	3,368
Depreciation	268	-
Renewal Provision	-	435
Heating and Lighting	1,871	953
Rates	539	443
Licences	69	70
Miscellaneous	4,318	1,968
Total Expenditure	25,767	10,604
Profit Before Charging	- 2,116	2,683
General Overhead Expenses		
Administration	895	490
General Charges	319	414
NET RECEIPTS	- 3,300	1,779

to purchase the Midland Hotel before offering it for general sale. In August, Hole, on behalf of the Hotels Executive, duly contacted Roger Rose, Morecambe's Town Clerk, asking if the Corporation would be interested in acquiring the hotel. Hearing of this possibility, the *Visitor* told its readers in no uncertain terms that the Corporation 'need not waste much time pompously discussing acquisition for the simple reason that there is no money in the Corporation Exchequer for this purpose and it is almost certain that no Government sanction would be forthcoming for any loan'. It also reminded the Corporation that it had a responsibility to ensure the building was not disposed of 'in such a way as to injure the amenities of the town'.

After considering the offer at its next meeting the Corporation, as the *Visitor* had anticipated, declined the offer to buy the Midland but requested an opportunity of further considering the question should the Railway Company decide to sell the property for purposes other than its present use as a residential hotel. Once news of the Midland's impending sale became public there was widespread speculation as to what would eventually happen to the hotel if it was not sold as a going concern. A variety of prospective uses began appearing in the local press – acquisition by a brewery for a 'drinking palace', conversion into administrative offices for the County Council and purchase by the Coal Board as a convalescent home for miners. Whatever the Midland's ultimate role, the *Visitor* took the Railway Company to task for reneging on its contract with the Corporation by not continuing to run it as a hotel – and it knew who to blame! 'The decision to get rid of this and one or two similarly owned hotels in the country is typical of the Socialist transport and shows the usual disregard for past agreements.'

Contrary to the *Visitor*'s conclusions, the Hotels Executive had no intention, at least initially, of upsetting Morecambe Corporation further by lifting restrictions on the terms of the Midland's sale. It instructed its agents, Herring, Son and Daw of Berkeley Square, London to test the market for purchasers wishing to continue operating the property as a hotel, forwarding to them a list of interested parties who had already made inquiries. An indication of the expected price was given in the *Bradford Telegraph and Argus* of 10 October, which informed its readers that 'The Hotels Executive of British Railways had put the Midland Hotel, Morecambe, on the open market … and are prepared to consider an offer in the region of £80,000.'

This decision prompted Morecambe solicitors Jobling and Knape to make representations to the Hotels Executive asking if consideration might be given to the offering of the hotel for sale by public auction as they had been contacted by several interested clients. Herring, Son and Daw supported this strategy, calculating that it could realise a higher price than a private sale. The Hotels Executive agreed and the hotel was advertised for auction as

'All that fully licensed Hotel called the Midland Hotel, with the garden, offices, garages, pleasure grounds, lands and hereditaments situate in the Borough of Morecambe and Heysham in the County of Lancashire. Together with all the fixtures, fittings, fixed plant and equipment, services, furniture and effects (hereinafter called 'the fixtures and furniture') as detailed in the Inventory and list which have been signed on behalf of the Vendors and deposited with the Auctioneers. All linen, glass, cutlery and electro-plate marked or badged with the railway monogram will be excluded.'

Before the above inventory had been finalised, Hole received an intriguing memo from Miss Oxenford. As the Company's Chief Officer for Domestic Services, she suggested that to save money all the high quality furniture and equipment might be transferred to other Company hotels and replaced with inferior pieces. Hole contemplated the idea but concluded that such a substitution would so alter the character of the hotel that the prospects of obtaining a satisfactory price would be diminished. However, he was not averse to swapping other items: bedspreads and eiderdowns were sent to Manchester's Midland Hotel in exchange for equal numbers of less good quality; pillows went to the York and Sheffield hotels to be replaced by second grade examples from Derby; nine special flower vases, three special flower bowls, four Hoovers and one Dustette were withdrawn from the hotel and sent to the St Pancras store – as were all the covered coat hangers!

Around 100 people gathered in the Midland Hotel for its auction on 12 December. Among the crowd was Mrs Maud Bourne, owner of Morecambe's Broadway Hotel and most people's tip for buying the Midland. A small, plump widow, she was an astute businesswoman who had made a fortune by buying up prime seafront land between Broadway and Thornton Road on which she had built several private hotels, later sold at a substantial profit. Bidding quickly reached £31,000, encouraging the auctioneer, H.W.Stevens, to ask for and receive an offer of £40,000. Gradually, the bids crept up to £59,000 and then stopped. 'Make it £60,000', appealed Mr Stevens, 'it's dirt cheap at that'. But despite his persuasiveness no more bids were forthcoming and he reluctantly announced 'I cannot sell at £59,000'. To everyone's surprise Mrs Bourne had taken no part in the bidding but immediately the auction was over she sought out Mr Stevens and made a private offer of £60,000. This was rejected by the agents who believed that a better price could still be obtained in a private sale – an error of judgement that would later return to haunt them.

Over the next few months prospective buyers came and went and the Midland remained unsold. As resident manager, A. V. Gill was growing increasingly worried about his position and conveyed his concern to Hole. Was the hotel going to open for the season? If so, what were the terms to be? Should he take bookings? The Labour Party Conference was to be held in Morecambe that September and Trade Union representatives were asking for accommodation. As the prospect of effecting a satisfactory sale in the near future seemed unlikely, Hole decided that the Midland should continue to function until 31 October and then close for the winter.

The situation changed in early May when Herring, Son and Daw received an offer of £55,000 for the Midland from Lewis Hodgson of the Devonshire Arms, a prestigious hotel at Bolton Abbey in Yorkshire. Keen to be rid of the building and doubtful of a better offer, the BTC took little time to accept. Sensing a certain amount of desperation on the part of the BTC, Hodgson's solicitors wrote to Herring, Son and Daw on 19 May in an attempt to get the price reduced.

You will know that our Clients are not only people of substance but in addition and what is of paramount importance they have a name second to none as Hoteliers. You may know that they regularly accommodate and cater for members of the Nobility and it would be their intention if they acquire the Midland Hotel, to conduct it to the highest possible standards. There is no doubt, in our view, that their acquisition of the Midland Hotel would be an asset to this town.

You will, however, know something of the very serious economic blizzard that has hit Lancashire and Yorkshire in the last few months. Our Clients have given most careful and anxious thought to the whole transaction, and they are firmly of the opinion that the maximum amount they could pay is £50,000 with a down payment of £25,000. They would be prepared to repay the balance of the purchase money by an annual payment of a minimum of £3,000 [although] it would be their intention to pay considerably more than this amount.

May we say that our Clients are satisfied that they would be involved immediately in an expenditure of something like £5,000 to carry out what they consider to be essential repairs, renovations and improvements and it is for this reason that our Clients have felt that they cannot make an offer in excess of £50,000.

With little room for manoeuvre, and seemingly without the resolve to prolong negotiations further, the BTC reluctantly agreed to the revised figure (despite what the *Visitor* told its readers). There can be little doubt that the BTC must have been extremely upset and disappointed with the outcome, mindful of the fact that it could have obtained £10,000 more for the hotel at the aborted auction five months earlier.

Contracts were signed and at midnight on 25 July 1952, almost exactly nineteen years after it first opened, the Midland Hotel passed out of railway hands and into the ownership of Mr and Mrs Lewis Hodgson.

"The Visitor," Morecambe & Heysham & Lancaster—July 16, 1952

MIDLAND SOLD FOR £60,000
To Tenant Of Devonshire Arms, Bolton Abbey

"THE VISITOR" understands that the Midland has been sold to Mr. and Mrs. Lewis Hodgson, tenants of the Devonshire Arms Hotel, Bolton Abbey, and they will take possession on July 25th.

This 41 bedroomed hotel, owned by British Railways, was put up for auction last December and withdrawn at £59,000. Since then it has been investigated by several potential purchasers but they gradually faded away.

Negotiations with the present purchasers have been going on for several weeks and the deal was settled yesterday through the agency of Mr. Harry Wood, well known local auctioneer, estate agent and valuer, in conjunction with Messrs. Herring, Son and Daw, auctioneers, London.

The

MIDLAND HOTEL

MORECAMBE

TEL. 2591 (3 lines)   Grams: Midland, Morecambe

A.A. 4 Star   Appointed   R.A.C. 4 Star

Situated centrally on the seaward side of the Promenade, the MIDLAND HOTEL is of modern design and structure, embodying all those features which go towards the making of a first-class Hotel and, therefore, assuring every comfort.

Many bedrooms have their own balconies overlooking the sea, and many have private bathrooms. Suites are also available.

We are proud of our cuisine, and the Restaurant caters for the most fastidious, providing both Table d'Hote and a la Carte Menus.

We are very conscious of the important role your Hotel plays in the success of your holiday and, with this in mind, we assure you of our best endeavours. Whether staying in the Hotel or calling for an aperitif or a meal, you may be sure of a welcome.

Open all the year round   Central Heating Throughout

Night Porter   Resident Director: RENNICK S. HODGSON

Chapter Eight
UNDER NEW OWNERSHIP

Having purchased the Midland Hotel, Lewis Hodgson decided to remain in charge of the Devonshire Arms in Bolton Abbey, entrusting his new acquisition to son Rennick and daughter-in-law Morag. It had been Lewis Hodgson's original intention to manage the Midland himself, which he did for a brief period but his wife Florence disliked Morecambe and persuaded Lewis to return to the Devonshire Arms and exchange positions with Rennick who had taken it over from his father.

Most of the Midland's existing staff were retained by the new owners, one notable exception being A. V. Gill who had run the hotel since its re-opening four years earlier. With Rennick Hodgson arriving as resident manager, Gill's services, through no fault of his own, were no longer required. Not wishing to lose his expertise, the Hotels Executive acted quickly to provide him with holiday relief work pending his transfer to another managerial appointment.

Rennick Hodgson, who had trained at Oddenino's, one of London's leading hotels, was determined to raise the profile of the Midland which had slipped in comparison to its pre-war eminence. Notices were placed in the local press advertising the change of ownership and steps were taken to improve the hotel's amenities. Within days of re-opening, plans had been submitted to enclose the open loggia at the south-west corner of the building in order to enlarge the Children's Room and create a Residents' Lounge – a modification which had been mooted before the war by Arthur Towle who had asked Oliver Hill to draw up a scheme for enclosure of the area, perhaps with glazed doors, to make the space more usable during periods of inclement weather.

On the accommodation front the first major test for the Hodgsons was the impending Labour Party Conference which was being held in Morecambe at the end of September, beginning with a civic luncheon in the hotel dining room. While most members of the Labour Executive, notably Clement Attlee, Aneurin Bevan, Hugh Gaitskell and rising luminaries such as Harold Wilson and Barbara Castle, would be

Advertisement for the Midland Hotel in the 1958 Morecambe and Heysham Holiday Guide.
(Morecambe Library)

staying at the Grosvenor Hotel, the Midland would be playing host to a number of prominent Trades Union officials. These included Arthur Deakin the President of the TUC, its General Secretary Sir Vincent Tewson, Will Lawther the Miners' President and Tom O'Brien from the TUC's International Committee.

During conference week some 2,000 party delegates and reporters crammed into the Winter Gardens for the speeches and debates, their presence in the town estimated to have been worth around £15,000 to local businesses – and perhaps even more than that in publicity for the resort. However, the event was to prove a one-off. Asked by a reporter what she thought of Morecambe's suitability as a conference venue, the well-known Liverpool MP Bessie Braddock replied 'All right, but not as good as Scarborough' – although she did like the Illuminations. She cited a lack of working space and inadequate accommodation as the town's main shortcomings, factors which no doubt influenced the Labour Party's decision to adopt the larger resort of Blackpool as its preferred North-West England conference location.

While the conference was in progress the Hodgsons learnt that planning permission had been granted for the structural alterations to the loggia and for conversion of what had originally been the Writing Room into a TV lounge. The work was completed in time for residents to watch the coronation of Queen Elizabeth II the following June. Television sets were still something of a novelty in 1953 and quite an expensive item.

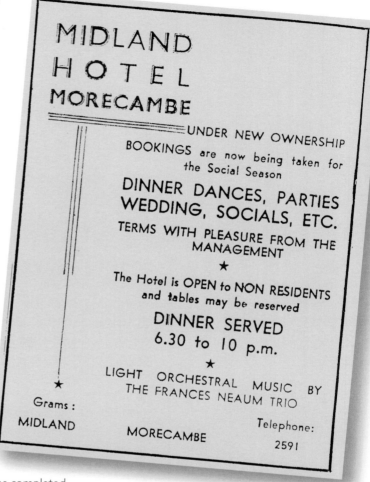

(Two years later, guests at the Midland Hotel would be able to see the new queen at much closer quarters. On 13 April 1955 Elizabeth II and the Duke of Edinburgh arrived at the Promenade Station for an official visit to Morecambe, pausing on the forecourt for a ceremonial welcome before proceeding to the Town Hall.)

1953 saw the appointment of a young Scotsman as assistant manager. Robert Speirs, fresh from Courtfield Catering College in Blackpool, was destined to enjoy a long and fruitful association with the Midland, returning to manage the hotel on two occasions in the 1960s.

When I first went to the Midland, Rennick and Morag Hodgson were in charge. They were a good couple to work for. I gained much useful experience towards management including administration, organising functions, the supervision of different departments, etc, and was encouraged to progress, using my day off to study nutrition part-time back in Blackpool.

Having spent three years learning the business and gaining further qualifications, Robert Speirs left the Midland to get married and to manage a Trust House Hotel in Berkhamstead, Hertfordshire – but he would be back. Joining the hotel staff a little later, but on the bottom rung of the ladder, was Beulah Drinkall. After leaving school in 1957 she obtained a job as a chambermaid, living in staff quarters at the hotel. Looking back with affection on her time at the Midland she paints a fascinating picture of life 'below stairs' in the late 1950s.

A chambermaid's day started early with the preparation of morning teas – no tea making facilities in the rooms then – and a hectic hour ensued taking trays to those bedrooms that had requested the service. The top floor trays had yellow crockery, the first floor ones had blue and getting them mixed up was *not* an option! At 8.00am we went down to the kitchen to collect our breakfast which we took upstairs to eat in the chambermaids' pantry – a glorified cupboard with table and chairs, a huge set

Directly opposite the Promenade Station, the top bedrooms and flat roof of the Midland Hotel afforded an unrivalled view of the Royal visit in April 1955 for privileged guests, staff and photographers.
(R. Hodgson)

of shelves where the trays of crockery were kept and a large water boiler. Never a morning went by without a ding-dong battle with the head still-room maid, a fearsome woman called Pru, who counted each slice of toast. Woe betide any 'Oliver' who asked for more than their allocation!

At 9.00am we had to be 'on the floor' ready for work. Each floor had two chambermaids and one corridor maid. Corridor maids were responsible for cleaning the bathrooms, toilets and corridors which were mopped and polished daily. The two chambermaids worked together to make beds and then split up to clean their own set of rooms. If guests were leaving then the beds were stripped and the towels removed. When all the dirty linen was gathered up and checked it was put in a big wooden trolley and wheeled into the lift to be taken down to the linen room. A favourite escapade of the chambermaids – if the housekeeper was out of sight – was to hitch a ride along the corridors of the hotel from one end to the other.

At lunchtime we took turns to eat as someone always had to be on duty in case there was a ring for room service. The pantry was fitted with a board of room numbers and if anyone rang, the number would register on the board – very 'Upstairs Downstairs'! The head chambermaid was a lovely lady called Ruth Holroyd who took me under her wing. She gave me some 1920s style dancing shoes and had me doing the Charleston in the pantry. This became a regular entertainment at break times.

Chambermaids were also required to do evening duties. We had to be ready at 7.00pm dressed in black with white apron and cap and as the guests went down to dinner we would go to each room and remove the silk bed covers and turn down the corners of the bedspreads. In winter some guests would request hot water bottles which we would fill from the boiler in the pantry. Any dirty towels would be replaced and after tidying up where necessary we would go off duty at 9.00pm.

In the hotel there was a pecking order – management, kitchen staff, dining room staff and so on – and although chambermaids were only one step up from cleaners, I loved my job. The head porter was called Wilf and looked like Mr Pickwick, all round and tubby in his gold braided uniform. In his charge were two bell-boys whose main duties were fetching and carrying and running errands. Both were about sixteen but very different. Barrie was a gangly youth who always seemed to get all the work. Tommy had a cheeky smile under a crew-cut of bright ginger hair and managed to do as little as possible.

The owners of the hotel were Mr and Mrs Rennick Hodgson who occupied a suite of rooms on the first floor. They employed a nanny to care for their children. She wore an imposing uniform and all the maids were a bit in awe of her. She had travelled all

Lord and Lady Docker were frequent guests at the Midland Hotel in the 1950s and are seen here descending the main staircase. (R. Hodgson)

over the world and at one time had been nanny to the family of the actor Robert Newton, he of *Treasure Island* fame – "Ah, Jim lad!" Nanny would sometimes pop into the pantry for a chat with the older maids but we young ones were warned not to say too much in her presence as apparently any gossip would be relayed to the management.

In the 1950s Morecambe was buzzing. The Winter Gardens had different shows and most of the stars appearing there stayed at the Midland – David Whitfield, Frankie

Vaughan, Michael Holliday, Shirley Bassey, Alma Cogan, Mike and Bernie Winters and many others. Joe Loss was a regular guest as his band were on at the Pier Ballroom on Wednesday nights. Working at the hotel and actually seeing all these stars was an amazing experience for an impressionable teenager. Some of the Miss Great Britain contestants would also stay the night before the contest. They would spend all morning slapping on fake tans and the corridor maids would have their work cut out cleaning the bathrooms after this cosmetic operation. Regular visitors to the Midland were Lord and Lady Docker; they always had the suite of rooms on the top floor and we were pleased to hear that they were in residence because we invariably got a £5 tip.

Two views of the inside of the Midland Hotel c.1955 – the Entrance Lounge (above) and the new Cocktail Bar (opposite). (R. Hodgson)

The
Midland Hotel
MORECAMBE
announce
CHRISTMAS AND
NEW YEAR
PROGRAMME

Christmas Eve
AFTERNOON TEA, Orchestra Music by the
Frances Neaum Trio.
DINNER DANCE—Music by Cyril J. Burnett
7.30 p.m. to 11.30 p.m., 21/-

Christmas Day
CAROLS by Frances Neaum Trio in the
Lounge, 11 a.m. to 1 p.m.
CHRISTMAS LUNCH from 12.30
Cyril J. Burnett will play light music during
dinner, from 7 p.m.

Boxing Day
CARNIVAL DINNER DANCE & CABARET
Music by Cyril J. Burnett, 8.30 p.m. to
2 a.m., 25/-

The Management offer the following
attractions and suggestions for

New Year's Eve
SUGGESTIONS:
For our guests: Dinner Dance
8.30 p.m. to 2 a.m. Savoury
snacks before retiring. Break-
fast from 10 a.m., 50/- incl.
ATTRACTIONS:
Grand New Year's Eve Dinner
Dance. Music by Cyril J.
Burnett, 8.30 p.m. to 2 a.m.,
25/-

May we respectfully request your
early reservations for Tables
TEL. NO MORECAMBE 2591

In summer the Midland employed a lot of additional workers who were laid off in September as the season came to an end. However, the hotel remained open through the winter months and hosted several dinner dances. Anyone attending these functions would use cloakroom facilities made available in one of the first floor bedrooms. Two chambermaids would be on duty to hang up the coats and issue tickets. We loved these events. After all the ladies had floated off down the spiral staircase to mingle for cocktails in the foyer, we would peer over the banisters and admire the fashions being paraded below, keeping one ear cocked for anyone in authority coming along the corridor. When the throng disappeared to dine we would return to the 'cloakroom', lock the door and amuse ourselves by 'modelling' the array of expensive fur coats left in our care – the only time I have ever worn mink.

Christmas was always a busy time and the hotel was usually full for the festive season. We all worked very hard but we had fun too. In one year a carpet of snow lay in front

of the hotel and although we were not supposed to venture into this area, we took a chance and had a super snowball fight.

At the north end of the building there was a café opening out to face the jetty. This was always full of mums and dads having pots of tea and kiddies with buckets and spades enjoying fizzy drinks and ice creams. There was also a little public bar next to the café which my mother ran during the season. The café looked out over the Harbour Band Arena and on summer days rows of deck chairs were filled by holidaymakers taking the air and enjoying the music. Sometimes, when the weather was nice, the younger members of staff would arrange a beach party, usually at night, on the end of the jetty. An old Ekco radio would be brought out to provide the music and the older teenagers would indulge in a couple of bottles of alcohol. We were daring young things!

Eventually, I decided to spread my wings and move on to bigger things (a decision I have always regretted). I went to work in the Midland Grand Hotel in Manchester but it

Waiters line up behind one of the Midland Hotel's lavish buffets … (R. Hodgson)

... admired by Rennick and
Morag Hodgson.
(R. Hodgson)

was nothing like working at Morecambe's Midland – no friendly, carefree atmosphere.
I loved my time there.

Throughout the 1950s the Hodgsons worked hard to make the Midland a success, investing a substantial amount of money on updating the hotel's facilities. Improved lighting was installed, including new fluorescent tubes between the double windows of the staircase tower, and new carpets were laid throughout the ground floor with the initials MH incorporated into the design (Midland Hotel or Morag Hodgson?). The Cocktail Bar was completely refurbished. All the bedrooms had telephones fitted, as did the bars and kitchen. Previously only a few bedrooms had the convenience of an internal telephone, most guests having to use one of the hotel's four public phone boxes. In the cellar the old solid fuel boilers were replaced by three modern and more economical oil-fired boilers to supply hot water and run the central heating system.

During this time the hotel provided a base for the Morecambe Car Club and also acted as headquarters for the Lancashire Automobile Club's annual National Rally. Rallying was then a very popular sport and the 'National' was an important event in the rallying calendar, drawing entrants from all over the country. For three days competitors wound their way through the Lake District and parts of Yorkshire before finishing on the promenade outside the Midland. In 1955 the event was won by local driver Bobby Parkes in an Aston Martin DB2. One of the top British rally drivers of his day, Bobby went on to drive for Jaguar in the Monte Carlo Rally, winning his class in 1959 and finishing eighth overall. He remembers the Midland as 'a marvellous place.'

Shortly after they arrived, I was introduced to the Hodgsons and we became great friends. My wife and I used the hotel as our local at week-ends and on Bank Holidays – I worked in Manchester during the week. The new Cocktail Bar was spacious and run to the highest standards. The two barmen, Peter and Arthur, wore white aprons to their ankles. They were both UK Bartenders Guild qualified and had their qualification pennants and pictures each side of the bar. The service was immaculate and it was the custom to give the barman sixpence after ordering a round of drinks.

All the top people stayed at the Midland – rich Yorkshire families, theatre performers and stars who came to judge the Bathing Beauty competitions or to switch on the Illuminations. I met Trevor Howard there. He had earlier starred in *Brief Encounter* which was partly filmed at Carnforth Station. He was a really nice man, keen on MGs. I had one then and we would go out on drives together. Laurence Olivier stayed when he was making *The Entertainer* which was shot locally and in the Winter Gardens. Another film star was Anthony Steel who was supposed to judge the Miss Great Britain contest. However, they had trouble getting him out of bed for it as he had been out late the previous night! Shirley Bassey I remember because she always came in the bar and read a book. Bud Abbott and Lou Costello did a season at the Winter Gardens in 1953. Lou was once thrown out of the Midland at four o' clock in the morning for 'misbehaving himself'. Morag Hodgson took umbrage and told him to go. He was put in a taxi and drove round Morecambe looking for somewhere to stay but it was 'Wakes Week' in the town and there wasn't a room available. He couldn't get in anywhere, so four hours later he came back on his knees and apologised and begged to be allowed in. They relented and let him back – and after that his behaviour was impeccable!

A more unusual visitor arrived in March 1956. The hotel had received a letter from the United Kingdom Atomic Energy Authority asking it to cater for a party of about thirty who would be arriving for afternoon tea on Sunday 25th. No details of the guests were given and hotel staff were puzzled by the air of secrecy. At 4.00pm on the day a coach drew into the Midland forecourt and disgorged a number of officials from the Central Electricity Generating Board. About twenty minutes later two long

A smiling Georgy Malenkov signs the Midland Hotel's guest book after his visit in March 1956. Looking on (front left to right) are Rennick Hodgson, Mayor Robert Allen and Malenkov's ever-present interpreter.
(R. Hodgson)

black ZIS limousines bearing *Corps Diplomatique* plates swept up to the front door and out of one stepped the chubby figure of Georgy Malenkov who, until the previous year, had been Premier of the Soviet Union. Now Russia's Minister of Energy, he was on a tour of Britain's power plants and that Sunday was en route from Fleetwood to the recently completed atomic power station at Calder Hall.

Waiting to greet Malenkov on the steps of the Midland was the Mayor of Morecambe, Councillor Robert Allen, who welcomed him to the resort. Malenkov shook hands warmly and through an interpreter said 'I am very glad to meet you'. Accompanied by several burly bodyguards and other members of the Russian delegation, he passed through the hotel foyer, filled with people taking afternoon tea, and into the dining room where a long table had been set for the distinguished visitors. Not surprisingly,

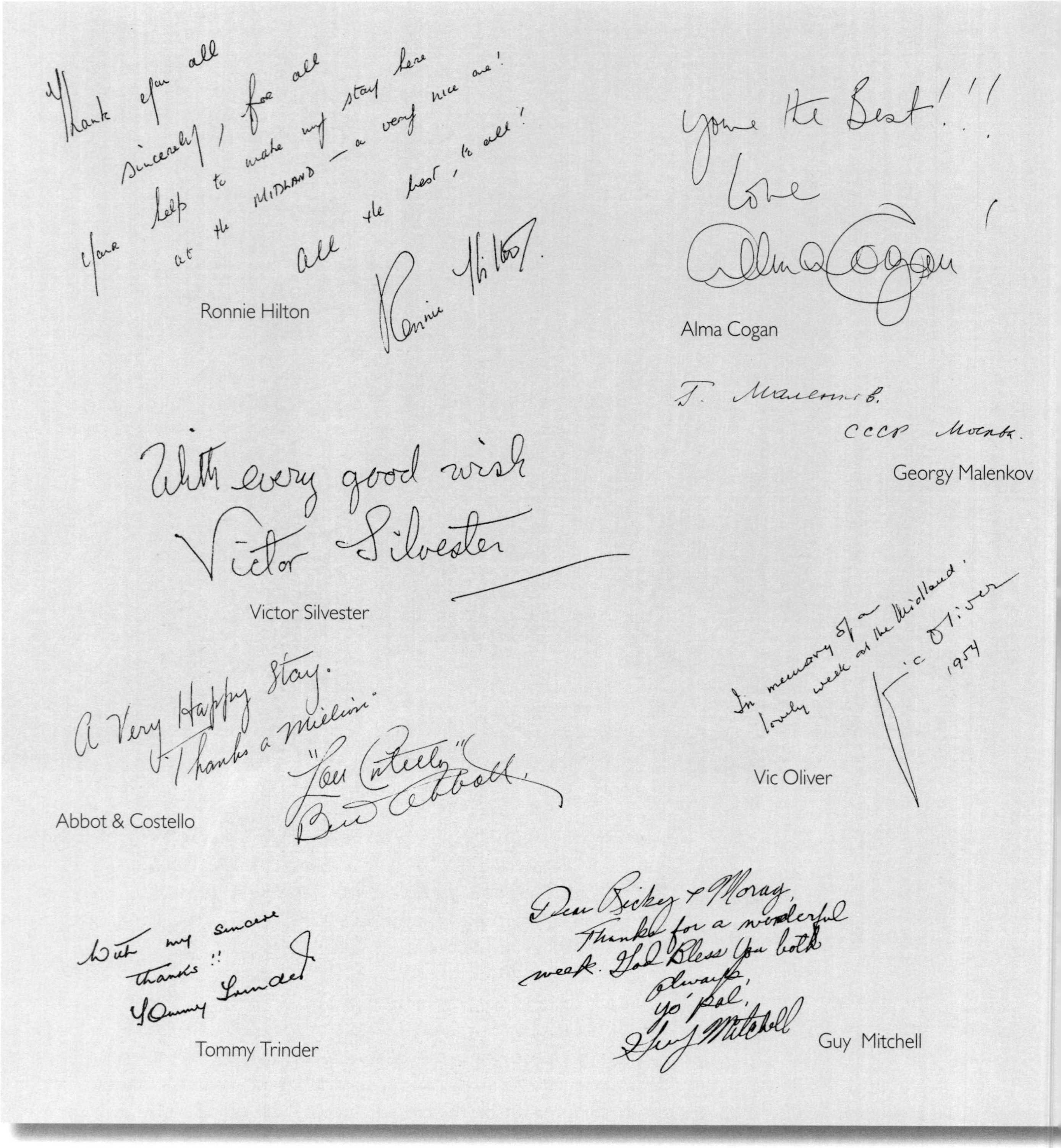

Thank you all
sincerely, for all
your help to make my stay here
at the MIDLAND — a very nice one!
All the best, to all!

Ronnie Hilton

You're the Best!!!
love
Alma Cogan

With every good wish
Victor Silvester

Г. Маленков.
СССР Москва.

Georgy Malenkov

A Very Happy Stay.
"Thanks a Million"

Abbot & Costello

In memory of a
lovely week at the Midland.
1954

Vic Oliver

With my sincere
thanks !!

Tommy Trinder

Dear Ricky & Morag,
Thanks for a wonderful
week. God Bless you both
always,
yo' pal,

Guy Mitchell

A selection from the Midland Hotel's guest book of the 1950s. (R. Hodgson)

Sorry you had to turn us out!! But we will come back. Regards Ezra ???.

Peter Brough

To Ricky & the "missus". Thanks — best digs in Morecambe.

Max Bygraves

The Midland Hotel Morecombe is the nicest & most comfortable Hotel we have stayed in. We thank Mr & Mrs Hodgson for being so kind to us & making our visit such a happy one.

Norah & Bernard Docker

Lord and Lady Docker

Happy Memories & Always Happiness. Sincerely Al Read "Right Monkey!"

Al Read

Thank you for the pleasant week. Sincerely Al Martino

Al Martino

Thank you for making our stay, though short, so very comfortable. Rowland Emmett

Rowland Emmett

the menu included Morecambe Bay shrimps together with Lune salmon, scones and jam and an assortment of fancy cakes. Lemons were provided for those who wished to take their tea Russian style. By this time, word of Malenkov's presence had spread and a large crowd of curious spectators had assembled around the hotel. When he noticed the people gathered at the rear of the building Malenkov went over to one of the large windows and waved to them. The original 'hush-hush' nature of the visit had now entirely dissipated and on his way out after the meal Malenkov smiled and waved at the bemused tea drinkers in the foyer, pausing for a few minutes to sign autographs and write his name in the hotel book.

Outside, he stood in the sunshine on the hotel steps and shook hands again with Councillor Allen, expressing his thanks for the reception and adding 'If you are in Moscow you must come and see me'. Then, instead of stepping into his waiting car which had drawn up in front of the hotel, he announced that he wanted 'to take a walk and see the sea'. To the ill-concealed consternation of his security men Malenkov strode across the hotel lawn to meet the excited crowd which had swollen to around a thousand. Hatless and with a curl of hair flopping over his forehead he exchanged greetings via his interpreter while shaking hands and happily signing any piece of paper that was presented.

With large numbers of people pressing round him, he walked past the War Memorial and turned down the side of the Swimming Stadium towards the sea. Noticing a young couple arm in arm he inquired if they were on their honeymoon but received the reply that they were not married. The interpreter explained that earlier in the day Malenkov had met a honeymoon couple on Blackpool Promenade and had presented them with a box of chocolates. Looking out over the bay Malenkov asked about the tides and the distance to the other side. A police superintendent, part of the low key police presence, pointed out the route round the bay the party would take to Calder Hall. After chatting to a couple of elderly ladies ('I hope you both live to be a hundred!') and patting a dog which had been rescued from the crowd, Malenkov headed back towards the Midland Hotel to rejoin his car and resume his journey – but not before another smile and several final waves to the crowd.

(Georgy Malenkov's roly-poly appearance and amiable persona belied an ambitious and sometimes ruthless politician. On the death of Josef Stalin in 1953, Malenkov became Premier of the Soviet Union with Nikita Krushchev as First Secretary. However, his programmes of reform were opposed by others in the Communist Party and he was forced to resign in 1955, being replaced by Nikolai Bulganin. Demoted to Minister of Energy, it was in this capacity that Malenkov visited Britain in March 1956. Ostensibly he had come to inspect various power plants and research establishments but the real reason for his trip was to test the temperature of British hospitality for the forthcoming visit of Krushchev and Bulganin. In 1957 Malenkov's participation in a failed attempt to depose Krushchev saw him expelled from the party and exiled to Kazakhstan.)

The Hodgson's last major project, completed in July 1960, saw the transformation of the rotunda café into a new bar and function room for the use of both guests and non-residents. Known as the Seahorse Bar – the special blue linoleum floor was decorated with seahorse motifs – it cost over £5,000 and was able to accommodate 100 people at the tables and a similar number standing. A long, curving bar occupied one side of the room, offering customers 'a touch of luxury above the ordinary'. Lancaster architects Jackson & Hodgson were responsible for the design with construction work carried out by W. Huddleston & Sons of Morecambe. The main alterations involved knocking through an internal wall between the café and existing bar to create a larger space and the installation of a suspended ceiling. The Seahorse Bar was officially opened on 28 July 1960 by comedian Albert Modley, 'Morecambe's own star of Stage, Screen and Television', and was to prove a popular local rendezvous for many years.

However, even before the Seahorse Bar was finished, the Hodgsons had decided to sell the Midland and move back to Bolton Abbey to take charge of the Devonshire Arms. Lewis Hodgson, who had been running the latter, had recently died after a long illness leaving his wife struggling to cope on her own, a situation which had persuaded Rennick to give up the Midland and return to Yorkshire.

Unlike the long, drawn-out saga of the Midland's previous sale, the hotel's transfer to its new owners, Scottish Brewers Ltd (later to become Scottish & Newcastle Breweries) went through with few complications. The company took over the building on 1 November having agreed a price of around £100,000, double the sum paid by Lewis Hodgson in 1952 – but the Midland Hotel it had purchased was now a far better proposition than eight years earlier. Over the course of their tenure Rennick and Morag Hodgson had spent in excess of £25,000 on extensions, improvements and refurbishments and increased the annual turnover from £42,000 to £84,000.

Delighted to be returning to the Midland after an absence of four years – this time as manager – was Robert Speirs, together with his wife and new baby.

> It was through some old Midland customers, particularly Harry Wood [the Auctioneer who had conducted the sale of the hotel] that my name was put forward to Scottish Brewers. I was asked to apply and was interviewed for the position of manager jointly with my wife Margaret.

The revival of the hotel's fortunes which had begun under the Hodgsons continued under the Speirs and the 1960s saw the Midland go from strength to strength. In addition to catering for the needs of its residents, the hotel provided the venue for a wide range of functions from dinner dances and balls to seminars and conferences, and was the centre of a vibrant social scene. Ensuring that all the above ran smoothly were some forty full-time members of staff, augmented on occasions by a number of part-time waitresses (known as 'extra ducks') who helped on special occasions and during busy holiday periods. In common with most hotels the basic organisation of the Midland was split into several sections: Reception, Kitchen, Dining Room, Porters, Housekeeping and Bars.

Reception normally had a staff of four who dealt with enquiries, reservations and accounts, operated the switchboard and served drinks to guests after hours from the Dispense Bar. The working day (divided into two shifts) usually ran from 8.00am until the books were balanced at the end of the evening. Main meals were prepared in the Kitchen, run by a head chef with four under-chefs and two or three kitchen porters, and served in the Dining Room presided over by the head waiter and his team of waiters and waitresses. Between breakfast and dinner Still Room staff provided light refreshments and the ever-popular Afternoon Teas.

During the day, two porters were on hand to look after guests and their luggage and operate the lift. The night porter looked after late arrivals and also polished guests' shoes and delivered morning newspapers to the bedrooms as requested. A Housekeeping staff of seven would start each day with a morning tea service before cleaning and preparing the bedrooms.

The Midland had two Bars, one for residents (the Cocktail Bar or American Bar) and one for the general public (the Seahorse Bar). Both had a staff of two. In addition, there was also a storekeeper/cellarman who was responsible for the liquor stocks and the food and sundries store. When Thistle Hotels (the hotel arm of Scottish Brewers) took over the Midland there was an attempt to introduce draught beer in the American Bar but after complaints that it was not 'proper' to serve pints in a respectable cocktail bar only half pints of beer were permitted! In the summer months a kiosk was erected outside the café for the sale of ice cream.

Most of the staff were locals but for others the hotel provided accommodation on the first and second floors at the northern end of the building. During the early 1960s it became increasingly difficult to recruit sufficient chambermaids and waiters, a problem that was eventually solved by obtaining permission to import qualified workers from Spain and Germany. University students and older school pupils were also employed in the summer months but normally had to leave before the hotel's season had finished.

Although the old Childrens' Room was now a Residents' Lounge, most guests preferred to relax in the Foyer where they could chat to friends and observe the comings and goings in the hotel. The Residents' Lounge tended to be used for a variety of functions, notably the formal dinners for two of Morecambe's most glamorous events, the Miss Great Britain Bathing Beauty Final and the Town Council's Illuminations 'Switch-On'. The resort's Illuminations, cancelled when war broke out, had been revived in 1949 when Yorkshire actor and presenter Wilfred Pickles became the first in a long line of celebrities to perform the ceremony. Most of those who followed stayed at the Midland, the roll call of famous personalities invited to switch on the Illuminations reflecting the changing public tastes in entertainment over the

Finalists of the twenty-fourth Miss Great Britain Bathing Beauty Contest gather on the staircase of the Midland Hotel and raise their glasses to the 1968 winner, Yvonne Ormes of Nantwich. The Midland frequently played host to the judges and finalists of this long-running competition. Each year legions of leggy lovelies paraded before the discerning gaze of famous celebrities deemed worthy of assessing their various attributes. Some winners went on to successful careers as models, in films or on TV, while for others this was their 'fifteen minutes of fame'. By the late 1970s, however, times and attitudes had changed and beauty contests were no longer regarded as harmless fun but as 'degrading cattle markets'. After the loss of TV revenue in the 1980s, Morecambe Council decided to withdraw its funding and the event was axed.

(Robert Speirs)

decades. In the 1950s variety artists, sportsmen and stars from radio shows such as *The Archers* and *Life with the Lyons* dominated proceedings. By the 1960s the emphasis had shifted to TV personalities – actors, comedians and chat show hosts – a trend which continued into the 1970s. In more recent years (the Illuminations ended in 1996) the 'celebrities' were drawn largely from the casts of popular 'Soaps' such as *Coronation Street*, *Emmerdale* and *EastEnders*.

In his first year as manager, Robert Speirs remembers the hotel chef marking the occasion of Stirling Moss switching on the Illuminations by baking a special 'Grand Prix Gateau' in the racing driver's honour. Another memory, from two years later, is of clarinettist Acker Bilk descending the hotel's spiral staircase playing his million-selling hit *Stranger on the Shore*. Robert was not initially impressed by the Town Council's choice for 1964, the DJ Jimmy Savile, but soon changed his opinion once the ceremony started.

> There was a great crowd in front of the Town Hall to witness him perform the switch-on. After he had thoroughly entertained everyone for about half an hour he pressed the button to light up the promenade and then … disaster! Nothing happened. Instead all the street lights went out – a complete black-out! This did not faze him and like a true professional and without any hesitation he carried on with his patter for a further twenty minutes or so until the fault was remedied. Big cheers! We also saw another side to Jimmy Savile. When he left the hotel the following morning he made an unannounced and unpublicised stop at a house in Morecambe to give some presents to a very sick girl. This was not mentioned in the local paper and showed his compassionate side.

The star who gave Robert most concern was Roger Moore who came the following year. Extremely popular at the time, thanks largely to his role as suave amateur sleuth Simon Templar in the TV series *The Saint*, he attracted huge crowds to the Midland.

> The numbers outside the hotel were unprecedented. It was virtually a state of siege and I felt that some of the foyer lounge windows would give way such was the pressure on them. The hotel was being painted at the time and fans were climbing all over the scaffolding – it was actually quite frightening. When the time came for Roger to leave for the switch-on a large open car forced its way to the front entrance but because of the large crowds it was felt it would be unsafe for him to use it and he was smuggled out of the hotel and into a normal saloon. And this was before his James Bond days!

James Bond provided the link to another but very different 'personality' staying at the Midland – not in one of the suites but in the yard outside. This was the gyrocopter known as 'Little Nellie' which was flown by 007 into the crater of a volcano in the film *You Only Live Twice*. Accompanied by its real pilot it was in Morecambe for a promotional appearance.

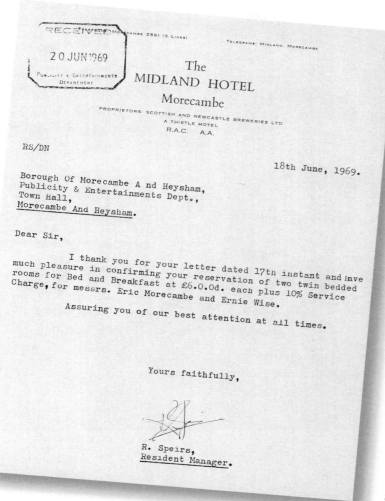

Morecambe 2591 (3 Lines)

TELEGRAMS: MIDLAND. MORECAMBE

RECEIVED
20 JUN 1969
PUBLICITY & ENTERTAINMENTS
DEPARTMENT

The
MIDLAND HOTEL
Morecambe

PROPRIETORS: SCOTTISH AND NEWCASTLE BREWERIES LTD
A THISTLE HOTEL
R.A.C.   A.A.

RS/DN

18th June, 1969.

Borough Of Morecambe A nd Heysham,
Publicity & Entertainments Dept.,
Town Hall,
Morecambe And Heysham.

Dear Sir,

I thank you for your letter dated 17th instant and have
much pleasure in confirming your reservation of two twin bedded
rooms for Bed and Breakfast at £6.0.0d. each plus 10% Service
Charge, for messrs. Eric Morecambe and Ernie Wise.

Assuring you of our best attention at all times.

Yours faithfully,

R. Speirs,
Resident Manager.

My own young boys were very impressed with the gyrocopter and during the night they sneaked down to have a closer look. Jonathan climbed into the cockpit and pretended to fly it but to his horror when he pressed a button on the joy-stick there was a fearsome Rat-a-Tat-Tat from its simulated machine gun. He leapt out and they both scampered back to bed – an escapade I only learnt about quite recently!

The 1969 Illuminations were switched on by Morecambe and Wise, the only celebrities who performed the ceremony twice (they returned in 1975) – if one discounts the risible 'Mr Blobby' who presided over the death throes of the event. Robert had laid on the usual special dinner in the Residents' Lounge but 'we had a job to get it started on time. The problem was caused by the irrepressible Eric Bartholomew who was too busy talking and joking with some of the waitresses who had been classmates of his at Euston Road School.'

Adam Faith, Jet Harris, Dusty Springfield and the Rolling Stones were among the many pop stars who stayed at the Midland in the Sixties, often in the company of more traditional entertainers like Max Bygraves who played to full houses at the Winter Gardens.

Max once got me into trouble with my Scottish Brewers' bosses for whom I had managed to get complimentary tickets. In his act he related his experiences in the Midland and said that one day there were no towels in his bathroom. Phoning down to reception to complain, he was told just to wave his hands out of the window. His response was to say that he was quite glad he had not had a bath! This was a well-rehearsed gag he used around the country but my bosses took it as fact and I was reprimanded for my lack of service to such an important guest.

Comedian Albert Modley and organist Harold Graham were two local entertainers who performed at the nearby Harbour Band Arena in the summer.

Robert Speirs had three spells at the Midland Hotel, the last two as manager. Being in charge of the Midland carried with it a certain kudos, as is noticeable in the Visitor's account of his return to the hotel in April 1968. 'Absent from Morecambe since the summer of 1966, Mr Robert Speirs, a former manager of the Midland Hotel, has returned to his old post. On Tuesday night Thistle Hotels, the company owning the Midland, gave a cocktail party in the main lounge to welcome Mr Speirs back. Over 200 people joined in the toast, including the Mayor and Mayoress of Morecambe, several local councillors, builders, theatre people, licensing trade friends and the Press. The Mayor, on behalf of the town, welcomed him and wished him every happiness and success.'
(Robert Speirs)

They would often come into the Cocktail Bar at lunch time. Albert was always friendly and a bit of a cheeky chappie. During the holidays an elderly lady and her daughter were regular guests and as the years progressed the mother became more and more infirm but refused a wheelchair. This meant she had to be 'escorted' into the Dining Room for meals, daughter taking one arm and our tall Head Porter, Bill Muggliston, the other, her feet not touching the floor. Observing this one day, Albert Modley remarked that he did not think the food in the hotel was that bad that our guests had to be dragged in to eat!

I can safely say that of all the famous personalities who stayed in the Midland in my time there were none who caused any problems. None demanded any special attention and were treated like any of our normal guests. Several became good friends.

For the well-to-do ladies of the town the Saturday coffee morning was a regular event. They would congregate in their finery (always with a stylish hat) to partake of pots of coffee and chocolate mint crisps while enjoying a musical interlude – initially by the Francis Neaum Trio (piano, violin and cello) but later replaced by pianist Norman Tobias offering a more updated repertoire. With the addition of bass and drums, Tobias provided the musical accompaniment for the hotel's popular Dinner Dances.

The highlight of the winter season at the hotel was probably Morecambe Golf Club's Annual Ball when the Foyer was set up with a lavish buffet, leaving the Dining Room for dancing. Another spectacular event was Colonel Donald Lang's T.A. Regimental Dance when the full Regimental Band took over the Foyer along with the Regimental Colours guarded by an armed escort. The band was so loud that all the guests packed into the Cocktail Bar until dinner was announced!

For several winters we also put on a very popular series of Latin American Dance Competitions. They were organised by two of the top Latin American dance teachers in Britain and contestants came from around the UK. The winning couples from each heat competed in a grand final for the Champion of Champions Trophy – a very enjoyable and colourful evening.

Celebratory cakes were something of a speciality of Midland Hotel chef Tony Brown and pastry cook Annie Wells, pictured with Manager Robert Speirs and two assistants. Made to commemorate its opening in 1964 is an edible replica of Marineland, an oceanarium which once stood at the landward end of the Stone Jetty. With its canopy roof, rows of seats and two pools in white icing and the ground floor entrance picked out in chocolate, the cake was exact in every detail, thanks to a set of plans provided by the architect Robert Jackson. (Robert Speirs)

In the summer of 1966 Robert Speirs left the Midland again, this time to take up an appointment at the Golden Lion Hotel in Stirling, a much larger establishment. It was, however, destined to be a relatively short absence and in April 1968 he and his family were welcomed back to the Midland by the Mayor and Mayoress of Morecambe at a reception attended by over 200 people – an indication of the status then enjoyed by the manager of the resort's premier hotel.

With hindsight, perhaps the end of the 1960s was not a good time to return to Morecambe. Times were changing and, as the decade gave way to the 1970s, Morecambe and the Midland Hotel stood on the brink of a dramatic transformation – one that would mark the beginning of a slow but inexorable decline for the resort and its leading hotel.

When it was built, the Midland Hotel was designed to lure wealthy travellers whose trips to the continent had been disrupted by the Depression. While successful in this aim during the 1930s and able to attract similar custom in the immediate post-war period, a small but growing percentage of its clientele was gradually rediscovering the attractions of foreign travel. Until the late 1960s, however, continental excursions tended to remain the preserve of those who could afford the time and the transport to reach their destinations.

All this was to change with the rise of the package holiday industry. Helped by the introduction of a new generation of larger and more efficient aircraft, travel companies began to offer relatively cheap all-in deals covering flights, accommodation and meals, to resorts in Spain, Greece and the south of France. The Mediterranean, with its warm seas, sandy beaches and guaranteed sunshine, was now within reach, geographically and financially, for a much broader spectrum of the population. Not surprisingly, the prospect of spending a fortnight in Morecambe with the likelihood of rain, even in the summer, no longer held quite the same appeal.

From the early 1970s Morecambe was on the way down – and the Midland with it.

(Bradford Telegraph and Argus)

Chapter Nine

FALSE DAWNS AND DECLINE

As the 1960s drew to a close, the British seaside resort was still the principal destination for 75% of all main holidays taken by Britons. Thirty years later the figure had fallen to 44%, a steady long-term decline that inevitably had a serious effect on the economy of seaside towns. Like many comparable resorts, Morecambe's popularity suffered markedly during the 1970s as more and more people began to desert their traditional holiday destinations in Britain for the sun, sea and sand of Benidorm, Torremolinos and Lanzarote.

While the nature of its clientele cushioned the blow to some extent, the Midland Hotel still felt the impact of changing holiday patterns – sufficient to worry the chairman of its owners, Scottish and Newcastle Breweries Ltd. He admitted that the hotels division of the company was going through a difficult period and that a number of its properties, including the Midland, would be looked at closely regarding possible disposal. Robert Speirs, in the interim, had taken the sensible decision to leave the Midland for the third and last time, accepting a management position with the Reo Stakis chain of hotels and restaurants based in Glasgow. In September 1974 Scottish and Newcastle put the Midland Hotel on the market. With an asking price of £180,000, several potential purchasers were rumoured to be interested, including a London financier, a Blackpool hotel group and a number of Morecambe business people, notably Licio Prada, proprietor of the town's Mayfair Hotel. However, no firm bids materialised and the Midland continued to operate throughout the 1975 season. During this time, tentative inquiries were received from the University of Lancaster which wanted the building as a hall of residence and a social and community centre for students lodging in Morecambe (with the possibility of running it as a hotel out of term time) – but local councillors were not in favour of this change of use.

In March 1976 the Midland was eventually bought by the Hutchinson Leisure Group (HLG), a company with a portfolio of cinemas, pubs, clubs, hotels and holiday centres, mostly located in north-west England and north Wales. The new management did not make an auspicious start. Within a short time, a dispute over union recognition led to half a dozen hotel staff walking out of the building and establishing a picket line at the main entrance. Several delivery vehicles were turned away before the two sides eventually met and resolved their differences.

Promising they 'would be pumping a lot of money into the hotel', HLG embarked on a programme of internal alterations designed to bring the Midland up to date. Unfortunately, most of these alterations proved to be totally out of sympathy with Oliver Hill's original concept for the hotel's interior. HLG's intention to remove the Eric Gill panel from the Entrance Lounge and replace it with a bar was of particular concern to Lancashire's Conservation Officer, John Champness. Worried what might happen, he wrote to the Department of the Environment on 4 October 1977.

Interior of the Midland Hotel after alterations by the Hutchinson Leisure Group. The partition wall, leafy carpets and floral patterned furniture overwhelm the original light and airy foyer and considerably lessen the impact of the sweeping staircase. (Anne Greenham)

On the other side of the partition wall the Eric Gill bas-relief has been replaced by a bar which, along with the late 1970s décor, reduces the once unique Midland to 'just another hotel'.
(Anne Greenham)

I have received word from the City Architect and Planner in Lancaster that a superb bas-relief by Eric Gill, which forms an integral part of the original design of the pre-war Midland Hotel in Morecambe, is about to be removed and sold across the Atlantic. I am therefore writing to you to urge you to spot list the hotel – which is per se of the highest interest – in the hope of thereby preventing the accomplishment of this threat.

Four days later, in a remarkably quick response, the Midland Hotel was listed Grade 2*, at the time an unusual achievement for a Modernist building, although there had been much campaigning on behalf of this style of architecture by organisations such as the Thirties Society (later the Twentieth Century Society). One result of the hotel being given such a high listing was to make it illegal to remove from the building any objects deemed to be fixtures or fittings. Lancaster City Council, however, did agree to HLG dismantling the panel and re-erecting it on a wall in the former Children's Room. In 1979 HLG applied for listed building consent to loan the panel to the Hayward Gallery in London for inclusion in its forthcoming Arts Council 'Thirties' exhibition. This was granted but with the stipulation that the panel be returned to the hotel and remounted in its new location. Once the exhibition was over, HLG asked if they could sell the panel to the Victoria and Albert Museum 'for permanent public display' and replace it in the hotel with a replica. Lancaster City Council refused, commenting that 'Its permanent removal would seriously harm the character of the building, and its replacement by a replica is considered inadequate as a substitute.' HLG appealed against the decision to the Secretary of State for the Environment whose judgement was published in May 1981 following a public enquiry. He dismissed the appeal on the grounds that

> despite alterations to the interior of the hotel premises, the character and architectural value of the building as a Grade 2 star listed structure relies both on its external design and on the remaining original decorative internal features which were specially commissioned by the architect of the hotel, Oliver Hill. The view is taken that these internal features constitute an integral part of the overall design and that in principle they should remain *in situ*. Whilst therefore removal elsewhere of the original mural

By the mid-1980s Gill's bas-relief had been relocated to the old Children's Room (renamed the Eric Gill Suite) which also contained his map of North West England. Both suffered from juxtaposition to each other, the wallpaper and the light fittings. (Anne Greenham)

Despite its uninspiring architecture, the sun-lounge quickly became a popular venue for morning coffee and afternoon tea. (Anne Greenham)

sculpture and its replacement by a replica might have little visual impact, this would undoubtedly diminish the architectural value and importance of the building as a whole.

This was a significant ruling as, according to Teresa Sladen of the Victorian Society, it established 'that a piece of sculpture, specially made for the interior of a particular building, was protected by the listed status of the building even when the sculpture was no longer in its original position in the building'.

Although the individual pieces of the panel had been returned to the hotel in June 1980, they had still not been re-erected over three years later. This inaction finally

A conservation officer examines the condition of the Eric Gill bas-relief after its return to the Midland Hotel in June 1980 from an exhibition in the Hayward Gallery, London.
(Lancashire Evening Post)

156

Jack Latty was the Midland
Hotel's longest continuous serving
manager, running the hotel for the
Hutchinson Leisure Group between
1977 and 1987.
(Lancashire Evening Post)

led Lancaster City Council to serve HLG with a listed building enforcement notice on 30 November 1983 giving them until the following June to reinstate the panel in its agreed position. This had the desired effect and in May 1984 local monumental masons Kenneth Fraser Ltd assembled the panel on the east wall of the old Children's Room, which was renamed the Eric Gill Suite. Hotel manager Jack Latty said the room would be used for dining and as a meeting place for local organisations.

As well as the internal changes carried out to the hotel during this period, few of which enhanced its appearance, one new external feature met with general approval. In January 1979 planning permission was granted for a glass sun-lounge to run along the seaward frontage of the building to provide additional space and a pleasant place to take afternoon tea while enjoying the view across the bay. In a way this was an acknowledgment that the management now saw the general public as much a part of the hotel's clientele as the residents.

In 1982 the few remaining vestiges of 1930s décor were effectively eliminated when the Seahorse Bar was transformed into the Royal Lancaster Suite, 'an elegant new function complex'. Resplendent with plush, deep-pile carpets, Regency chandeliers and gold curtains, it was described as 'tastefully and luxuriously capturing the mood of the Midland' but was more redolent of the interior of one of the town's better Working Men's Clubs. Oliver Hill must have been turning in his grave.

While these 'improvements' met with some modest success, the Midland was still battling against the tide. If anything, Morecambe's decline was getting progressively worse. Without the influx of summer visitors to compensate for the traditional problems of seasonal unemployment, the resort's economy was hit hard. Less money was available for investment in the new attractions which were desperately needed. In 1977 the Super Swimming Stadium had been demolished, winter storms had broken the back of the West End pier leaving the landward half a tangle of twisted metal, and the Winter Gardens, once the resort's premier theatre, had closed its doors for the last time – left to act as a decaying reminder of Morecambe's once prosperous past.

Little was done to replace what had been lost. Those responsible for Morecambe's tourism seemed unable to grasp the fact that the traditional seaside holiday was dying and lacked the foresight and imagination to plan for a different future, for a different type of holidaymaker with different demands. Many blamed the apparent lack of political will to do anything about a steadily deteriorating and inadequate infrastructure on the absorption of Morecambe and Heysham by Lancaster City Council following the reorganisation of local government in 1974 – a sore which continues to fester today. There is the belief that, since amalgamation, Morecambe has lost out to Lancaster in terms of investment for regeneration, the council preferring to spend its money on the centre of Lancaster where it is easier to attract private sector developers.

The 1970s had been a difficult period, with the three-day week, industrial action and rising unemployment all leading to an economic recession in the later years of the decade. The 1980s were little better. As John Walton pointed out in his book *The British Seaside*:

> There was a sharp decline in main domestic holidays in Britain between 1975 and 1985, driven by recession and competition, in which the seaside took more than its fair share … by 1981 more main holidays were allegedly taken abroad than at home.

In 1987 Hutchinson Leisure Group was taken over by the Oxford based company Apollo Leisure. As a 'leading force in the entertainment and leisure industry' it was more interested in acquiring HLG's cinemas and clubs rather than the hotels it 'inherited' as part of the takeover. Unsure of the Midland's viability, Apollo Leisure was reluctant to invest in any major developments and two years later, in February 1989, the hotel was put up for sale. A spokesman said that the decision to sell had been made for purely commercial reasons 'in line with the company's aim to target a more specific market'.

Within a few weeks the Midland had been bought for £895,000 by Family Hotels, a newly formed company run by Anne and Rob Greenham.

> We came to Morecambe with the intention of buying the Broadway Hotel but our agent said that the Midland had just come on the market and did we want to go and have a look? But the trouble with the Midland is that once you look you're hooked!

They were confident of reviving the hotel's fortunes, convinced that 'the great English seaside holiday is back. There is nothing wrong with Morecambe. We have got it all up here and now people are putting money into the place and it's really going to take off.' Their intention was to reinstate some of the original style and quality of the hotel commensurate with the needs of present day guests. Architect Tony Dugdale and his wife Pat, a designer, were engaged to oversee a major, yet sensitive, rehabilitation of the hotel. Well versed in the style of the 1930s, they had previously worked on the refit of the luxury liner *Queen Elizabeth 2*, the reception area for the Orient Express at Victoria Station and the Lloyds building in the City of London. The Midland Hotel project was ambitious in its conception, involving removal of the 1970s partition walls, uncovering and restoration of floor and wall surfaces, redesign of furniture and textiles and replacement of items originally made for the hotel but since lost, such as the Marion Dorn rugs. Future developments would include a purpose-built conference centre and indoor swimming pool sited on the grassed area adjacent to the hotel.

The Dugdales' objective was not to produce an exact copy of the 1930s Midland. 'It's a working hotel, not a museum, so while remaining faithful to much of its original design, realistic compromises have to be made.' The furniture provided an example of such a compromise. As all of Oliver Hill's original tub chairs and sofas had long since disappeared from the hotel, replicas would be made, but using sustainable timber and veneers rather than endangered tropical hardwoods.

One of Pat Dugdale's achievements was the re-creation of Marion Dorn's large circular rugs, a difficult task as the complex designs had been lost and contemporary photographs showed the rugs only as ellipses. However, using computer software she was able to transform the pattern from an ellipse into a circle, imposing rigid geometry onto flowing lines. The two rugs were hand tufted by Atelier Interiors Ltd of Halifax using colours chosen from a typical Dorn tuft box but with a different tonal range from the originals. Once finished they were positioned in the hotel's entrance lounge on top of a new carpet. It was thought sensible to keep the terrazzo floor covered as the delicate silver mosaic waves had deteriorated and started to break up, while trials had also shown that an exposed floor created unacceptable echoes.

Another reconstruction resulted from the Midland Hotel being chosen by London Weekend Television as the location for an episode of its popular detective series *Agatha Christie's Poirot*. For the programme LWT built a replica of the circular café at its studios in Twickenham, complete with mural. Some months after filming, set designers Mike Gromnell and Wyndham Giles travelled to Morecambe to paint a version of the mural in the hotel. While the scenes generally corresponded to those of Ravilious, their quality reflected the fact that they were done by set painters rather than a leading artist. To complement the refurbishment of the café, its original wooden flooring was rescued from beneath the patterned carpeting.

Sadly, the Greenhams' ambitions were never fulfilled. In autumn 1990, boardroom changes at Family Hotels brought the appointment of a new managing director who considered that the Midland was not being run efficiently enough, despite a substantial increase in turnover. Accusing the Greenhams of losing thousands of pounds a month, he attempted to remove them from the hotel and install a replacement manager. It later transpired that the decision to oust them had been taken at a board meeting attended only by the chairman and managing director, a meeting Rob Greenham believed was probably in breach of company law. Although Anne Greenham had earlier resigned from the board for personal reasons, she still owned 52% of the company's shares and was determined to fight the decision. 'We have not sweated and slaved for the last eighteen months to let somebody run away with our hotel.'

The Greenhams strongly refuted any claims of mismanagement.

> When we took the Midland over there was no life or soul in the place – it was just like an empty shell but we put the heart back into it. Most of the town's functions had gone to the Carleton but we gradually got them back. The place had been neglected by the previous owners – they didn't really want hotels – and the rooms had only about 25% occupancy. We got the turnover up from £600,000 to £800,000 in our first year and nearly £850,000 in the second.

Staff at the hotel urged the Greenhams not to quit. Local magistrates turned down an application by the Family Hotels' new managing director to take over the licence of the hotel and the City Council offered help to keep the couple in business. An Extraordinary General Meeting of the company was called and, with the support of shareholders, Anne and Rob Greenham were able to remain at the Midland until the hotel was eventually sold.

> We thought of going to court but couldn't face it, so decided to move on and start again. The annoying thing was that we could have afforded to buy the Midland outright in the first place but were persuaded, against our better judgement, to use our money to create Family Hotels plc and get investors to buy shares – under the Business Expansion Scheme you could get up to £40,000 set against income tax. But the whole thing turned into a nightmare. Our accountant was bent and all the board of directors wanted was to make as much money as possible out of the hotel. We should have pulled the plug at the beginning but made the big mistake of carrying on. Things came to a head when our accountant failed to include VAT on a business projection and blamed it on us. We managed to get a bank loan to keep the company afloat but the board just took the money and sent us into bankruptcy.

Mounting pressure from its bank gave Family Hotels no other option but to sell the hotel. Advertised for sale by public auction on 17 April 1991, the Midland was described in the estate agent's brochure as a

> Fully licensed three star resort hotel with full functions facilities and 48 en-suite bedrooms, strategically located in the very heart of Morecambe, overlooking the bay to the Cumbrian Hills. Magnificent 'art deco' architecture in nautical 'liner-style' … a certifiable masterpiece.

Anne and Rob Greenham
with a message of support from
staff at the Midland Hotel
following their dispute with
directors of Family Hotels.
(Lancashire Evening Post)

The actual auction proved to be something of a non-event. About forty people – a mixture of the curious and genuinely interested – crammed into the Eric Gill Suite at the hotel to hear the auctioneer from the Skipton firm of Dacre, Son and Hartley attempt to start the bidding at £750,000. Following a lengthy pause he dropped the figure to £650,000, a move which elicited a response from a man at the rear of the room. An appeal for further bids was met by a stony silence. In frustration he was prompted to observe: 'We have come with the intention of selling the Midland today but we didn't exactly want to give it away. It's not Christmas yet!' There were still no takers and the auctioneer, while admitting that the offer was 'not a million miles away' from the reserve price, stated that he could not sell the hotel for £650,000 and brought the proceedings to a close.

It later came to light that after the auction the mystery bidder had met the auctioneer and agreed a private deal to buy the hotel although the price paid was not

disclosed. The next week he was identified in the local press as Les Whittingham, a nursing home owner from North Wales. Rob Greenham remembers discussing the hotel with him before the auction.

London Weekend Television's mock-up of the Midland Hotel's circular café in its Twickenham studios. The mural has been painted onto canvas and pinned to the wall.
(Anne Greenham)

> Les was a character. The first time I met him was at the sale. I had all these statistics for the last ten years' trading, who stopped at the hotel, what the weather was like, and so on. Les didn't want to know. He just got out his fag packet, ripped it down and scribbled some figures on the back. After the auction he did a deal to buy the hotel but without having the money in place. He phoned his bank manager down Chester somewhere, but as I found out later Les used to scam people and he must have had something on this bank manager – he just rang up saying 'I've bought it, you'd better put the money up'. Then he drove off in his Mercedes.

Les Whittingham's seven and a half year ownership of the Midland Hotel was to prove both colourful and controversial, characterised by frequent and often acrimonious altercations with the local council. In retrospect, it is difficult to understand his reasons for buying the hotel. Did he have a genuine belief that he could make it successful – no easy task given the state of Morecambe's tourist trade in the early 1990s – or was there some other motive? One person who knew him said he just liked big buildings! He already owned two impressive properties in North Wales, one of which was the Grade I listed Hafodunos Hall designed by Sir George Gilbert Scott. Whatever the truth, Les Whittingham was no ordinary hotelier. Often described as a likeable rogue, he could be in turn amusing, brusque, solicitous and rude – but the word used by most people who met him was eccentric.

After they sold the Midland, Anne and Rob Greenham used to go in occasionally to lend a hand at busy times. Rob recalls passing reception one day

> when this fellow came to check in for one of the suites. A bit later I was in the kitchen helping with the washing up when Les comes rushing in. 'Where's probe? Where's meat probe?' He was after one of the probes used to test the temperature of meat being cooked. I said 'Why? What's up?' Anyway, he gets it and runs off and we follow. What had happened was this fellow had complained about no hot water in the bedroom. So Les went all the way up to his suite and stuck this probe under the tap. The fellow said 'There you are – it's cold.' So Les marches him outside and points to the sign saying 'What does that say there? – Bed and Breakfast. It doesn't say anything about hot water!'

> On another occasion a lady came into reception when he was there having a fag. She asked 'Have you got a lunch menu?' Les said 'Yes, it's there on the board – and if you don't like it you can **** off down to the Strathmore.' The fellow was eccentric, bizarre – I honestly never met a bloke like him.

Despite his unconventional behaviour and Basil Fawlty-like manner, Pam Brook found him friendly and hospitable when she visited the Midland in 1992 to catalogue the works of art in the hotel. Also staying at the hotel was a freelance photographer who had been commissioned by the *Daily Telegraph* to do a photo shoot of the Midland. (The photographs were eventually published to accompany an article entitled *Keeping up Appearances* which appeared in the newspaper's colour supplement on 13 February 1993.)

At the time, the mosaic seahorse by Marion Dorn was hidden under the lounge carpet and an approach was made by Pam Brook to Les Whittingham for the carpet to be lifted so the seahorse could be measured and photographed.

> He murmured something that sounded like consent but then typically proceeded to be elusive during the day. In late afternoon he finally announced his intention to uncover the seahorse claiming he knew exactly where it was located. He decided that cutting a flap in the carpet would prove least disruptive. As the hotel handyman had gone home and all the shops that could provide the necessary tools for this operation

Poirot Investigates at The Midland

In September 1989, one of fiction's most celebrated detectives pursued his enquiries at the Midland Hotel in Morecambe. The hotel was chosen by London Weekend Television for location filming of an episode of its popular *Agatha Christie's Poirot* series, starring David Suchet as the Belgian sleuth. Originally, LWT had intended to film elsewhere, using a seaside hotel in the south of England. However, on learning of the existence in Morecambe of one of the country's finest Modernist hotels, the television company not only decided to come to the resort but also re-wrote part of the script to accommodate the change of location.

In the televised episode, entitled *Double Sin*, Hercule Poirot decides that his trusty friend Captain Hastings needs a holiday and where better to go than the health-giving seaside resort of Whitcombe. Once there, it is not long before Poirot is called upon to exercise his 'little grey cells' in order to solve the audacious theft of a set of valuable antique miniatures. The exterior of the Midland is seen on several occasions, the most impressive of which is the programme's final shot when Poirot's car sweeps out of the drive with the hotel in the background gleaming white against a bright blue sky. Although many of the inside scenes for the episode were filmed in the company's studios in Twickenham, there were shots of the hotel's spiral staircase, Eric Gill's ceiling medallion and the mosaic seahorse designed by Marion Dorn. Picturesque Kirkby Lonsdale doubled as the actual town of Whitcombe (Morecambe was presumably considered visually unsuitable!) while extensive use was made of the Lake District around Windermere for other scenes.

The episode's denouement takes place in a studio mock-up of the circular café for which scenic artists recreated Eric Ravilious' ill-fated mural *Day and Night*, sadly damaged beyond repair soon after its completion. As a permanent reminder of the filming the same artists travelled up to Morecambe a few months later to reproduce the painting on the wall of the café itself.

When *Double Sin* was broadcast on 11 February 1990 it gave the Midland Hotel a nation-wide audience (12 million people regularly watched *Poirot*). The following day the hotel was inundated with telephone calls from incredulous people asking "Is it for real?"

Captain Hastings (Hugh Fraser), Poirot (David Suchet) and Chief Inspector Japp (Philip Jackson) outside the Midland Hotel. (Lancashire Evening Post)

were closed, Les attacked the carpet with a Stanley knife. The blade disappeared under the carpet after the first incision but he solved the problem of the lost cutting tool by disappearing into the kitchen and returning with the chef's boning knife, closely followed by a disgruntled looking chef holding a poker-shaped steel sharpener. After managing to cut through the carpet, Les lifted it up with a broom handle and then shone a torch into the darkness until the seahorse was spotted. During this operation the boning knife required frequent sharpening which Les accomplished by running the blade up and down the steel held at arm's length by the chef – whose face remained expressionless throughout! The photographer got his picture and I was able to measure the seahorse.

While Les Whittingham could get annoyed with anyone who upset him, most of his vituperation was reserved for Lancaster City Council, especially its planning department. His first run-in with authority came soon after he took over the hotel and began organising regular tabletop sales on the lawn to the side of the sun-lounge. This dismayed planning officers who threatened court action unless the sales were halted, claiming that 'this kind of activity detracts from the character of the resort in general and the listed Midland Hotel in particular'.

In response, he went on the offensive, reminding the council that the covenants which came with the hotel when it was built allowed him to do what he liked in the grounds. Furthermore, he accused the council of breaching the same covenants which prevented land adjacent to the Midland from being used for any purpose which would 'interfere with the amenities of the hotel'. 'Should you wish to read the covenants you will see that the café you have leased without any planning permission on the stone jetty is not permitted. Neither is your rather stuffy roller skating rink or your road train and whatever else you have managed to sneak on there.'

In May 1994 he again crossed swords with council officials following the repainting of the hotel in bright yellow trimmed with turquoise. The funding for this new colour scheme came from the Disney Corporation who requested the change as it wanted to use the hotel in a film called *Funny Bones*, a quirky British comedy starring Lee Evans and Jerry Lewis. (In the event, most of the footage shot at the Midland ended up on the cutting room floor.) The hotel's lemon image did not find favour with Lancaster City Council which served Les Whittingham with an enforcement notice giving him two months to

Les Whittingham, in typical working attire, did not fit most people's image of the proprietor of Morecambe's premier hotel. (Morecambe Visitor)

Dame Thora Hird in front
of the Midland Hotel.
(Morecambe Visitor)

In May 1996 Dame Thora Hird
returned to her home town of
Morecambe to film a programme
exploring the history of the Midland
Hotel for the BBC Two television
series 'One Foot in the Past'.
Growing up in the resort, she could
remember the old Victorian hotel
being demolished and the dramatic
impact its modern replacement had
at the time.

'The Midland Hotel was a
revolutionary piece of architecture
which changed the town. It really put
Morecambe on the map. Modern
times were here. Of course, the
hotel really was for the crème de
la crème, and while I was having
fun on the pier the gilded youth of
Manchester and Bradford – the
fast set – were living it up here. It
was fit for movie stars – Hollywood
had come to Morecambe!'

restore its original white appearance. Arguing that English Heritage were happy with the change, he thought the council's order 'very stupid, really, because everybody likes the new colour', adding that if he was forced to comply he would paint it pink with big yellow blobs to fit in with the resort's plan for a 'Mr Blobby' theme park (one of Morecambe's less successful enterprises!).

By the early 1990s Morecambe was at last waking up to its plight and was starting to make some attempt to improve its image. It still had serious problems. Apart from the view across the bay, a tired looking fairground and a handful of amusement arcades, there was little to attract visitors to the town. In a belated attempt to stem the spiral of decline the council identified an extensive tract of derelict land next to the Promenade Station as the focus for the regeneration of the resort. This would eventually result in a mix of commercial and tourism based developments, including a supermarket, bowling alley, multi-screen cinema and indoor market, as well as a new road layout, all of which, it was hoped, would act as a catalyst for future investment. In addition, the council had won substantial Government funding for improvements to Morecambe's coastal defences (a huge civil engineering project which would secure the town against flooding) while a £1 million lottery grant would finance a series of public artworks along the promenade, themed around the birdlife of Morecambe Bay.

Unfortunately for Les Whittingham, once this work began, the Midland found itself surrounded by construction activity, not only across Marine Road but also on the promenade where the peace and quiet of the hotel was shattered by a constant stream of heavy lorries delivering boulders to shore up the sea defences.

Frustrated by all the noise and disturbance and convinced that the council were persecuting him, he submitted a planning application to convert the Midland into a nursing home, stating that the building would be ideal for such a use 'as it was a RAF hospital during the war and is purpose-built with a great view'. He did not share the council's confidence that Morecambe would again become a successful holiday destination and cited economic reasons for the proposed change.

> I've had three years of hassle and disturbance since buying the hotel. It's been an absolute nightmare. Morecambe looks more like Bosnia than a holiday resort. My visitors are woken up early in the morning by construction work and many have said they just won't be coming back.

In the end nothing came of the nursing home plan as just before Christmas the Midland Hotel was taken over by the Lancaster based company Progressive Leisure Corporation Ltd. Its two partners, Jared Brook and Lincoln Fraser, were associates of Les Whittingham and had lease-purchased the hotel with the intention of later buying the building outright. They had also offered to enter into a £7.2 million project with Lancaster City Council to redevelop the hotel and the adjacent Bubbles leisure complex. The following July, council officials aborted the deal after Progressive Leisure was found guilty of financial irregularities and issued with a winding up order at Preston County Court.

Les Whittingham returned to manage the hotel but was still intent on selling if he could find a suitable buyer. During the brief tenure of Progressive Leisure the Midland's kitchens had been inspected by environmental health inspectors and condemned as unhygienic, with preparation areas covered in grease and cigarette ash, uncovered food and pools of dirty liquid on the floor. Although he was not running the hotel at the time, Les Whittingham was still charged with breaching environmental health laws and fined £2,700 with £1,280 costs at Lancaster Magistrates' Court.

Three months later, he had 'sold' the hotel again, this time to city councillor Diane Huddleston, stating that he would be leaving Morecambe altogether, 'glad to see the back of a town that has caused me nothing but trouble'. Mrs Huddleston had great hopes of turning the Midland into a profitable business venture but her plans collapsed in the summer of 1996 when Les Whittingham returned to reclaim the hotel stating that she had failed to complete the deal, estimated to have been in excess of £2 million.

Seemingly having a change of heart about the economic prospects for the Midland, he put forward plans for its total refurbishment, including a new reception area, revamped restaurant and cocktail bar and, possibly, a glass structure on the roof to take

As the Midland Hotel moved downmarket, garish advertisements offering cheap deals began to disfigure its walls and were sometimes draped the full height of the staircase tower. In 1996 Les Whittingham was fined £200 with £724 costs for breaching planning rules by erecting a banner on a listed building without consent. (Lancashire Evening Post)

advantage of the panoramic view across the bay. What might also have influenced his decision was the Government's intention to relax its laws on gambling. This would allow casinos to open up in places where they had previously been banned, a prospect which Les Whittingham, thinking of the Midland, found very attractive. While the planning department appreciated that a casino in Morecambe might be controversial, it explained that any application had 'to be considered strictly in planning terms and from this point of view, the location is a good one for this kind of development'. Les Whittingham was delighted. 'It's bound to make a hell of a difference to Morecambe. The building itself looks as though it was designed as a casino not a hotel.'

However, any hopes of turning Morecambe into the Monte Carlo of Lancashire were dashed when the Government, faced with mounting criticism of its original decision, was forced to revise its gambling reforms, effectively ending Les Whittingham's plans for a money-spinning casino in the Midland. It was peculiarly ironic that the only time he and the council were in agreement, nothing came of the scheme.

Of all the disputes between Les Whittingham and Lancaster City Council, the longest running and most contentious concerned the ownership of the hotel's stone panel carved by Eric Gill. Early in 1992 Les Whittingham was visited by John Hoole of the Barbican Centre in London who was planning an exhibition on the sculptures of Eric Gill. He wanted to inspect Gill's bas-relief *Odysseus Welcomed from the Sea by Nausicaa* with the possibility of including it in the exhibition. No decision was made at this stage as Hoole was concerned about its condition and worried that removing it (the panel was now cemented to the wall rather than hung on pegs) might cause further damage.

Despite the ruling of the Secretary of State in 1981 that the panel was a permanent fixture at the hotel, Les Whittingham realised that the forthcoming exhibition might provide him with an opportunity to sell the work for a substantial sum of money. Taking matters into his own hands he arranged for it to be dismantled by workmen from Momart (an art storage firm) and removed from the building. By chance, John Champness was driving along the seafront past the Midland when he saw pieces of the panel being loaded into a lorry. Contacting the City Council, he discovered that Les Whittingham had not applied for permission to detach the panel and became alarmed that it was about to be sold. On 1 April 1992 he sent an urgent fax to English Heritage.

> I am writing to inform you immediately that I understand that the Eric Gill bas-relief has been removed without Listed Building Consent from the Midland Hotel, Morecambe, and is now in the warehouse of the specialist transport firm, Momart, in London. Mr Whittingham claims that the bas-relief is going to be repaired and then displayed in the exhibition of Gill's works later this year at the Barbican Centre, but the Centre has not yet made any formal agreement with the hotel's owner to display it. In view of the reputation of the owner, one is entitled to be suspicious.

Lancaster City Council issued a writ against Les Whittingham instructing him to return the panel. This precipitated a legal battle which was to continue for several years. To establish its legal position, Lancaster City Council liaised with the Twentieth Century Society and other bodies in an attempt to stop what it regarded as 'cultural asset stripping'. However, the removal of the panel for exhibition purposes was not entirely without its supporters. As president of the Art Critics Association, Keith Patrick observed, somewhat optimistically, that

The pieces of the Eric Gill bas-relief safely in store at Lancaster Police Station, having been recovered after a lengthy undercover operation. (Lancaster Guardian)

> There is no implication that this piece will not return to the hotel. A great deal of people will be given the chance to see this piece because of the altruism of its owner.

At the end of April both parties in the dispute agreed to let the panel stay in London pending a High Court trial in the autumn to determine if it was actually an integral part of the hotel or, as Les Whittingham claimed, free-standing. In November the panel was one of the highlights of the Barbican exhibition 'Eric Gill: Sculpture' but did not arrive with the rest of the works when the exhibition travelled to Leeds Art Gallery the following April, remaining in storage with Momart.

Another year and a half elapsed before the case finally came to court. Over three days in September 1995, at Liverpool Law Courts, Les Whittingham tried to convince the presiding judge that the panel was not a fixed part of the building and thus his to dispose of as he saw fit. He based his argument on the fact that it had been moved once before and had originally been attached to the wall with brackets so that it could be lifted on and off. He also contended (incorrectly) that the panel had not been sculpted in the hotel but was a last minute replacement for an earlier version (*High Jinks in Paradise*) which, he said, Arthur Towle

> played holy hell about [when he] realised the LMS had gone into pornography … and decided that this thing should be ripped out and the other one put in. Eric Gill had got the design for Adam and Eve which was quickly whipped into being Nausicaa and somebody else by extending it. It was partially worked on in mid-Wales and brought over and finished in the lounge.

Les Whittingham's convoluted and implausible answers under cross-examination and his surreal questioning of various expert witnesses transforms the court transcript of the case from a mundane record into a potential comedy script. Not unexpectedly, Judge Maddocks found for Lancaster City Council. In his opinion

> Once a 'structure' or 'object' becomes part of a listed building, that structure or object or fixture is embraced by the listed building regime. In this sense, once a fixture always a fixture.

Les Whittingham argued that it would be unsafe to re-erect the panel in the hotel because coastal defence work carried out by the local council had caused cracking in the wall where it was to be fixed. This was dismissed due to lack of evidence. An appeal against the ruling was lodged but, for some reason, not pursued, and in April 1998 he finally agreed to reinstate the panel after being threatened with imprisonment if there was any unreasonable delay. It was returned to Morecambe but remained in pieces in wooden crates, stored in the sun-lounge.

A further twist to the saga came at the end of August when Les Whittingham suffered a heart attack and died shortly before celebrating his fiftieth birthday. A month later, when conservation officers called at the hotel to examine the Eric Gill panel they found that it had mysteriously disappeared. Not surprisingly, the police were suspicious – it seemed just too much of a co-incidence that the panel should vanish so soon after Les Whittingham's death. 'Witnesses' talked of an unmarked

Chairperson of the Friends of the Midland Hotel, Sue Thompson, is glad to see the Eric Gill bas-relief back in its rightful home after an absence of over seven years.
(Lancaster Guardian)

blue van parked outside, while inside, workmen were seen wheeling wooden crates from the sun-lounge towards the lift, ostensibly to take them down to the basement. Whatever the truth of this, the trail had gone cold and there was no trace of the Gill panel or the blue van.

Following Les Whittingham's demise, his estate was found to be insolvent. The administrators, Sills and Betteridge of Lincoln, were charged with selling all his assets, including the Midland, for the best price they could obtain. The hotel was offered for sale with an asking price of £1.5 million, a figure which many thought far too high, especially as there was no longer any possibility of a casino licence. For the time being, it was placed in the hands of a management company with instructions to continue operating it until a sale was agreed. Six months later no firm offer had been received and rumours started circulating that the building might be turned into luxury apartments or even a Department of Social Security hostel.

With the hotel's prospects uncertain, a number of concerned individuals met in its sun-lounge in early April 1999 to form a support group which became the Friends of the Midland Hotel. Its spokeswoman Sue Thompson said:

> A lot of people feel for this building and we're quite willing to act as an unpaid advert for it. We want to help the hotel while it's having a hard time and see it back on its feet.

(Beginning with only a dozen individuals, the Friends of the Midland are still going strong with a countrywide membership over over 500. More information about the group can be found on page 209.)

In the summer, Sills and Betteridge reduced the asking price to £850,000 in the hope of attracting more interest. Keeping the Midland open so it could be sold as a going concern was proving a drain on the estate's assets and serious thought was being given to closing the hotel and boarding it up.

One piece of good news came in August when police announced that they had recovered the stolen Eric Gill bas-relief. Following months of undercover work, officers finally tracked it down to a blue van parked in a service area near the West Yorkshire town of Pontefract. Two men were arrested and later released on police bail. Although there was the suspicion of a conspiracy involving a number of Les Whittingham's associates, nothing could be proved. Both men claimed they had the deceased owner's permission to take the panel but as this was impossible to verify the Crown Prosecution Service felt there was insufficient evidence to pursue the case and no charges were brought. In October1999, after an absence of over seven years, *Odysseus and Nausicaa* were finally restored to their rightful position in the hotel, a little chipped but generally none the worse for their adventures.

With the approach of the Millennium the Midland was still without a buyer – and it was beginning to show. Streaks of rust stained the now dirty white façade, a number of windows had been broken and weeds were advancing across the forecourt. In the New Year the Architectural Heritage Fund offered a grant to the Friends of the Midland to finance a feasibility study for the hotel, to ascertain whether it actually did have a future. In an attempt to improve the Midland's chances of attracting funding, the Twentieth Century Society recommended (unsuccessfully) that its listing be upgraded from 2* to 1. Spring had turned into summer when Sills and Betteridge announced that the hotel had at last been sold. As the purchaser preferred not to reveal his identity, stories began to spread of who it might be and what was in store for the Midland – ranging from a businessman who wanted to convert the hotel into accommodation for refugees to a recluse who had bought it for a luxury home. There was even a rumour that Les Whittingham had come back from the dead to buy it for himself! In the end all the speculation became irrelevant as the mystery buyer called off the deal before completion, a decision welcomed by the Friends of the Midland who had heard that the person in question had plans to turn the hotel into time-share apartments.

Towards the end of the year the Midland suffered two more blows. As the result of an inspection by environmental health officers the kitchen was found to be unsafe (parts of the ceiling had started to collapse) and was condemned, leaving the hotel open for room bookings only. A few weeks later, the heating system broke down and the building was forced to close.

Although the asking price had again been reduced – offers around £450,000 would be considered – Sills and Betteridge were beginning to despair of ever selling the hotel. 'It is clear from hotel groups whom we have approached that the building is not viable any more as a hotel alone.' They partly blamed English Heritage and Lancaster City Council who were both against any change of use for the building, a stance which, according to the agents, had deterred a number of would-be purchasers. Sills and Betteridge broached the possibility of the council compulsorily purchasing the Midland at a price established by an independent valuer but before any meaningful discussion could take place, the agents reported that they had received a firm offer for the hotel.

In June 2001 contracts were exchanged and Kalber Leisure Ltd, a Grimsby based company, became the new owners of the Midland Hotel. Emerging from the past, as directors of Kalber Leisure, were Jared Brook and Lincoln Fraser, whose short-term 'purchase' of the hotel from Les Whittingham seven years earlier had ended in a Preston courtroom. Since leaving Morecambe they had founded a financial investment company called Imperial Consolidated which they claimed to have sold in order to fund the purchase and restoration of the Midland. It was their intention to spend some £4 million on transforming the building into a 1930s themed 5* luxury hotel.

Not everyone was convinced. Critics pointed to their bankruptcy following the collapse of Progressive Leisure and alleged that Imperial Consolidated was little more than a cover of convenience for the dubious activities of a number of companies, an accusation strenuously denied by Brook and Fraser. The first warning signs appeared in July when both men were disqualified at Blackpool County Court from acting as company directors for four years, a result of their financial mismanagement when last in charge of the Midland. This, they claimed, would not affect their plans for the hotel. In the meantime, a detailed survey had revealed the building to be in a far worse state than originally thought, more than doubling the estimate for its renovation to £9.6 million.

At the beginning of January 2002 Kalber Leisure submitted its ambitious plans for the renovation of the Midland. Chief among them was a three-storey extension to the south end of the building to contain a leisure complex, swimming pool, function room and additional bedrooms. A new sun-lounge with circular bar would replace the existing structure which was in very poor condition. The rest of the building would undergo extensive refurbishment. While appreciating that the proposed extension and other changes might not to be to everyone's taste, the Friends of the Midland accepted that the hotel had to be able to survive in a commercial world and reluctantly conceded that more bedrooms were probably necessary to make it financially viable. The Twentieth Century Society also had concerns, disapproving of the extension's 'pastiche style' which, it said, lacked the subtlety and detailing of the original building. Lancaster City Council, relieved that someone was at last willing to take on the challenge of the Midland, was favourably disposed towards the scheme and when Kalber Leisure's proposals came before its Planning Committee on 18 March they were passed with hardly a dissenting voice.

To publicise its 'Vision for the Future', Kalber Leisure took over an empty building opposite the Midland and converted it into a café/bar and exhibition centre with the past, present and future of the hotel displayed through posters, photographs and video. This was followed by an lavish launch party at the Platform Arts Centre at which invited guests could meet the hotel's management team while nibbling canapés

Kalber Leisure's design for a restored and extended Midland Hotel, and its 'Vision for the Future'. (Deighton International)

Lincoln Fraser and Jared Brook, former 'owners' of the Midland and the men behind Kalber Leisure. (Morecambe Visitor)

A Vision for the Future

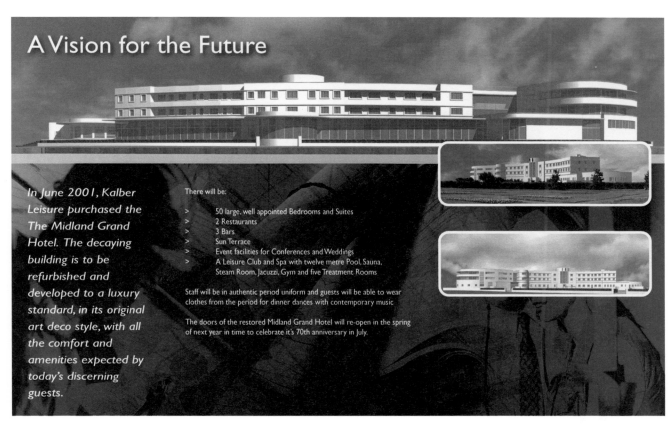

In June 2001, Kalber Leisure purchased the The Midland Grand Hotel. The decaying building is to be refurbished and developed to a luxury standard, in its original art deco style, with all the comfort and amenities expected by today's discerning guests.

There will be:

> 50 large, well appointed Bedrooms and Suites
> 2 Restaurants
> 3 Bars
> Sun Terrace
> Event facilities for Conferences and Weddings
> A Leisure Club and Spa with twelve metre Pool, Sauna, Steam Room, Jacuzzi, Gym and five Treatment Rooms

Staff will be in authentic period uniform and guests will be able to wear clothes from the period for dinner dances with contemporary music

The doors of the restored Midland Grand Hotel will re-open in the spring of next year in time to celebrate it's 70th anniversary in July.

and sipping champagne – all to the accompaniment of a string quartet. Kalber Leisure could not be faulted for its PR.

Settling its bills was a different matter. After a relatively short existence the café was threatened with closure when catering suppliers were not paid; the firm employed to remove asbestos from the hotel was requesting money, as were the architectural consultants who had drawn up the plans for the building's restoration. With costs spiralling upwards several key backers began withdrawing their financial support, leaving the whole project in jeopardy. Months earlier, even before Kalber Leisure had bought the Midland, the Serious Fraud Office had started to look into the finances of its parent company Imperial Consolidated. Over the ensuing weeks a tangled web of intrigue started to emerge, taking in a Syrian arms dealer linked to Osama bin Laden, a gold mining scam in Argentina, money laundering via a private bank in the Caribbean and angry creditors world wide.

Matters came to head at the beginning of June when UK clearing banks, following advice from financial regulators, stopped dealing with Imperial Consolidated. The company collapsed and receivers were called in. Many investors lost large amounts of money. After extensive investigations by the Serious Fraud Office, Jared Brook and Lincoln Fraser, as managing director and chief executive of Imperial Consolidated, were later brought to court on charges of conspiracy to defraud. One of their unpaid debts was £470,000 owed to the Southampton based design firm Deighton International for its work at the Midland Hotel.

Abandoned by Kalber Leisure, the hotel was prey to vandals. The perimeter fencing offered little deterrent, resulting in smashed windows, graffiti-daubed walls and constant break-ins. Despite the council pressing the absentee owners to secure the site, nothing was done and fears grew that vagrants and thieves could cause further damage to the interior, especially to the works of art in the building. With no response from Kalber Leisure, the council took matters into its own hands and instructed workmen to board up the doors and windows in order to prevent unlawful access. At this stage the Midland appeared without hope. There were calls from certain councillors to bulldoze the hotel and market the prime seafront site for redevelopment. That anyone could contemplate demolition of such a landmark building brought a deluge of letters to the town's local newspaper. The Friends of the Midland considered it would be 'an act of cultural vandalism' and vowed to fight any attempt to raze the hotel. Even the satirical magazine *Private Eye* joined the war of words with a thinly veiled criticism of Lancaster City Council.

It is interesting how quick our elected representatives are to discard beautiful things or recommend destruction … anywhere else the Midland would be cherished and restored.

When not actively planning the destruction of the Midland, the council was lending a sympathetic ear to proposed changes of use and, once again, the spectre

For the Midland Hotel the writing was on the wall — literally, its physical appearance stark testimony to years of neglect. On the seaward side, vandals have reduced the sun-lounge to little more than an empty shell. (Barry Guise)

Peeling paintwork and crumbling render lend an air of decay to the rotunda whose dancers have long gone, replaced by docks and dandelions. (Barry Guise)

The hotel's rusting fire escape spirals pastdiscoloured walls and boarded-up windows. (Barry Guise)

of conversion into apartments loomed over the hotel. Stung by earlier criticisms, the council claimed that its primary aim was 'to see the building restored and retained for future generations rather than be demolished'.

Another suggestion was that the council should compulsorily purchase the hotel for a nominal sum (Kalber Leisure having failed to comply with listed building repair notices) and then hand it over to a restoration trust which would guarantee its future. The Friends of the Midland had been liaising with Heritage Trust for the North West with the intention of forming such a body, which could then obtain grants to carry out the necessary refurbishment. Lancaster City Council, however, with unpleasant memories of previous business ventures in Morecambe still fresh in its mind, was averse to risking even a 'nominal sum' in the hands of amateurs.

All discussion was put on hold in early November when a sale was reported to be on the horizon.

"Yes, I know it's a Listed Building – it's on the List of Buildings the Council wants to Forget About ..."
(Peter Millen/ Lancaster Guardian)

Chapter Ten

A BRIGHT NEW FUTURE

arly in 2003, it emerged that the Midland Hotel had been bought by Urban Splash. On 13 January, Tom Bloxham, chairman of the award-winning property regeneration company, issued a press release.

> I have known the building for years, visited it on many occasions and watched its gradual decline with sadness. When I heard that the latest restoration scheme had fallen through … I decided to buy the building. It is a fantastic building. I hope we will be able to restore it back as a hotel and restaurant but it will be very difficult, expensive and will no doubt take several years. For now we have to take stock, look carefully at what needs doing.

Despite this latter note of caution, the news was met with delight – and no little relief. The *Visitor*, in its front-page article of 15 January, was of the opinion that 'With the company's track record so far, it may be more than just another false hope, something the town has seen too many of in recent years.'

Sue Thompson of the Friends of the Midland welcomed the fact that Urban Splash had said 'they want to keep it as an hotel because that is what we've always wanted. The hotel has great untapped potential and its redevelopment could be the kick-start that Morecambe needs.'

Equally up-beat was Lancaster City Council.

> In Urban Splash we have an established and nationally recognised company with a strong reputation for securing development of unused buildings. We look forward to receiving their planning applications for the development of this central Morecambe feature in due course.

The council had to wait some time for these. True to his word, Tom Bloxham was indeed 'taking stock'. Months passed while the building slipped further into decline

A long queue waits at the door of the Midland on 22 November 2003 when Urban Splash opened the hotel to the public. (Barry Guise)

and waves of disquiet began to ripple through Morecambe. There were rumours that Urban Splash was in talks with the council regarding the area of the seafront adjacent to the hotel and this was causing the delay. In August the *Visitor* broke the news that the company had been granted an 'exclusivity agreement' on this site, giving it two years to come up with ideas for the development of this important part of Morecambe – but there was still no word on the Midland.

However, the people of Morecambe had been fretting unduly – Urban Splash had been hard at work, along with their chosen architects, Liverpool-based Union North, and on Friday 21 November, nearly eleven months after buying the property, Tom Bloxham revealed his plans for the Midland. In contrast with the Kalber Leisure 'launch', this was a low-key affair, with the local Member of Parliament, city councillors, reporters and representatives of Friends of the Midland packed into the slightly gloomy atmosphere of the temporarily lit and heated foyer of the hotel.

A comparison was drawn with Brighton which had also been 'a run-down seaside resort that had seen better days' but which had 're-invented itself and is now a successful, modern and happening place'. (This aside caught the imagination of the press and for weeks Morecambe was heralded in news

(The Guardian, 20 March 2004)

Morecambe fights decline with Mars bar effect

The regeneration of the Midland Hotel has focused attention on Morecambe. Urban Splash, along with partners selected as a result of an international design competition, has plans for the area next to the hotel and the local council hopes to see the town – not quite in the words of Mars – a 'good place to live, work and play'.

We've bought The Midland

Back to its best

A bright new Midland Hotel

SIGNPOST TO THE FUTURE

They're all set to Splash the cash

Newspaper headlines from 2003.

reports as the 'Brighton of the North' – contrasting with the time a century ago when the resort was known by the equally fanciful soubriquet, the 'Naples of the North'.)

Although the Midland Hotel was a building of national importance, Mr Bloxham regretted that it no longer met the needs of the modern market. When it had been built, its style reflected the sense of optimism and confidence which Morecambe displayed as a modern, thriving holiday resort. It was Urban Splash's intention to honour that spirit by looking forward rather than reflecting on past glories. A restoration was planned which would be sympathetic to the building's design but the Midland would definitely *not* be a museum. All that was of merit would be restored but for anything new there would be no pastiche of the Thirties' period. The additions and alterations of the 1970s, such as the sun-lounge and bedrooms, would be swept away and replaced by modern designs. On the roof a glass-covered bar and terrace were to be added while on the south side of the hotel, but separate from it both physically and stylistically, was to be a stainless steel bath-house, complete with sauna, hot tub and cocktail bar. The Midland would have a revolutionary heat and power system whereby

By February 2005, security fencing surrounded the hotel. A curious passer-by pauses to look at Urban Splash's vision for a restored Midland Hotel (with the optimistic completion date of 2006). (Barry Guise)

Artist's impression of the front elevation of the future Midland Hotel.
(Urban Splash)

Artist's impression of the seaward façade of the future Midland Hotel.
(Urban Splash)

it produced no nett emissions of CO_2, thus becoming the first carbon neutral hotel in the United Kingdom.

On the following day, the hotel was opened once again so that the general public could view the proposals. An estimated three thousand people passed through the doors to see the future pinned to display boards around the entrance lounge. They were able to gain an insight into Urban Splash's previous ventures, chat to Development Director, Bill Maynard and Development Manager, Paul Jones and sneak another look at the Midland from which they had been barred for so long.

As expected, planning permission was granted by Lancaster City Council at its Planning Committee meeting at the end of January 2004. In the *Lancaster Guardian*, Ron Sands (Councillor with responsibility for Tourism and Leisure) welcomed this 'flagship project that sends a strong signal to other entrepreneurs and will attract investment', a sentiment echoed by Jim Trotman (Principal Tourism Officer) who said: 'We are still working to improve Morecambe's image … and a top-class re-opened Midland will bring more positive publicity to the resort.'

At this point it was hoped that work would start on the hotel in April with a completion date pencilled in for July 2005. Meanwhile, assistance with funding of the project was being sought as the costs were estimated to be around £8 million. Tom Bloxham explained that Urban Splash was not expecting much financial reward – in fact it would be a 'labour of love'.

April passed with no sign of activity on the Midland site. Local people, by now accustomed to disappointment, began to get restive. Rumours of demolition resurfaced in the *Visitor* in June, followed in July by a more prosaic and rather more accurate explanation that 'funding delay holds up work'. The *Citizen* of 19 August carried reassurances from local Member of Parliament, Geraldine Smith, that the North West Regional Development Agency (NWDA) had agreed to help finance the restoration project and were just deciding 'how much'.

Eventually, on 2 December, a press release from NWDA confirmed an investment in the Midland Hotel redevelopment. Helen France (NWDA Executive Director of Development and Partnerships) stated 'The Midland Hotel is a unique asset and the restoration of this landmark building will be a huge step in the renaissance of Morecambe.' Local and national papers reported that £7·3 million had been earmarked for the hotel (£4 million from NWDA, £0·6 million from the Heritage Lottery Fund and £2·7 million from Urban Splash). Work could begin at last!

Six months later, the *Visitor* of 1 June 2005 was able to proclaim that 'today, the first phase of the £7 million, twenty-two month project got underway'.

Appointed to oversee the project was Senior Construction Manager Kieran Gardiner. 'We recognise that the Midland is a building close to many people's hearts and we shall be doing a full and proper job – but that takes time. It's going to be a very complex restoration; when it's finished we're going to be able to walk away with great satisfaction. The first phase will involve clearing the area in front of the hotel and protecting the various pieces of artwork inside the building. Demolition work will then follow, beginning with the sun-lounge and the fire escape – I think everybody wants them down! I am hoping that by September we can start to get the scaffolding up to make a start on the exterior.'

A complete refurbishment of the interior was planned. On the ground floor, the best of the existing features would be retained and restored but as Development Manager Paul Jones pointed out: 'We will be demolishing anything on the first and second floors that isn't structural. All the original corridor lines will be the same but we will bring the rooms up to a suitable standard for modern hotel operators.'

Urban Splash was talking to a number of specialist hoteliers but if nobody satisfactory could be found the company was more than willing to run the Midland itself. Director of Development Bill Maynard said: 'We have been quite keen to set up a division looking at hotels and if that's the way we have to go, we'll do it. There would be no better building to start off with.' (As it transpired, no suitable end-user was forthcoming and the Midland became Urban Splash's first venture into the hotel business, with Olivier Delaunoy appointed as General Manager in January 2007.)

By October, demolition work at the hotel was almost complete. Piles of rubble littered the grass while, on the forecourt, portakabins and skips occupied the parking places once reserved for visitors' cars. The building's leaking roof had been made watertight and temporary drains put in for the removal of rainwater. Inside, the terrazzo floor was under protective covering, as were Eric Gill's bas-relief and pictorial wall map. Upstairs, the first and second floors had been completely gutted – corridors, walls, doors, fixtures and fittings (mostly dating from a 1970s makeover) had all gone. Removing the plaster had revealed that all the metal ties holding the brickwork of the outside walls together had corroded and would need to be replaced – just one of the many unforeseen problems that would emerge over the ensuing months.

Even at this early stage, Kieran Gardiner's forecast that the project would be 'very complex' was beginning to look remarkably prescient. As work progressed, more and more problems continued to emerge with the result that the completion period, estimated (rather optimistically) at 22 months, was constantly undergoing revision. In the end it would be three years before the Midland Hotel re-opened its doors to the public.

In the initial phase the main focus of activity was the hotel's basement which, ever since the Midland opened in 1933, had been susceptible to periodic flooding. The aim was to turn what was a damp, sometimes waterlogged, area into a functional space to accommodate most of the hotel's back-of-house services. Key to this was the construction of a central corridor – no small task as some of the walls to be cut through were 600mm thick – off which various rooms could be built. Then the whole basement needed to be made watertight. This was achieved by an elaborate 'tanking out' system which involved the fitting of a waterproof membrane to the walls and floor. Any waste water outside the membrane would be collected in sumps

Kieran Gardiner: Senior Construction Manager

When Kieran Gardiner first saw the Midland Hotel after Urban Splash had bought it he knew he wanted to be involved in its restoration.

'I really wanted this particular job. When I got home following a site visit I wrote down all my feelings and thoughts about the Midland – the Jazz Age, its modern looks, imagining all the people coming down that lovely staircase. I could almost hear the sound of the tea-dance coming through the door...'

Kieran's feeling for the hotel has its roots in his love of old buildings and the conservation jobs he has worked on in the past. Originally from County Galway on the west coast of Ireland, Kieran followed his father into the building trade. 'He dragged me round building sites from when I was small. He would sit me in JCBs when I was five or six, so I suppose it's always been there. Leaving school I worked with two old Geordie guys in a five-year apprenticeship as a roof slater and tiler. They were very thorough and taught me that in any job the important part was the groundwork – get that right and everything will fall into place. So I'm very methodical in my approach. I try to be ordered and structured and I do my research. That's the hard bit but if you do it properly then everything will work as it should.'

After finishing his apprenticeship Kieran worked in Britain and Ireland for fifteen years, followed by short stints in Germany and Spain. During this time he also studied for his HNC and HND. When a three-month contract with Urban Splash came up he applied and was successful; a year later he was given a full time position. Before coming to Morecambe he was Senior Site Manager for a more typical Urban Splash project, the transformation of a redundant factory building in Altrincham into luxury apartments.

Kieran regards the restoration of the Midland as the most challenging job he has worked on. 'The building has a persona – I could feel it from the very first day I walked in – but it didn't give up its secrets easily. The more we got to know it intimately, how it was put together and how it worked, the more we realised what a difficult task lay ahead. But until you strip away the fabric you don't know what's underneath.' From the very beginning, problem after problem began to surface – asbestos in the walls, dry rot in the woodwork, loose render, a leaking roof and, later on, new windows and doors which failed and had to be replaced, not to mention some of the worst storms in recent years.

Kieran admits that 'there were some very dark days when I felt the building didn't want us to complete. We had a main programme for the renovation which worked on logic but you can't always factor in delays and bad weather. Difficulties will invariably arise but a site manager has to be organised and resourceful in order to overcome them. If we had a problem, could we do things differently? Push on in another area? Move things around?' This flexible approach, helped by bottles of holy water sent from Ireland by his mother, stood Kieran in good stead as completion day crept ever nearer and the fitting out of the hotel proceeded apace.

'Trying to put twenty-first century technology into a 75-year-old building has not been easy but now that everything is finished I am happy with the way the old has been married to the new and pleased that we have been able to maintain the integrity and original ethos of the Midland. It is a fabulous building.'

(Anna Goddard)

THE MIDLAND HOTEL

Work began with the removal of virtually everything from the first and second floors of the building. [Some undamaged pieces of furniture – dressing tables, mirrors, sinks, etc – were auctioned to raise money for the National Children's Home and the Friends of the Winter Gardens.]
(Barry Guise)

and pumped via new pipe-work into Morecambe's main sewerage system. Concrete screeds were then laid to provide a more uniform floor surface. Once this was done the main services such as water, gas and electricity were installed and partition walls constructed to create a range of rooms including kitchen, food and beverage stores, crockery and linen stores, staff rooms, toilets and a small health spa.

(As all this work was taking place largely out of sight of the public, it appeared to passers-by that very little was actually happening at the Midland. By early 2006 no scaffolding had been erected and rumours began to spread questioning Urban Splash's commitment to the project. Concerned letters started to appear in the *Visitor*. With hindsight, it might have been politic for Urban Splash to have provided the local press with regular updates of progress, a move which would probably have countered the negative publicity it received at the time.)

In the basement the new central corridor begins to take shape as the partition walls are installed.
(Ian Thompson)

186

The transformation of the basement into a usable space containing many of the services which once occupied parts of the floor above has been crucial to the economic viability of the hotel. It freed up a significant area of the ground floor which could then be put to more commercial use. Urban Splash had realised that the financial success of the Midland could be compromised by the number of relatively small rooms on this floor. With the existing configuration it would have been difficult to cater for large parties or hold conferences of any size – a drawback which would have effectively restricted the potential client base of the hotel. Enlarging the rooms on the south side of the entrance foyer seemed the answer as one or two walls would be easy to remove and the space once occupied by the now redundant toilets could also be incorporated. The stumbling block to the scheme was the wall containing the pictorial map of North West England, carved by Eric Gill and painted by his son-in-law Denis Tegetmeier. There was no possibility of it being dismantled and rebuilt. The question was, could it be moved in its entirety without damaging the plasterwork of the map?

The erection of scaffolding signalled to the people of Morecambe that restoration was underway.
(Barry Guise)

Mike Hawkins and Brian Cardy check the protective covering of the wall map before attaching the wheels for its move.
(Ian Thompson)

Brian Cardy, an expert in the conservation of works of art, and engineer Mike Hawkins believed it was feasible. After expressing some initial concern about the plan, English Heritage was persuaded and gave its permission. The first step was to protect the map and ensure that the plaster would not crack during the move. Brian Cardy explained what was done: 'Immediately over the picture we pasted two layers of Japanese mulberry tissue and then a layer of very strong brown Kraft paper to give it strength and prevent any cracking. On top of this went a cotton scrim and then another layer of brown paper. I then put on a self-adhesive scrim and covered it with foam held on by squares of cardboard which gave it tremendous rigidity.'

Mike Hawkins and his colleagues then took over. The bottom half metre of the wall was cut away and replaced by a series of blocks, with a steel support beneath the remaining wall to give it strength. Two lengths of steel were then welded at right angles to the support beam and fitted with wheels. More reinforcing steel was attached to the back of the wall to prevent it from collapsing during transit. Once this was completed, the top and sides of the wall were cut round using a diamond-tipped saw. Standing free, the wall was ready to be moved. The blocks on which it was resting were replaced by four hydraulic jacks which slowly lowered it and the wheels to the floor. Fingers were crossed and gradually, following the gentle curve of the building, the wall was guided the fifteen metres or so to its new position. It was then jacked up so the wheel-bars could be removed before being eased into its final resting place. Remarkably, the actual moving process had taken less than 45 minutes and gone without a hitch, a tribute to the skill and expertise of those involved.

The relocation of this wall has turned the south end of the ground floor into what is, effectively, one large 'L'-shaped room, capable of accommodating up to 180 people and serviced by its own kitchen, bar and toilets. It can also be adapted for smaller groups by the use of sliding partitions which subdivide the space.

Having overseen the picture wall's successful transit, Brian Cardy turned his attention to the map itself which, over the years, had been touched up with household paint in colours unrelated to the original shades. Careful cleaning was followed by several weeks of painstaking restorative brushwork using modern equivalents of Denis Tegetmeier's paints. The result is stunning.

Equally impressive is his renovation of the ceiling medallion, also painted by Tegetmeier, but noticeably discoloured by damp and cigarette smoke. A tower of scaffolding in the stairwell allowed him access to a small wooden platform set two metres beneath the ceiling. Although the medallion had been covered during building work some flaking of the paint had occurred and a certain amount of remedial work was necessary before repainting could begin. Like the map this also took a number of weeks to complete but was physically more demanding as all the painting was carried out above head height.

Plan showing the new layout of the ground floor at the south end of the hotel. See page 61 for the original configuration. (Urban Splash)

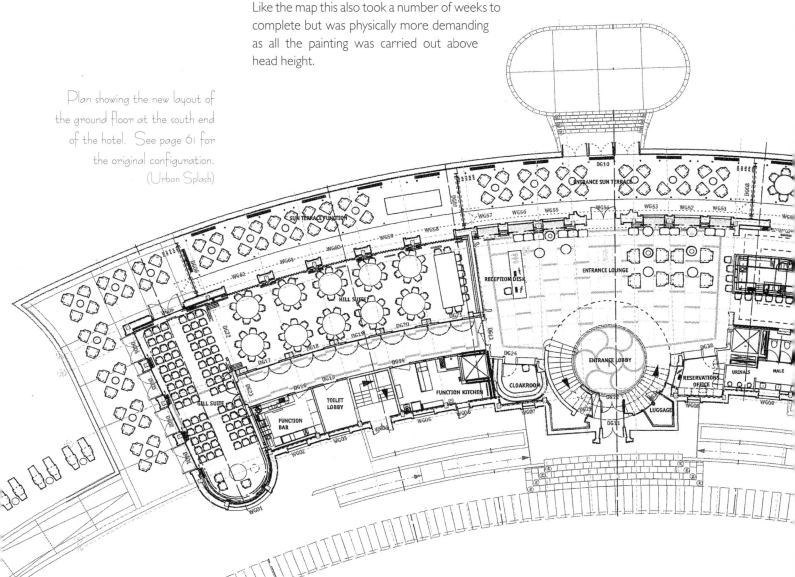

Scenes from
Eric Gill's Map
of North West
England after its
restoration.
(Anna Goddard)

The central section is dominated by the Midland Hotel.

The rural idyll of the Lake District is
represented by mountains, lakes and woods.

Liverpool's two cathedrals are shown
wreathed in industrial smoke.

Gill's ceiling medallion restored to its original colours. (Anna Goddard)

Brian Cardy at work on the medallion. (Barry Guise)

During restoration work on the pictorial wall map in the Midland, the small figure of a child and the initials J M T were revealed in the space just below the depiction of the hotel. Never incised, it had disappeared from view (as had a compass rose) as a result of later overpainting. The figure's unexpected reappearance gave rise to some speculation as to its origin. Although the wall map is usually referred to as 'Eric Gill's map of North West England', its painting was done by Gill's son-in-law, Denis Tegetmeier. In the summer of 1933, a visit by his wife Petra and two-year old daughter Judith Mary (J M T?) may have prompted Tegetmeier to leave a personal memento of his young child's visit to the seaside.

Denis Tegetmeier (1895–1987) has been somewhat overlooked as an artist and craftsman, possibly because of his close association with Eric Gill. He first met Gill in the early 1920s while still a student at London's Central School of Arts and Crafts and later joined him at Pigotts, near High Wycombe. Despite a talent for cartoons and book illustration, with which he enjoyed considerable success between the two World Wars, Tegetmeier is probably best known for his engraving and lettering, carried out firstly alongside Gill and then with Laurie Cribb, Gill's chief letter-cutting assistant. Leaving Pigotts in 1962 he moved to Wiltshire and in retirement found a greater freedom of expression in painting, sometimes in watercolour but mainly in his preferred medium of oils on gesso.

Olivier Delaunoy: Operations Director, Urban Splash Hotels

Brussels born Olivier Delaunoy trained as a chef in his native Belgium before coming to England at the age of 22. After working as a bricklayer on building sites for a while – 'because it was the only job I could find' – he moved back into catering, running the restaurant of a country house hotel in Sussex. From here he became food and beverages manager at the George Hotel in Stamford before opening his first restaurant in Sheffield. Its success led to an approach by Rocco Forte to take charge of his restaurants in London. After this, Olivier worked for Raymond Blanc helping him set up a chain of *Le Petit Blanc* restaurants.

Wanting to gain hotel management experience, Olivier offered to organise the food and beverage operation for a large hotel in Birmingham in exchange for being taught how to run a hotel. He then went into partnership with a friend to form a company called 'Night Night' whose concept was 'to put the most luxurious facilities into the smallest possible hotel bedroom space.' Following the death of his business partner and a disagreement with shareholders, Olivier left the company and not long afterwards was introduced to Tom Bloxham of Urban Splash, a meeting which eventually led to his appointment as General Manager of the Midland Hotel. (When Urban Splash decided to enlarge its portfolio, buying and renovating other hotels in different parts of the country, Olivier was given the task of overseeing this development, together with the new title of Operations Director, Urban Splash Hotels.)

Like everyone else, Olivier was captivated by the Midland and is determined to make it a success. The key to this, he believes, is to utilise every space to the best of its potential. 'All the different areas have to be sustainable in their own right – the conference section, the restaurant, the bar and the rotunda. Normally in a hotel you generate your revenue through your bedrooms but because of the configuration of the Midland you have to do 50/50 with the catering which is a difficult strategy. This means that the quality of the food and the quality of the service are very important. Most of the food will be sourced locally, with the main restaurant and the rotunda offering different culinary experiences.' For Olivier, selecting the right staff for the hotel is crucial to its long term success. 'My approach is to employ people who have personality. If they have the personality to give each customer a great experience then I will employ them; if they have no skill I can train them from scratch. If guests like the surroundings and are treated well and with warmth they will come back again.'

'What we have achieved is a truly functional building but one with a heart and soul, a place where our guests will instantly feel great when they walk through the door. The Midland will bring a lot of pleasure to a lot of people.'

(Simon Webb Photography)

Matt Redhead: House Manager

As House Manager of the Midland, Matt is responsible for the service procedures within the hotel – the practicalities of its day-to-day operation.

Born and brought up in Cornwall, Matt has spent all his working life in the catering and hospitality industry. After gaining a Higher National Certificate at South Devon College in Torquay, he learnt his trade in local hotels before taking a job as a waiter on the luxury liner *QE2* at the age of 21. Over the next ten years he worked his way up through various posts, including restaurant manager and assistant food and beverages manager, eventually becoming corporate trainer for Cunard. In this capacity he oversaw the training of new staff for Cunard's *Queen Mary 2*.

Returning to dry land, Matt was appointed deputy manager at the Headland Hotel and Cottages in Newquay. However, with the general manager a long way from retirement, there was little chance of promotion. An application to a catering agency led to a meeting with Olivier Delaunoy, Operations Director of Urban Splash Hotels, and two interviews later Matt was offered the House Manager's position at the Midland.

'I knew from the initial interview that this was something I wanted. When I wake up in the morning I can't wait to get to work. The impact of the building on me was just amazing.' He is full of enthusiasm for the challenge of making the Midland a first class hotel. 'A whole lot of passion has gone into its renovation and it's my job to make sure our team is filled with the right people to be able to complement such an outstanding building. All 50 staff have been personally selected and trained to ensure that every guest, whether staying in the hotel or just enjoying a drink at the bar, has the best possible experience.'

Many other people have also played their parts in the restoration of the Midland Hotel but deserving of particular mention are Site Manager Paul Huett, Assistant Site Manager Luke Birch and Site Supervisor Gary Falkingham.

(Anna Goddard)

Down in the entrance foyer a second wall was constructed behind the picture wall to provide extra support and to facilitate the return to its original location of the Midland's most famous work of art – Eric Gill's bas-relief of *Odysseus and Nausicaa*. Its constituent stone panels had experienced some slight damage on their travels but proved relatively straightforward to repair. It now looks across the restored terrazzo floor, with its silver mosaic inlays and Marion Dorn seahorse, to the new bar occupying the centre of the original dining room. Here, extensive dry rot was discovered in the wooden flooring which had to be removed. It has been replaced by boards of a sustainable hardwood called jatoba, laid down in a herringbone pattern, the same wood also being used for the floors in the main function rooms. Beyond the bar is a small dining/meeting room serviced, along with the rotunda restaurant, by an adjacent kitchen. The rotunda is dominated by a central 'chandelier' designed to evoke the lighthouse-style mirrors of the original light fitting. As in the past, this part of the Midland is open to the public and can be accessed directly from the promenade, via steps up to a newly constructed terrace.

The removal of everything but the supporting pillars from the first and second floors provided a 'blank canvas' for the layout of the new bedrooms. On each of the two floors a fresh concrete screed was laid (asbestos having been found in the old screed) and the lines of the corridor marked out, mirroring the sweeping curve of the building. Individual rooms of varying sizes were then constructed separated by specially insulated and sound-proofed walls which, according to Kieran Gardiner, would block out the noise of the entire cast of *Riverdance* going full blast next door!

Only radiators and a solitary bath remain after the first floor has been cleared.
(Ian Thompson)

One of the hotel
bedrooms.
(Anna Goddard)

The bathroom
(below left) is hidden by
the wooden panelling.
(Simon Webb)

A rooftop suite showing
the lounge area with
panoramic views of
Morecambe Bay.
(Anna Goddard)

THE MIDLAND HOTEL

Each floor now contains nineteen bedrooms, some with balconies and well over half having a sea view. While all the rooms have been planned with similar space-saving features, there is no overall uniformity and a variety of colour schemes has been employed.

As restoration progressed, the original plans for the hotel underwent constant modification in order to take account of changing circumstances. On the roof, for reasons of health and safety (and commercial considerations), the proposed bar was replaced by six guest suites, bringing the room total for the hotel up to 44.

Although Oliver Hill had designed the Midland with a future fourth storey in mind, Urban Splash's architects could not utilise the existing stud columns to support the additional weight on the roof. Because of planning constraints and to make them as unobtrusive as possible, the new rooms had to be set back at least one metre from the parapet. This presented the problem of how the extra weight could be transmitted to the main load-bearing structure of the building. The solution was to strengthen a number of the roof beams and lay out a steel base to which was fixed a lightweight metal framework holding the predominantly glass walls – opaque on the landward side and clear facing the sea, affording guests panoramic views across Morecambe Bay to the distant mountains of the Lake District.

Pictured under construction, the additional storey would eventually contain six suites, storage and service facilities and a small gym. (Barry Guise)

A workman carefully applies the
hotel's bespoke new render.
(Morecambe Visitor)

The potential danger to guests
of the relatively low parapet
necessitated the addition of
handrails. These are in stainless
steel and accentuate the nautical
appearance of the hotel.

The erection of scaffolding around the Midland in the spring of 2006 not only indicated to the people of Morecambe that work on the hotel was really underway, it also enabled a detailed examination of the building's façade to be carried out. After layers of peeling paintwork had been power-washed away (using tiny glass beads rather than sand) the render underneath was discovered to be in a far worse state than anticipated, with many loose patches and a number of serious cracks, all of which had to be made good before a new surface could be applied. On the rotunda, the render was in such poor condition that it had to be removed down to the brickwork.

Sourcing a suitable replacement render – one that could withstand the worst of Morecambe's weather – proved a difficult task. Over 30 different samples were tested (trial squares appeared all over the hotel walls) before an aggregate was found that satisfied Kieran Gardiner's stringent requirements. It was, he explained, 'a modified polymer render with three types of glass and 39 different components. It's bespoke for the building and should protect it better than the original render.' Samples of the coloured glass used in the window ledges and soffits were sent for chemical analysis so that these blue-green highlights – a distinctive feature of the hotel when it opened in 1933 – could be replicated.

Rendering the 2,500 square metres of the Midland's exterior has taken over twelve months and could only be done when conditions permitted. The temperature had to be at least 5°C but, on the other hand, it could not be too hot or too windy (the render must not dry too quickly) or too wet. After setting hard, the render was acid etched, washed and electrically polished so that the building once again sparkles in the sunlight.

The Midland Hotel's glistening
façade in close-up.
(Anna Goddard)

Once the scaffolding was up to roof level it was relatively easy to reach the two stone seahorses set high above the main entrance. For some reason these had been painted red in the past and were also showing the effects of over 70 years of exposure to the salty air. Chemical solvents were used to strip off the unbecoming colour and the figures were then cleaned and repaired by craftsmen from Stonebridge Masonry.

Stonemason Tony Gregory makes
the final touches to his renovation of
Eric Gill's seahorses.
(Morecambe Visitor)

The rotunda bar at night,
illumininated by its pink toned
'chandelier'.
(Simon Webb)

A long bar occupies most of the
old dining room. Part of the
original burr-ash panelling has been
used to face two of the walls.
The main restaurant is now located
in the adjacent sun-lounge.
(Anna Goddard)

Running virtually the full length of the seaward side of the building is the new sun-lounge. There was no such structure in the original 1930s plan but the addition of a single storey glazed extension in 1979 proved to be both popular with the public and beneficial for the hotel in terms of offering some protection against the weather – two reasons why Urban Splash decided to build a replacement. Considerably more robust than its predecessor, the sun-lounge has floor to ceiling glass on three sides giving it a light and airy appearance, more in sympathy with the building as a whole. Accessible from the hotel and the promenade, it offers additional dining space and will be, for many visitors, a pleasant and convivial spot to enjoy afternoon tea or to take an evening drink while watching the sun go down across the bay.

Seven and a half years after its closure and five and a half years since its acquisition by Urban Splash, the Midland Hotel is once again open for business. Not all of Tom Bloxham's original ideas for the hotel have come to fruition and only time will tell if Morecambe ever truly becomes the 'Brighton of the North.' However, what is undeniable is that the end result of three years of restoration is a magnificent building of which Urban Splash – and Morecambe – can be justifiably proud.

After all the trials and tribulations of recent years, it now seems that the Midland Hotel can look forward to a bright new future – a 1930s icon fit for the twenty-first century.

CATALOGUE OF THE
WORKS OF ART AT THE
MIDLAND HOTEL

Title	Seahorses (two virtually identical objects)
Location	On the exterior façade of the building at the top of the central tower.
Artist/Designer	Eric Gill with Donald Potter.
Date	1933.
Medium	Portland stone.
Size	67" (170 cms) height × 10.5" (27 cms) width × 20.5" (52 cms) depth.
Description	Two monumental figures of seahorses following an 'S'-shaped curve with scaled bodies and rounded tails, carved *in situ* and overlooking the hotel forecourt.
Discussion	For a full discussion of the objects see pages 65 and 67.
Condition	They have been painted in the past but have been cleaned and restored to the original stonework by Stonebridge Masonry for Urban Splash.

Title	Neptune and Triton
Location	Ceiling at the top of the circular staircase in the central tower.
Artist/Designe	Eric Gill with Denis Tegetmeier.
Date	1933.
Medium	Polished natural ivory coloured 'Marplax' surface raised a quarter of an inch below the surrounding ceiling and then painted.
Size	10' (305 cms) diameter.
Inscription	AND HEAR OLD TRITON BLOW HIS WREATHED HORN
Description	The central figure in the ceiling medallion portrays Neptune wearing a crown and enthroned amongst waves. The bearded crowned figure of Triton emerges from the sea, his golden horn clasped in his hand. To the left a mermaid appears to touch the waist of Neptune with her left hand. Another female embraces Neptune from behind the throne. The hair of the figures, the waves, the folds of the cloak and the mermaid's fishtail all combine to create a rhythmic, decorative pattern. The colours are blue, blue green, yellow and shades of red brown.

Discussion	For a full discussion of the designs for the medallion see pages 66–67, 71–72.
Condition	Damage had occurred from damp causing white patches at the edge and on some of the figures. This has been repaired and the medallion restored to its original colours by Brian Cardy for Urban Splash.

Title	Odysseus Welcomed from the Sea by Nausicaa
Location	Originally on a wall of the Entrance Lounge but later moved to a wall in the Eric Gill Suite, formerly known as the Children's Room. Now back in its original location.
Artist/Designer	Eric Gill with Laurie Cribb.
Date	1933.
Size	10' 5" (318 cms) height × 16' (488 cms) length.
Medium	Shell bed Perrycot Portland stone supplied by H. T. Jenkins & Son Ltd, carved *in situ* on nine slabs and polished by a representative from the company.
Inscription	THERE IS GOOD HOPE THAT THOU MAYEST SEE THY FRIENDS, HOMER/Ody, ΝΑΥΣΙΚΑΑ, ΟΔΥΣΣΕΥΣ, Eric G.
Description	Carved bas-relief panel depicting Odysseus being welcomed from the sea by Nausicaa, who greets him by clasping his hand. She is attended by three female servants, the first of whom carries a bowl of fruit, the second a jug and goblet and the third a garment. The bearded Odysseus covers himself with a branch as he steps out onto land from waves depicted by curvilinear forms. Branches and foliage arch above the figures. The message is of welcome and friendship, comfort and refreshment for both Odysseus and guests of the hotel.
Discussion	For a full discussion of the designs for the bas-relief see pages 72–75 and for an account of its attempted sale and theft see pages 153–4, 156, 169–172.
Condition	Good with slight damage which has been repaired by Urban Splash.

Title	Map of North West England
Location	On the north wall of the Eric Gill Suite, formerly the Children's Room. A communicating door was in place before the relief was carved. The wall and map have been relocated to the south side of the Eric Gill bas-relief.
Artist/Designer	Eric Gill with Dennis Tegetmeier.
Date	1933.
Medium	Oil paint on a polished natural ivory coloured 'Marplax' surface on a plaster ground.
Size	8' 6" (259 cms) height × 17' 2" (523 cms) width.
Inscription	BIRKENHEAD, LIVERPOOL, Adelphi Hotel, SOUTHPORT, PRESTON, BLACKPOOL, FLEETWOOD, THE MIDLAND HOTEL, Tarnbrook Refuge, HEYSHAM, LANCASTER, MORECAMBE, THE ROYAL SCOT,

KENDAL, Arnside, Cartmel, Ulverston, Dalton, Millom, Furness Abbey, BARROW-IN-FURNESS, BROUGHTON, St Bees, WHITEHAVEN, PENRITH, KESWICK, Langdale Fells, Airy Force, HAWESWATER, ULLSWATER, THIRLMERE, GRASMERE, Ambleside, WINDERMERE, CONISTON, DERWENT WATER, Lodore, Bassenthwaite, Scafell, WASTWATER, CRUMMOCK WATER, Buttermere, Borrowdale Fells, LOWESWATER, ENNERDALE WATER.

Description	The map is an incised low relief painted by Dennis Tegetmeier and shows the coastline from Whitehaven in the north to Birkenhead in the south with each centre represented by a dominant feature. The LMS connection is suggested in the Midland Hotel, the Adelphi Hotel and the Royal Scot train. Gill pays homage to a romantic vision of the Lake District and depicts the industrial centres wreathed in smoke. The map is inscribed with circular lines emanating from its centre where the Midland Hotel is located. There is a pentimento (under drawing) of the Midland Hotel and the final version has been moved upwards slightly. There is also evidence of a typographic error on the word THIRLMERE which appears to have been initially mis-spelt with a 'U' instead of an 'I' and later corrected. Airy Force is a mis-spelling of Aira Force.
Discussion	For a full discussion of the map see pages 76–77.
Condition	The map had experienced slight damage and suffered from inappropriate overpainting. It has been restored by Brian Cardy for Urban Splash.

Title	Day and Night at the Seaside
Location	On curved internal wall of the Tea Room/Café.
Artist/Designer	Eric Ravilious with Tirzah (Garwood) Ravilious.
Date	1933.
Medium	Oil paint mixed with wax on plaster. Although referred to by Oliver Hill in his correspondence as a 'fresco', this was not correct in a strict art historical sense.
Size	11' 7" (353 cms) height x 53' 5" (1628 cms) width (calculated on a semicircle in a room with a radius of 17' (518 cms)).
Description	The mural depicts day and night scenes at the seaside with abstract architectural forms, flags, planes and, in the night scene, fireworks. The tubular forms to the foreground of the mural form a *trompe l'oeil* effect with the original tubular Bauhaus-like furniture in the room. The walls had not been allowed to dry sufficiently when Eric and Tirzah Ravillious began work on the mural which was later damaged by damp from a leaking roof. It was eventually painted over in 1935.
Discussion	For a full discussion of the mural and the conjectural reconstruction made in 1990 by set designers from London Weekend Television see pages 77–79, 82–83, 86, 159, 162.
Condition	No longer in existence.

Title	Circular rugs (two identical objects)
Location	Originally in the Entrance Lounge.
Artist/Designer	Marion Dorn.
Medium	Hand tufted wool – made by H. and M. Southwell.
Size	15' 6'' (472 cms) diameter.
Description	Circular frame in tones of brown and brick red with an interlocking pattern comprising two bold stripes of waves. The colours were intended to complement the floor, the furniture and Eric Gill's Perrycot Portland stone bas-relief. The waves end in a curve that strongly relates to that at the base of the seahorse tail and echoes the seaside theme apparent throughout the original lounge area.
Discussion	For a full discussion of these objects, including their conjectural reconstruction, see pages 86–87, 159.
Condition	The rugs and their original designs have not been located.

Title	Seahorse
Location	Set in the floor of the Entrance Lounge.
Artist/Designer	Marion Dorn.
Date	1933.
Medium	Tesserae and glass mosaic manufactured by James Powell Ltd inlaid in polished terrazzo slab.
Size	28'' (71 cms) height x 11'' (28 cms) width, set in a composite slab measuring 34.5'' (88 cms) x 28.5'' (72 cms).
Description	The mosaic depicts a seahorse partially following an 'S'-shaped curve. The tesserae are coloured in two shades of green, two blue and a red-orange with silver leaf enclosed in clear glass, giving off a mother of pearl sheen. Two ribbons of the glass mosaic form waves or ripples beneath the figure of the seahorse. This theme is followed through the floor with ribbons of glass mosaic inlaid in the 'sand' covered terrazzo, suggesting waves on a beach.
Discussion	For a full discussion of the mosaic see page 87.
Condition	The mosaic is in very good condition with no apparent damage, the carpeting of the floor having helped to preserve it.

PRINCIPAL CONTRACTORS FOR THE MIDLAND HOTEL (1933)

Listed overleaf are the principal contractors to the LMS Midland Hotel in Morecambe during its construction 1932–3, together with the payments for their work. With one exception, those firms receiving less than c. £100 have not been included. Most companies had head offices in London although the actual manufacture of their products was carried out elsewhere. Not surprisingly, many have ceased trading or been absorbed by larger companies over the intervening years but a few are still in business.

Between 31 October 1932 and 2 November 1934, fourteen Certificates of Payment totalling £57, 349 were issued by Oliver Hill. These constituted payments to the General Contractor, Messrs Humphreys Ltd, and the various sub-contractors responsible for the building of the Midland Hotel. Of this total, £27, 218 went to Humphreys and £30,131 to the sub-contractors.

THE NEW L.M.S.
HOTEL AT
MORECAMBE

•

GENERAL
CONTRACTORS

HUMPHREYS
LTD.
KNIGHTSBRIDGE
LONDON
S.W.7

Telephone: KENSINGTON 8255

1.	ASPHALTING	Limmer & Trinidad Asphalting Co.	£392
2.	BIANCOLA PAVING	Art Pavements & Decorations Ltd.	£1,862
3.	CARPETS	H. & M. Southwell Ltd.	£741
4.	CEMENT GLAZES	Hoyle, Robson, Barnett & Co.	£142
5.	CONSTRUCTIONAL STEELWORK	Banister, Walton & Co. Ltd.	£4,184
6.	DECOLITE FLOORING	Asbestos Cement Building Products Ltd.	£275
7.	ELECTRICAL WORK	Arthur R. Farrar & Co.	£1,330
8.	EXTERNAL RENDERING	F. Bradford & Co. Ltd.	£2,765
9.	FABRICS	Donald Brothers Ltd.	£98
		and Edinburgh Weavers	£249
		and Allan Walton Ltd.	£124
10.	FURNITURE AND PANELLING	Frederick Tibbenham Ltd.	£4,980
		and B. Cohen & Sons Ltd.	£1,148
11.	GENERAL CONTRACTORS	Humphreys Ltd.	£27,218
12.	GLASS	Pilkington Brothers Ltd.	£124
13.	HEATING & HOT WATER SYSTEMS	G. N. Haden & Co.	£3,500
14.	HOLLOW TILE FLOORING	Bolton & Hayes Ltd.	£2,625
15.	INTERNAL GLASS SCREENS	Crittall Manufacturing Co. Ltd.	£126
16.	IRONWORK	Roanoid Ltd.	£138
17.	KITCHEN EQUIPMENT	Carron & Co.	£368
		and William Still & Sons	£104
18.	LIGHT FITTINGS	Troughton & Young	£746
19.	MARBLE AND PORTLAND STONE	H. T. Jenkins & Son	£595
20.	MARPLAX	James Robertson & Co. Ltd.	£429
21.	METAL FURNITURE	Cox & Co.	£411
22.	METALWORK	Fred K. Braby & Co.	£250
		and James Gibbons Ltd.	£911
		and Comyn Ching & Co. Ltd.	£186
23.	PASSENGER LIFT	Marryat & Scott Ltd.	£595
24.	REFRIGERATION	L. Sterne & Co.	£341
25.	REVOLVING DOOR	Samuel Elliot & Sons	£480
26.	ROOF LIGHTS	Haywards Ltd.	£104
27.	RUBBER FLOORING	Dunlop Rubber Co.	£216
28.	SANITARY FITTINGS	Doulton & Co.	£988
29.	STEPS AND FRONT PAVING	Carter & Co.	£171
30.	TILE PAVING	Thomas Foster & Co.	£263
31.	UPHOLSTERY	Skellorn, Edwards & Co. Ltd.	£263
32.	WINDOW CASEMENTS	Henry Hope & Sons Ltd.	£1,338
33.	VENTILATION	James Keith & Blackman Co.	£289

THE FRIENDS OF
THE MIDLAND HOTEL

The Friends of the Midland Hotel was formed in April 1999 with the aim of trying to help preserve the building and to raise awareness of its architectural importance both locally and nationally. A committee was appointed and held its first meeting later that month. It discussed possible membership fees, the production of a newsletter and ways in which the hotel's plight could be disseminated to a wider audience. Further meetings followed and a constitution was drawn up. A newsletter (called *Seahorse*) was issued in July to thirty Friends.

Today there are over 500 members – from Cornwall to Essex, Cumbria to Kent, in Wales and Scotland, across the Channel in France and as far away as New Zealand – an indication of the high regard in which the Midland Hotel is held. In the past, the Friends have produced limited editions of Midland Hotel mugs, plates and calendars which have sold well and intend to bring out further items of Midland memorabilia in the future.

Since the purchase of the hotel by Urban Splash in 2003, the Friends have established a good relationship with the company and were pleased with its plans for the restoration of the hotel, realising the need for certain changes in order to make the Midland a viable economic proposition for the twenty-first century. Bill Maynard, Paul Jones, Kieran Gardiner and Olivier Delaunoy from Urban Splash have all spoken at Friends' AGMs and have organised tours of the building to keep members up-to-date with progress during its restoration.

During its existence the group has actively campaigned for the hotel's future. Its chairwoman, Sue Thompson, has given (apart from considerable amounts of her time) numerous radio interviews and appeared on television programmes such as ITV's *Derelict Discoveries* and BBC One's *Inside Out* as well as helping with research for an episode of BBC Two's *Coast* – all to promote the Midland Hotel.

While the focus of the Friends has changed since the purchase of the hotel by Urban Splash, there is still a role for such a group. It might have been relieved of the worry about saving the building for posterity but it can still play a part in helping to ensure the Midland's success in the future – and it will always be there if needed.

New members are welcome.

Telephone: (01524) 851351

Email: friends@midlandhotel.org

Write to: The Membership Secretary
23, Broadlands Drive
Bolton-le-Sands
Carnforth
Lancashire LA5 8BH

Website: www.midlandhotel.org

Committee members of the Friends of the Midland outside the hotel in 1999, the year the support group was formed. From left to right: Peter Wade, Barry Guise, Sue Thompson and Ian Thompson. (*Morecambe Visitor*)

CHAPTER
REFERENCES

Several chapters have drawn information from local and regional newspapers which provide an invaluable source of historical and contemporary detail. Those used are: the *Citizen*, *Lancaster Gazette*, *Lancaster/Morecambe Guardian*, *Lancashire Evening Post* and, particularly, the *Visitor* (originally the *Morecambe and Heysham Visitor and Lancaster Advertiser*).

Individual issues are identified in the text.

Chapter One

British Railway Hotels 1838–1983 by Oliver Carter. Silver Link Publishing (1990)

Gothic and Exotic: The Victorian and Edwardian Buildings of Morecambe by Peter Wade. Published by the author (2001)

Lost Resort? The Flow and Ebb of Morecambe by Roger Bingham. Cicerone Press (1990)

Poulton-le-Sands: A History of Morecambe by John Spalding. Unpublished typescript in Morecambe Reference Library (1974)

The National Archives:

    BT 41/876/5176 Morecambe Bay Harbour Co. & Rly Co.

    RAIL 1007/148 Minutes of North West Railway Company.

    AN 109/636   Hotels and Catering Services Minutes: Rebuilding and opening of hotel; sale of excess land.

    AN 109/637   Tender for rebuilding and refurbishing new hotel.

'Railway News Section' *The Railway Gazette* February 1925, p. 171

Sharpe, Paley and Austin: A Lancaster Architectural Practice 1836–1942 by James Price. University of Lancaster Centre for Northwest Regional Studies (1998)

Shipbreaking at Morecambe: T. W. Ward Ltd. 1905–1933 by Ian Buxton and Nigel Dalziel. Lancaster City Museums (1993)

'The Hotels, Refreshment Room and Restaurant Car Department of a Great Railway', by J. F. Cairns, *The Railway Magazine* June 1916, pp. 241–256

The Little North Western Railway by Martin Bairstow. Published by the author (2000)

Chapter Two

Bauhaus 1919–1933 by Magdalena Droste. Taschen (2000)

Echoes of Art Deco: Art Deco in Morecambe by Peter Wade. Published by the author (1999)

Far Horizon: Buildings of Today by Oliver Hill. Collins (1950)

International Style: Modernist Architecture from 1925 to 1965 by Hasan-Uddin Khan. Taschen (2001)

'What was Moderism?' by Christopher Wilk in *Modernism: designing a new world 1914–1939* edited by Christopher Wilk. V&A Publications (2006)

Oliver Hill: Architect and Lover of Life 1887–1968 by Alan Powers. Mouton Publications (1989)

Oliver Hill Papers (RIBA):

HiO/56/3, HiO/57/1–2, HiO/58/1–2, HiO/59/1–3, HiO/60/1–2	Oliver Hill's correspondence with the Controller of LMS Hotels, Quantity Surveyor, Clerk of Works, Structural Engineer, Main Contractor and various Sub-contractors.

'Paradise lost for high jinks hotel' by Kenneth Powell *Sunday Telegraph* 9 May 1999, p11

The National Archives:

RAIL 418/164	Minutes of Morecambe Hotel Rebuilding Committee
RAIL 1057/2730	LMS New Hotel at Morecambe

'The Architecture of Oliver Hill' by Roderick Gradidge in *Britain in the Thirties* edited by Gavin Stamp. Architectural Design, Profile 24 (1979) pp. 30–41

'The Modern Movement by Oliver Hill' *Architectural Design and Construction* September 1931, p. 461

The Thirties: Recalling the English Architectural Scene by David Dean. Trefoil Books (1983)

Chapter Three

'London, Morecambe & elsewhere' by Lord Clonmore, *Architectural Review* September 1933, pp. 193–99

'Morecambe Hotel: The LMS as Maecenas' *Country Life* 18 November 1933, pp. 539–544

'The Midland Hotel, Morecambe' by H. W. Martin-Kaye (ed) *Architecture Illustrated* September 1933, pp. 72–101

Chapter Four

Art Deco and Modernist Carpets by Susan Day. Chronicle Books (2002)

Eric Gill by Fiona MacCarthy. Faber and Faber (1989)

Eric Gill: Sculpture by Judith Collins. Lund Humphries/Barbican Art Gallery (1992)

Eric Gill: The Sculpture by Judith Collins. The Herbert Press (1998)

Eric Ravilious: Memoir of an Artist by Helen Binyon. The Lutterworth Press (1983)

Oliver Hill Papers (RIBA):

HiO/56 – HiO/60	Oliver Hill's correspondence with the artists Boris Anrep, Edward Bawden, Mary Bone, Marion Dorn, Eric Gill, Edward McKnight-Kauffer, Eric Newton, Eric Ravilious and Edward Wadsworth.

The Architect of Floors: modernism, art and Marion Dorn's designs by Christine Boydell. Schoeser (1996)

The Odyssey by Homer. Senate Books (1996)

'The Stone and the Shell – Eric Gill and the Midland Hotel, Morecambe' by Alan Powers *The Book Collector* Vol. 47 No 1, Spring 1998

Chapter Five

A Day in the Sun: Outdoor Pursuits in the 1930s by Timothy Wilcox. Philip Wilson (2006)

'Keeping up Appearances' by Elisabeth Dunn *Daily Telegraph* magazine 13 February 1993

Oliver Hill Papers (RIBA):

    HiO/56 – HiO/60   End of maintenance report; accounts and statements for certificates.

Railway Posters 1923–1947 by Beverley Cole and Richard Durack. Laurence King/NRM (1992)

The British Seaside by John K. Walton. Manchester University Press (2000)

'The Healthy Body Culture' by Christopher Wilk in *Modernism: designing a new world 1914–1939* edited by Christopher Wilk. V&A Publications (2006)

Chapter Six

Lancashire Airfields in the Second World War by Aldon P. Ferguson. Countryside Books (2004)

Morecambe Wings RAF Station Magazine (published between November 1940 and October 1941)

The National Archives:

    RAF Morecambe Operational Record Books:

    AIR 29/490   No. 3 WAAF Depot, Morecambe.

    AIR 29/501   No. 7 Recruit Centre, Morecambe.

    AIR 29/711   No. 4 Motor Transport School, Morecambe.

    AIR 29/745   No. 9 School of Technical Training, Morecambe.

The RAF and Morecambe 1940–1946 by Trevor Jordan. OU Thesis (no date)

The formation and story of 3 WAAF depot, Morecambe by A. M. Thompson. RAF Museum X001–6486/001 (no date)

Chapter Seven

LMS Miscellany Volume 2 by H. N. Twells. Oxford Publishing Company (1984)

The National Archives:

    AN 13/1506   Midland Hotel Morecambe: proposed sale.

    AN 109/638   American Bar: development proposals.

    AN 109/639   Floodlights: installation.

    AN 109/641   Sale of hotel negotiations.

    AN 109/861   Sale of hotel: correspondence and press cuttings.

Staffordshire Pottery by Robert E. Cluett. Schiffer Publishing (2004)

Chapter Eight
Some liked it hot: The British on Holiday at Home and Abroad by Miriam Akhtar and Steve Humphries. Virgin Publishing (2000)

Chapter Nine
Coming Unstuck: The Removal of Fixtures from Listed Buildings by Teresa Sladen. Victorian Society Report (1992)
Conservation Today by David Pearce. Routledge (1989)
'Nooks and Corners' by Piloti *Private Eye* 5 September 2002
Shifting Sands: Design and the Changing Image of English Seaside Towns English Heritage/Cabe (2003)

Chapter Ten
'Morecambe fights decline with Mars bar effect' by Helen Carter the *Guardian* 20 March 2004
'New lease of life for the Midland Hotel'. Press Release from the Northwest Regional Development Agency, 2 December 2004
'Statement from Urban Splash re Midland Hotel, Morecambe'. Press Release from Urban Splash, 13 January 2003

About the authors

Barry Guise is a founder member of the Friends of the Midland Hotel and has recently retired as Senior Lecturer in Geography at St Martin's College, Lancaster. He lives in Bolton-le-Sands, near Morecambe with his wife, Lesley and two black and white cats, Dill and Tansy.

Pam Brook is a committee member of the Friends of the Midland Hotel and is currently Curriculum Team Leader for Art and Design at Bradford College. She catalogued the art works in the Midland as part of her Masters degree in Art History in 1992. She lives in Oakworth, near Keighley.

INDEX